TOEFL / TOEIC Express

WRITING

GIVING AN EXPLANATION
MAKING AN ARGUMENT

Florent GUSDORF

ellipses

Du même auteur dans la même collection

TOEFL/TOEIC Express. Auto-évaluation. Writing: Stating a Preference (niveau 2), 2013, 224 p.
TOEFL/TOEIC Express. Auto-évaluation. Writing: Agree/Disagree (niveau 2), 2013, 192 p.
TOEFL/TOEIC Express. Auto-évaluation. Speaking (niveau 2), 2012, 192 p.
TOEFL/TOEIC Express. Auto-évaluation. Grammaire (niveau 2), 2009, 208 p.
TOEFL/TOEIC Express. Auto-évaluation. Vocabulaire (niveau 2), 2008, 208 p.
English Academy. Les 50 fautes d'usage les plus fréquentes en anglais (niveau 2), 2008, 128 p.
Complete to compete. Réviser son vocabulaire anglais. Thèmes de société (niveau 2), 2007, 128 p.
Key Words English. Vocabulaire de la vie de tous les jours (niveau 2), 2007, 128 p.

Dans la même collection

Alexandra Nantet, Pascal Jacquelin, *Help! Grammaire et vocabulaire. 2e édition revue et corrigée* (niveau 1), 2005, 128 p.
Jean-Luc Bordon, *High Five! Vocabulaire thématique. Pour enfin maîtriser le vocabulaire incontournable de l'actualité et enrichir son expression* (niveau 2), 2012, 112 p.
Jean-Luc Bordon, *Well done! Entraînement à la compréhension écrite et à la lecture en anglais* (niveau 2), 2012, 128 p.
Rosine Joussein, *Vocabulary. Words & games. Jeux pour apprendre ou réviser le vocabulaire anglais de base* (niveau 1), 2012, 128 p.
Jean-Luc Bordron, *Easy-peasy. 500 expressions idiomatiques courantes pour comprendre la presse et enrichir son expression* (niveau 2), 2011, 128 p.
Jean-Luc Bordron, *Full Stop! Pour enfin maîtriser les 100 pièges classiques de l'anglais* (niveau 2), 2010, 208 p.
Kay et Daniel Rodd, *Xpression. Plus de 1 300 expressions idiomatiques de l'anglais d'aujourd'hui* (niveau 2), 2008, 160 p.
Pascal Jacquelin, *English Why not ? Les bases de l'anglais* (niveau 1), 2007, 112 p.
Corinne Carrillon, *Fifty-fifty. Réviser son vocabulaire en s'amusant.* Spécial sciences, 2007, 160 p.
Pascal Jacquelin et Alexandra Nantet, *Check In. Communiquer efficacement en anglais* (niveau 2), 2005, 128 p.
Diane Lafayette, *Express yourself! 15 chapitres thématiques pour connaître l'essentiel du vocabulaire courant en anglais*, 2003, 176 p.

ISBN 978-2-7298-86981

32, rue Bargue 75740 Paris cedex 15

www.editions-ellipses.fr

PRÉFACE

TOEFL/TOEIC* Express *WRITING* - *Giving an Explanation / Making an Argument est le troisième et dernier volume dans la série *Writing* du TOEFL/TOEIC. Il s'adresse aux candidats qui se préparent à l'épreuve d'expression écrite (*independent task)* des examens internationaux (TOEFL, TOEIC, IELTS).

TOEFL/TOEIC* Express *WRITING* - *Giving an Explanation / Making an Argument comprend 52 chapitres. Les thèmes abordés sont tirés de banques officielles de sujets.

Chaque chapitre comprend trois parties :

- le vocabulaire essentiel pour traiter le sujet (*Key words*) ;
- un aperçu de l'argumentaire (*Talking points*) ;
- deux réponses correspondant à chaque point de vue (*Possible answers*).

Les réponses fournies sont aussi **variées** et **complètes** que possible. À cet égard, nous avons choisi de traiter plus de trois ou quatre arguments afin d'offrir au lecteur un large éventail de points de vue, libre à lui de poursuivre le développement de certains d'entre eux. C'est la raison pour laquelle les essais offrent en général entre 400 et 500 mots, ce qui est supérieur à ce que l'on attend d'un essai classique au TOEFL (300-350 mots environ).

Le vocabulaire s'articule autour des notions et concepts de base, mais fournit également des pistes pour les réponses susceptibles de servir de support.

Les sujets traités ou les réponses données ne sauraient en aucun cas refléter les opinions personnelles de l'auteur, ce dernier se contentant de suggérer des exemples de réponse mettant en jeu les qualités requises (vocabulaire, grammaire, articulation, exemples) afin de produire une prestation à la hauteur des exigences attendues dans ce type de test.

L'ÉPREUVE ÉCRITE AUX EXAMENS INTERNATIONAUX

L'écrit du TOEFL

Les épreuves du TOEFL comprennent une partie rédaction. Celle-ci se présente sous la forme d'un essai dont la durée est de 30 minutes. La longueur de l'essai est de 300-350 mots, rarement davantage. Il convient donc de bien gérer son temps.

La partie expression écrite est notée entre 0 et 30 (soit un quart du score global). Score : 24-30 : bon - 17-23 : Moyen - 1-16 : limité. Selon ETS, l'organisme organisateur, « Plusieurs évaluateurs rigoureusement formés notent les tests anonymement. Les évaluateurs ETS sont continuellement contrôlés pour garantir équité et qualité. » ETS dispose également d'une « technologie de score automatisée utilisée en parallèle de l'évaluation humaine pour noter les tâches d'expression écrite intégrées et indépendantes. En associant le jugement humain pour le contenu et la compréhension avec le correcteur automatisé pour les fonctions linguistiques, nous garantissons des scores cohérents et de qualité. » (ETS)

L'essai fait l'objet d'une double correction. Si un écart entre deux lectures est supérieur à deux points, l'essai est soumis à un troisième correcteur.

Les types d'essai

Il existe quatre types d'essai au **TOEFL**. Cet ouvrage, qui fait suite à ***TOEFL/TOEIC Express WRITING - Agree/Disagree*** et ***TOEFL/TOEIC Express WRITING - Stating a Preference***, a pour objet de traiter les **troisième** et **quatrième** types, ***Giving an Explanation*** et ***Making an Argument***.

Giving an explanation

Dans ce type de question, on demande de décrire un objet, un événement, dire si quelquechose est bon ou mauvais. Il faut fournir une explication, établir des critères de jugement et les utiliser dans la démonstration.

Les questions sont du type suivant : *Describe / Explain / What do you consider more important? / What have you learned by doing? / Why do you think something happens? / What are the qualities of? / Choose an event and tell why you enjoyed it / How has (something) changed? / Why is (something) important? / How does (something) affect (something else)? / How is something different (from)?*

Exemples :

- *Many parts of the world are losing important natural resources, such as forests, animals or clean water. Choose one resource that is disappearing and explain why it needs to be saved. Use specific reasons and examples to support your opinion.*
- *People attend college or university for many different reasons. Why do you think people attend college or university? Use specific reasons and examples to support your opinion.*

Making an argument

Les questions sont du type suivant : *if / how / in your opinion / if you could change something, what would you change? / What is the best way to do something? / What should be the main focus? Which of the following should you do? / Which of the following is most important to you? / How would you do sth?*

Exemples :

– *If you could make one important change in the school that you attended, what change would you make? Use reasons and specific examples to support your answer.*
– *When students move to a new school, they sometimes face problems. How can schools help these students with their problems? Use specific reasons and examples to explain your answer.*

L'idée principale de ces types d'essai est d'exprimer un point de vue sur un sujet et d'appuyer la démonstration à l'aide d'arguments et d'exemples. L'argument est appelé *thesis statement.*

Avant de commencer à rassembler des idées, ou même de rédiger, il convient de se poser la question : Qu'est-ce que je veux prouver ? (*What is my point?*). Il est donc nécessaire d'indiquer clairement, dès l'introduction, le parti-pris que l'on a adopté et que l'on entend défendre dans l'essai.

La réfutation d'un argument doit être étayée par un exemple concret et précis. Il ne suffit pas de nier un argument pour avoir raison. Attention : il convient de veiller à faire une phrase entière quand on introduit *for example* ou *for instance. There are many reasons why people attend college. For example, deepening their knowledge* est un exemple de ce qu'il ne faut pas écrire. Toute phrase en anglais doit avoir un verbe conjugué. *There are many reasons why people attend college. For example deepening their knowledge is one of them.*

Une des façons de renforcer la solidité des arguments est d'utiliser le contre argument. Le candidat démontrera ainsi qu'il possède une connaissance intime du sujet, une capacité à anticiper les objections et à réfléchir en profondeur.

■ Les **éléments suivants** à prendre en compte dans la rédaction d'un essai :

- Comprendre la question et la tâche qui est demandée (le *prompt*) ;
- Indiquer clairement sa préférence ;
- Prendre quelques minutes pour chercher des idées que l'on écrira sur un brouillon (*brainstorming*) ;
- Organiser l'essai en paragraphes avec une introduction et une conclusion ; développer les arguments dans le corps de l'essai ;
- Étayer la thèse à l'aide de deux ou trois arguments appuyés par des exemples. La conclusion reprend la thèse principale ;
- Veiller à la cohérence de l'ensemble en reliant les parties entre elles afin que l'argumentation soit fluide ;
- Développer graduellement la thèse ;
- Rédiger dans une syntaxe au-dessus de tout reproche ;
- Utiliser un vocabulaire riche et précis afin de montrer la profondeur de la pensée et la pertinence de la démonstration ;
- Prendre le temps de relire sa copie à l'issue de l'épreuve ; bien vérifier la correction grammaticale, l'orthographe, la ponctuation, l'emploi des majuscules.

Pour ETS, l'organisme qui gère les examens du TOEFL, la qualité est plus importante que la quantité. Néanmoins, un essai long bien rédigé se verra attribuer un score supérieur à un devoir court. Quoi qu'il en soit, si une réponse longue peut garantir un score plus élevé, une réponse courte est sûre de se voir attribuer une note moins élevée.

■ **Le sujet** (*prompt*)

Il indique sur quoi portera l'essai. Il convient de lire le sujet très soigneusement.

Il n'y a qu'un seul choix. Le sujet est rédigé dans un anglais compréhensible pour tous. S'il y a un mot difficile, celui-ci est généralement expliqué.

Les sujets sont d'ordre général et ne requièrent aucune connaissance spécialisée. Il n'y a pas de sujet prêtant à controverse, comme la religion, la toxicomanie, ou la politique. Les sujets portent en général sur :

l'amitié
l'art et la culture
l'avenir
l'éducation
la carrière
la communication
la famille
la langue
la technologie
les affaires
les distractions
(TV, films, livres)
les gens célèbres
les sports et les jeux
les transports
les voyages

La recherche d'idées

La recherche d'idées et d'exemples à propos d'un sujet s'articule autour de plusieurs supports : l'expérience personnelle, la lecture (journaux, magazines), les choses lues et entendues en classe ou à la télévision.

Le plan de l'essai

La première étape est de choisir la thèse ou le point de vue que l'on va adopter. La thèse ou le point de vue constitue l'épine dorsale de l'essai. Il n'y a pas de bonnes ou mauvaises réponses dans le choix du parti pris. Les correcteurs d'ETS n'attachent aucune importance à l'opinion du candidat, quelle qu'elle soit. Pour cette raison, il est sans doute préférable de choisir la thèse ou l'idée qu'il est le plus facile de défendre. Mais une fois un point de vue choisi, il est nécessaire de l'argumenter et de l'illustrer. Se référer à ses notes pour construire l'essai.

Sélectionner quelques arguments et bâtir votre essai en trois parties. En suivant le plan, on pourra ainsi élaborer un essai cohérent, avec un début et une fin.

- *Introduction*
  My opinion is the following... (§ 1)
- *Body of the essay*
  My opinion is justified for reason 1 (§ 2)
  A second reason why I support this opinion is that... (§ 3)
  A third reason that justifies my opinion is that... (§ 4)
- *Conclusion*
  All in all, for those reasons (1, 2, 3) my opinion is that... (§ 5)

L'introduction

Une fois les idées rassemblées, il reste une vingtaine de minutes pour produire une réponse d'environ 300 mots (15 à 20 mots par minute).
L'introduction, qui ne doit pas dépasser deux ou trois lignes, répond à plusieurs fonctions :

- Attirer l'attention du lecteur ;
- Reformuler l'idée du sujet ;
- Présenter le cadre général du sujet ;
- Indiquer les points principaux qui seront traités dans l'essai ;
- Présenter clairement la thèse défendue dans l'essai.

Le corps de l'essai

Le corps de l'essai comporte les paragraphes qui vont aider au développement de la thèse. L'auteur apporte les informations et les exemples à l'appui de sa démonstration pour convaincre le lecteur.

Chaque paragraphe débute par une phrase qui annonce le contenu du paragraphe (la *topic* sentence) et comporte des détails, raisons, exemples, anecdotes tirées de l'expérience personnelle, en rapport avec le sujet traité.

La conclusion de l'essai

Tout comme l'introduction, la conclusion doit être courte et simple. Elle comporte généralement deux ou trois phrases. La conclusion doit résumer les points principaux et clore le débat. Une bonne conclusion doit comporter les points suivants :

- Présenter la thèse si cela n'a pas été fait dans l'introduction ;
- Reformuler la thèse, ou la rappeler ;
- Résumer les points principaux contenus dans l'essai ;
- Mettre en relief la signification des points présentés ;
- Introduire une dernière idée forte justifiant la thèse de l'auteur.

La relecture

Il convient de garder quelques minutes à la fin de l'épreuve pour se relire soigneusement.

- S'assurer que l'on a répondu correctement à la question posée ;
- Supprimer tout argument parasite et qui ne soutiendrait pas la thèse ;
- Vérifier la grammaire, notamment les accords sujet/verbe, l'emploi des pronoms, l'usage du singulier et du pluriel, les solipsismes et barbarismes ;
- Vérifier la ponctuation et l'emploi des majuscules.

Rappel grammatical

- Les mots suivants sont suivis soit d'un **singulier**, soit d'un **pluriel**.

Déterminants suivis d'un **singulier**	Déterminants suivis d'un **pluriel**
a / an	*two / three / four, etc.*
one	*dozens of / hundreds of / thousands of*
a single	*a few (of) / few*
each	*many (of) / plenty of*
every	*a number (of)*
this	*the number of*
that	*a couple (of)*
	several (of)
	every one of
	each of
	one of (the)
	these / those

Exemples :

Each contestant won a prize.
The Metropolitan *is one of the largest museums in the world.*
These flowers are red roses.
He's only played one game this season.

- Les mots suivants ont un **pluriel irrégulier**.

child	*children*
criterion	*criteria*
foot	*feet*
fish	*fish*
man / woman	*men / women*
mouse	*mice*
phenomenon	*phenomena*
series	*series*
sheep	*sheep*

- Les mots suivants sont **indénombrables**. Ils s'emploient avec un verbe au singulier et des quantifieurs indénombrables (*much, little*).

evidence : preuves - *furniture* : meubles - *information* : renseignements - *luggage* : bagages - *news* : nouvelles, infos - *progress* : progrès - *research* : recherches

Expressions utiles

• *Personal experience*

in / according to my experience	d'après mon expérience
some experiences from my own life	des expériences personnelles
to support (that)	montrer (que)
as for me	en ce qui me concerne
I will never forget the time when	Je n'oublierai jamais le moment où
to influence	influencer
to make a difference (in)	faire la différence (dans)
a life-changing experience	un tournant (dans l'existence)
with the benefit of hindsight / in hindsight	avec le recul

• *Rhythm*

to keep pace (with)	suivre, tenir l'allure
to gain / to gather momentum / traction	prendre de la vitesse
to lose momentum / traction	perdre de la vitesse
to keep abreast (of)	être au courant (de)
to be ahead of the curve	avoir une longueur d'avance
to have a headstart (on)	avoir une longueur d'avance (sur)
it is a major shift (in)	c'est un changement majeur (dans)

• *Responsibility*

to assume the responsibility (of)	assumer la responsabilité
to shoulder the responsibility (of)	endosser la responsabilité
to go a long way (towards + ING)	contribuer largement (à)
to be a burden (on)	être un poids (pour)
to put the onus (on)	faire porter le poids (sur)
to be in charge (of)	être responsable (de)
the person in charge	la personne responsable
to be in control (of)	être maître (de)
to exact a toll	faire payer
to trace back (to)	faire remonter (à)
to be overly dependent / reliant (on)	dépendre exagérément (de)
to be subject (to)	être sujet (à)
to be a panacea (for)	être une panacée (pour)
to fall prey (to)	devenir la proie (de)
to be the hallmark (of)	être la marque de fabrique (de)

- ***Cause***

to contribute to (sth)	contribuer à (qch)
to be a contributing factor (to)	être un facteur supplémentaire (à)
to be ascribed / attributed (to)	être mis sur le compte (de)
to be the main driving force (behind)	jouer un rôle moteur (dans)
to be in line (with)	être dans le droit fil (de)
to bring about / to generate / to entail	provoquer, entraîner
to impel / to prompt sb to	pousser qn à

- ***Opportunity***

to open up opportunities	offrir des occasions
to open up new worlds (on)	ouvrir de nouvelles perspectives (sur)
to expand one's outlook / vision / scope	élargir son point de vue
to broaden one's horizon	élargir son horizon
to rise to the occasion	se montrer à la hauteur
to be a far cry (from)	ne rien à voir (avec)
to live up to sb's expectations	être à la hauteur des attentes de qn
to lower one's expectations	réviser ses ambitions à la baisse
beyond expectation	au-delà des attentes
to remove the barrier (for)	supprimer la barrière (à / de)

- ***Progress***

to promote the development (of)	promouvoir le développement (de)
to give / to have a competitive edge	donner / avoir l'avantage
to be ahead of the curve	avoir une longueur d'avance
to explore every avenue (toward)	explorer tous les moyens (pour)
to boost efficiency / productivity	encourager l'efficacité / la productivité
to be a good vehicle (for)	être un bon moyen (de / pour)
to pave the way (for / to)	ouvrir la voie (à)

- ***Awareness***

awareness / understanding / realization	la prise de conscience
to raise / to heighten people's awareness	sensibiliser les gens
to encourage / to foster awareness	encourager la prise de conscience
to awaken the conscience (of)	éveiller la conscience (de)

- ***Trouble***

to be at risk	être en danger
at the expense of	au détriment de

to spin out of control	se dérégler
to cause grave concerns	être l'objet de graves préoccupations
a growing concern	une préoccupation croissante
an overriding concern	un souci majeur
to go from bad to worse	s'aggraver
to be poorly, ill-informed (about)	être mal informé (au sujet de)
to be uninformed (about)	ne pas être informé (de)
to be confronted with	faire face (à)
to spell trouble (for)	entraîner des problèmes (pour)
to spell disaster (for)	annnoncer la catastrophe (pour)

- ***Worth***

to be worth (+ ING)	valoir la peine de
to be worthwhile (to)	valoir la peine (de)
to be at stake	être en jeu
a litmus test	une mise à l'épreuve
an acid test	une épreuve de vérité

- ***Opposition***

to be at odds (with)	être en contradiction (avec)
to run contrary to	aller à l'encontre de
far from being	loin d'être
to frown on / upon	mal voir

- ***Doubt***

there's no guarantee that	il n'y a aucune garantie que
concerns have arisen (about)	des inquiétudes sont apparues (sur)
it is not entirely unfounded	ce n'est pas dénué de tout fondement
in all likelihood	selon toute vraisemblance
to take for granted	tenir pour acquis
to take at face value	prendre pour argent comptant, prendre au premier degré, prendre au pied de la lettre

- ***Whole and part***

to be part and parcel (of)	être partie intégrante (de)
a variety / a wide range / an array of	un ensemble de
to be an alternative (to)	être une alternative (à)
in accordance (with)	être en accord (avec)

to be the cornerstone (of)	être la pierre angulaire (de)
on the basis of	sur la base de
it is no exception	et ce n'est pas une exception

- ***Exaggeration***

it is no exaggeration to say that	il n'est pas exagéré de dire que
it is hard to overstate the significance (of)	il est difficile de surestimer l'importance (de)
it is beyond man's wildest expectations	cela dépasse toutes les espérances
the bottom line is	tout cela pour dire que

- ***Miscellaneous***

to stand sb in good stead	être d'un grand secours pour qn, rendre un grand service à qn
to give priority (to)	donner la priorité (à)
to unravel the mystery	faire la lumière
to satisfy / to meet the needs (of)	satisfaire les besoins (de)
to get into the swing of things	entrer dans la danse
to be a lifelong process	qui dure toute la vie
to sharpen sb's intellect	aiguiser / affûter l'esprit de qn
to catch a glimpse (of)	avoir un aperçu (de)
to take sanctuary (in)	se réfugier (dans)
to be in short supply	être difficile à obtenir / à trouver
to be bent upon	être déterminé à
to condemn rather than condone	condamner plutôt que tolérer
it is wrong to equate... with...	il est faux de faire un parallèle entre... et...

Abréviations utilisées

-ING : forme verbale du verbe
a : adjectif
adv : adverbe
INF : infinitif
inv : invariable
nd : nom dénombrable
ni : nom indénombrable
pl : pluriel
prov. : proverb
qch : quelque chose
qn : quelqu'un
sb : somebody
sg : singulier
sth : something
UK : anglais britannique
US : anglais américain

TABLE OF CONTENTS

I - Giving an explanation

II - Making an argument

I. Giving an explanation

01 HAS THE EASE OF COOKING IMPROVED LIFE?

Nowadays, food has become easier to prepare. Has this change improved the way people live? Use specific reasons and examples to support your answer.

1. Key words

food habits	les habitudes alimentaires
food science	la diététique
to be health conscious	faire attention à sa santé
to prepare a meal	préparer un repas
to prepare lunch / dinner	préparer le déjeuner / le dîner
to whip up / to rustle up a meal	préparer un repas en vitesse
canned food / preserves / to can	les conserves / mettre en conserves
a meal / lunch tray	un plateau-repas
to cook a meal	faire cuire un repas
to bake / to roast	faire cuire (au four) / rôtir
the cooking time	le temps de cuisson
food preservation	la conservation de la nourriture
foodstuffs / ingredients	les denrées alimentaires / les ingrédients
(pre)processed food	la nourriture industrielle
organic food / junk food	la nourriture bio / la malbouffe
to deep-freeze / deep frozen food	surgeler / les aliments surgelés
fresh produce / vacuum packaging	des produits frais / l'emballage sous vide
to process food	traiter / transformer la nourriture
preservatives	des agents de conservation
to introduce additives	injecter des colorants
artificial flavorings	des parfums / assaisonnements artificiels
a food processor	un robot ménager
time-saving	qui fait gagner du temps
a micro-wave oven	un four à micro-ondes
a pressure cooker	une cocotte minute
to freeze-dry / to decay, to rot	lyophiliser / se gâter, pourrir
a deep freeze / a cold room	un congélateur / une chambre froide
ready made food	les plats tout préparés
a meal ready to go	un repas tout préparé
a ready / ready to serve meal	un plat cuisiné
to be the worse off (for sth)	perdre au change

2. Talking points

1. The ease of cooking has improved life.

- The development of food devices, kitchen appliances and the progress of technology have led to many useful inventions, among which the refrigerator, the microwave oven, and the deep-freeze.
- Food has become easier to preserve and store thanks to the deep freeze, the refrigerator or processes such as freeze-drying, vacuum packaging or canning.
- Food conditioning (pre-packaged or pre-processed) has made it possible to instant-cook.
- For the housewife, modern kitchen appliances mean less time spent in the kitchen preparing meals. As a consequence, more time has been freed for other activities, including sports, entertainment, work, etc. Women are no longer tied to the sink.
- Access to some foodstuff, such as strawberries in winter or grapes in the spring, fresh vegetables all year round—once the preserve of the elite—has been made easier and cheaper.

2. The ease of cooking has worsened life.

- The development of homogenized and pre-processed food means a loss of culinary habits and therefore of tradition. Cooking is an art that is dying out / on the way out.
- Food quality has gone down: prepackaging and pre-processing means a loss of freshness, of natural vitamin content and antioxidants and an increase in preservatives and artificial flavorings.
- The development of standardized, homogenized, bland dishes sold has become common practice by caterers or food processing companies.
- Children now resort to snacking and gorging on unhealthy or junk food such as pizzas and French fries. Less quality food means more health problems, especially obesity for children.
- Less time at the family table means less conviviality and less quality time between parents and children.
- Man caught in the rat race can no longer afford to waste time eating. Man has lost his taste for good food in the race against the clock. Food is no longer considered as enjoyable. It is no longer seen as an art as well.

3. Possible answers

1. The ease of cooking has improved life.

Progress, and in particular the progress of technology, has spread to every aspect of our life. One area is the kitchen. Actually, food has become much easier to prepare than it used to be. Our lives have therefore been changed for the better.

Gone are the days when the mother would spend hours in the kitchen preparing elaborate dishes following old-fashioned recipes. The ingredients then were fresh cabbages, zucchini and other veggies from the kitchen garden, apples gathered in the orchard, potatoes harvested in the field nearby, strawberries or blackcurrants handpicked to eat for dessert or to can for the winter. The meat would be carved out from slaughtered animals, the game came from a recent hunt. The food was then locally produced and locally consumed.

The progress of technology has allowed food to be prepared more quickly. As well, it has prevented part of it from being wasted. On the one hand, the electric or gas cooker means we do not have to wait for hours before reaching the right baking temperature. On the other hand, thanks to the refrigerator and the deep freeze, we can actually preserve the food in perfect condition and for long periods of time. We now eat in winter what has been harvested in the summer.

Preservation methods have changed too. Today, prepackaged food is being sold in supermarkets and other specialized shops. The food is kept deep-frozen in cold rooms for months on end before distribution to the consumers.

Such changes in food preparation have brought considerable benefits. Preparing food is cost- and time efficient. People now spend far less time in the kitchen to prepare the evening meal or lunch. Foodstuffs are also cheaper owing to the development of transportation modes. Above all, the way food is prepared has enabled people to spend less time eating and more time for other pursuits, be it leisure activities, playing sports or pursuing hobbies. In the same way, such food preparation has made it easy for the housewife to rustle up a meal when her kids invite their friends around. She just has to defrost the pizza and heat it up in the oven. Dinner is ready in a matter of minutes, thus sating the appetite of hungry teenagers.

What is more, food is now available the year round and no longer dependent on local seasons. Food has gone global. We now consume strawberries in winter, grapefruit in the spring, and fresh vegetables all year round. Some exotic produces that were out of the reach of the average man are now available in the shop next door. In a word, such luxuries are no longer the realm of the well-off but can be enjoyed by a large part of the population. So, all in all, because cooking has become much easier, our diet has improved as well but also the way we live and consume.

2. The ease of cooking has worsened life.

From the hunter-gatherer's days to the high tech entrepreneur's, man's lifestyle has changed altogether and so have his eating and cooking habits. If, on the one hand, food preparation has changed woman's life, on the other, in the frantic world which man lives and works in, cooking has taken a backseat to other concerns, such as getting an education, making money, starting a company, finding a job or edging competitors out of the market. The changes in food habits have meshed with some of the concepts that define today's world: faster, simpler, and more efficient.

Global standardization and food pre-processing have led to a loss of care and tradition in the art of cooking. We no longer take time to prepare food according to yesteryear recipes. Caught in the rat race man can no longer afford to waste time eating. In the race against the clock, man has lost his taste for genuine food. The hurried parents that come home in the evening cannot afford to spend another two hours poring over cookbooks and coming up with the original and varied meal that is so necessary to a balanced health. Culinary art is dying.

The quality of the food that is prepared in haste or sold has gone down as well. What matters is to fill our stomachs, whatever the ingredients. Prepackaging and pre-processing means a loss of freshness, a decline in natural vitamin content and antioxidants and an increase in preservatives and artificial flavorings so that the food can remain on the shelves as long as possible. To that end, food-processing companies have dumbed down quality. Food has lost its freshness, its originality and become homogenized, artificial and bland through the introduction of additives to preserve flavor or enhance taste and appearance.

The loss of quality and freshness has made life worse for kids. First, unable to make a difference between good and bad food, children resort to junk food with the attendant consequences on health. No wonder obesity has been a growing problem in the rich countries. Second, kids have lost track of what fresh and healthy fruits or vegetables taste like. We buy our food in bulk from the supermarket and not from the local market because it is cheaper and we are obsessed with conserving it as long as possible.

Eating all-ready meals means that families no longer spend lunch or dinner together. Children for example retire to their rooms and snack in front of the video game console or other electronic devices, chatting on FB and paying no attention to what they eat. Food is no longer considered as an opportunity to get together and enjoy life. The culinary traditions have gradually frittered away as cuisine is no longer considered as an art but as a basic necessity. We eat to live, we no longer live to eat. Gone are the days when we looked forward to a hearty meal at Grandma's house with the whole family gathered together. Food is no longer considered as enjoyable. It is no longer considered as an art either.

02 WHY ARE MOVIES POPULAR?

Movies are popular all over the world. Explain why movies are so popular. Use reasons and specific examples to support your answer.

1. Key words

a form / a source of entertainment	une forme / une source de distraction
the cinema / the audience	le cinéma (genre) / le public
American / Italian cinema	le cinéma américain / italien
to watch a movie	regarder un film
the motion / film industry	l'industrie cinématographique
a movie theater / a movie house	un cinéma
a motion picture / a blockbuster	un film / un film à grand spectacle
a box office hit / a feature film	un film à succès / un long métrage
a hit / a flop / a remake	un succès / un navet / un remake
a thriller / a romance / a horror film	un film à suspense / d'amour / d'horreur
a musical / an animated cartoon	une comédie musicale / un dessin animé
an action-packed film	un film d'action
a actor / an actress / to portray	un acteur / une actrice / jouer le rôle (de)
stardom / the star system	le vedettariat, la célébrité
a moviegoer / a film buff / a film fan	un cinéphile
to release a movie / a release	sortir un film / une sortie
to be on / to show / a screenplay	être à l'affiche / un scénario
a moviemaker / a film director	un réalisateur / un metteur en scène
to shoot / shooting / a shoot	tourner / le tournage / un tournage
a shot / a take	une prise de vue, un plan
to perform (in) / to star (in)	jouer / briller (dans)
to bring excitement (into)	apporter de l'excitation (à)
to express one's emotions	exprimer ses émotions
to suspend disbelief	accepter l'invraisemblable
to escape (into) / to get away (from)	s'évader (à / dans) / de
escapism	l'évasion
glamour / glamorous	le prestige, le charme / chic, de star
a role model	un modèle à imiter
to inspire / inspirational	inspirer / qui inspire
a break from the humdrum life	une rupture avec le train-train
to take people's minds off	distraire les gens

2. Talking points

1. Essay 1

- The cinema is a cheap form of entertainment. It is a pastime affordable to all. The cinema is also a convenient form of entertainment: indeed, movies are easily accessible to all and there are theaters in every district. The ubiquitous presence of movie theaters all over town makes it easy to attend a movie. So do the special rates that some categories of people enjoy.
- The cinema is an easy way of reducing stress (when compared to other forms of entertainment). The exciting appeal of the image over text makes it easy to relax after a long day at the office or when you are traveling, by airplane, for example.
- The cinema is a communal experience: it is a form of socialization. You watch movies with friends and family. A movie fosters conversation and encourages dialogue. Films tell us that we're not alone: by the collective reaction in the audience we realize that we are not the only ones wrestling with life's secrets and meaning.
- Movies cater to everyone's needs and desires. The universal appeal of movies lies in the fact that we will always find a movie that corresponds to our tastes, passion or interests.
- Driven by clever advertising campaigns and teasers, such as trailers, movies are also the talk of the town and give the impression that people should not miss out on watching them.

2. Essay 2

- The cinema is a form of escapism. Hollywood is nicknamed the Dream Factory: it conjures up glamorous actresses, handsome actors, and gives us a glimpse of a world out of our reach.
- The cinema helps to relieve the pressure of everyday life. Thanks to movies, we can escape into different worlds and dimensions: we experience romance by watching romantic comedies, we express our inner fears by watching scary movies, we release our energy by attending action movies.
- The cinema is a source of knowledge of our country but also of foreign countries (history, civilization, culture, language). War movies re-enact a nation's moments of glory (*Gettysburg*) or shame (*All the President's Men*) whereas biopics shed light on the complexity of man's character or explain a period of history. Films are educational tools for the student as well as pedagogical aid for the teacher.
- A movie is part of man's journey through life, a way of identifying oneself, of being or becoming who we are.

3. Possible answers

1. Essay 1

Like many people, I have watched a good number of movies across a wide range of genres: horror movies, dramas, westerns, action films, war movies, comedies, and blockbusters. I have seen films from the early days of Hollywood when film was black and white to the modern day era cinema high tech 3D images and high paid performers. Why some movies are more popular than others is a matter of personal taste, yet there are many reasons why the cinema is so popular today.

First and foremost, films are a cheap form of entertainment. Whereas going to the opera or the theater may cost a pretty penny, not to mention the fact that we need to book a long time in advance, going to a movie is easy and inexpensive. In addition, there are movie theaters all over town and even in shopping malls, accessible to all. Going to the movies is therefore one of the most common pastimes. It is an affordable and enjoyable way of spending a couple of hours. Special rates for students or senior citizens, or cheaper matinee prices are an added incentive for people to go, all the more so as there are new releases every week.

Watching a movie reduces stress and does not demand much effort, especially if we compare it with other forms of entertainment, like reading or playing a musical instrument. Watching a movie is relaxing: it only requires that you sit and let yourself be carried away by the images, lulled by the music and entertained by the plot. Watching a movie is a passive way of entertainment; as such it appeals to many people because they can kick back after a long day at the office or during a long journey. Airline companies offer a wide range of recent movies precisely to that effect: keep the passengers happy and quiet during long flights.

The cinema is also a unique form of socialization. When you go to a movie, you usually go with friends or family: you share the same emotions, debate with one another and sometimes even argue. Not only is it a way of getting together, it also means sharing a communal experience that is likely to strengthen the bonds of friendship. Watching a movie is an invitation to dialogue and a venue for congeniality.

The success of the film industry owes much to the diversity of the movies it produces. Films cater to everyone's needs and desires, be it the thriller, the romance, the western or the science fiction movie: they satisfy our tastes. The war movie lover will be attracted to the genre because he is a patriot, he is fond of historical facts, or he is interested in the planning of military campaigns. Besides, thanks to well-orchestrated advertising campaigns, it is almost impossible to miss a movie for the simple reason that it is the talk of the town, of the classroom or the dinner party. Like it or not, some movies have the uncanny ability to arouse passions and stir debates.

2. Essay 2

From Hollywood to Bollywood, no country has escaped the grip of the movie industry. Whatever country we visit, the cinema occupies a major part of the local entertainment and contributes to the local industry. Actually, it looks like man's thirst for pictures can never be sated, begging the question: why are movies so popular?

First, films represent a form of escapism. Isn't Hollywood nicknamed the Dream Factory? One of the basic reasons why people go to the movies is to touch with their eyes the glamorous actresses, the handsome action heroes, set foot in a world that is out of their reach yet that the cinema exposes for a fleeting moment, holding the captive audience in thrall. Movies are seen as alternative worlds that we can only dream of.

Through films, people can escape their humdrum lives, relieve the pressure of work, flee to or take shelter in a dream world. They can take their minds off their problems. If they don't have romance in their own lives, a romantic movie will help them escape into a happy-ever-after world that they have always imagined. Scary movies are popular because they give people a surge of adrenaline or energy. The implication of the theory of course, is that fear is an emotion that needs an outlet. Excitement and thrill are the main reasons why moviegoers adore action films. Beyond, they introduce us to iconic heroes that we can glorify, such as Stallone and Jackie Chan. People root for Rambo when he clobbers the enemy communists and they applaud Jackie Chan's martial art skills for showing justice upon a group of mobsters. Both actors embody the victory of good over evil and thus make people feel good about themselves.

People go to movies because they find in them a source of inspiration and knowledge. Many movies indeed re-create periods of history, re-enact episodes of the war, expose scandals. *Gettysburg* recounts the horrors of a key battle of the American Civil War. Spielberg's *Amistad* brings to light the tragic plight of slaves whose fate was as much dependent on the will of nations as the rigors of American law. *Guess Who's Coming to Dinner* highlights discrimination and segregation. Biopics—*Malcolm X, Nixon, W., Patton, Lincoln*—shed light on the lives of great men. Some moviemakers also use the genre as a way of explaining history. Oliver Stone's *JFK* is a case in point. In that respect, films are educative tools, whether they conform to history or not.

Movies are also part of a man's journey through life, not just screen versions of his existence. Like music, they depict the true emotions of actors and actresses whom a person can look up to and identify with; movies help us connect the dots in our life, filling the gaps of inexperience, plumbing the holes of knowledge, be it intellectual or emotional and making us part of a whole. The cinema is like a modern, secular cathedral. As humans, we enter that darkened theatre seeking to expand our emotional bandwidth, seeking sensations we hardly ever experience in our everyday lives. Films are also a way of reminding us of what man is capable of in terms of both good and evil.

03 GROUPS AND ORGANIZATIONS

Groups or organizations are an important part of some people's lives. Why are groups or organizations important to people? Use specific reasons and examples to explain your answer.

1. Key words

a team / a team sport	une équipe / un sport d'équipe
a student association / club	une assocation étudiante
student government	le bureau des élèves
a trade union (UK) / labor union (US)	un syndicat
a trade association	une association professionnelle
a lobby / a pressure group	un lobby / un groupe de pression
a political party	un parti politique
a choir / an orchestra, a band	un chœur / un orchestre
a prayer group / a church	un groupe de prière / une église
a religious creed / faith	une croyance religieuse
a community / a village	une communauté / un village
a classroom	une salle de classe, une classe
a class / class of 42	une promotion / la promotion 1942
a youth movement	un mouvement de jeunes
the boy scouts / cub scouts	les boy scouts / les louveteaux
a gang / to join a gang	un gang / s'enrôler dans un gang
a clique / a herd	une bande / un troupeau
a bunch of drinking buddies	des compagnons de boisson
a social network	un réseau social
to join / to become a member	devenir membre
membership / to adhere (to)	l'adhésion / adhérer (à)
to integrate / integration	intégrer / l'intégration
tight-knit / united together	uni / solidaire
to socialize / socialization	se socialiser / la socialisation
to ostracize / ostracism	ostraciser / l'ostracisme
to be accepted / rejected (by)	être accepté / rejeté (par)
to compete with / competition	faire concurrence à / la concurrence
to share mutual interests	partager des intérêts communs
to support / support	soutenir / le soutien
to comfort / comfort	consoler / le réconfort

2. Talking points

1. Essay 1

- Man is a social animal. Regrouping is necessary for survival (see our ancestors in prehistoric times or the Indian tribes on other continents); there is strength in numbers. Evolution has taught us that it is beneficial to live in tribes, where we can share out the work of daily survival.
- The basic unit is that of the family, it is the first group known by a child and the one that will endure throughout the ages.
- The need to find support and comfort leads people to join a church, attend mass, take communion.
- The need for socialization (school, college, the firm, leisure) is another reason why people join a church, a prayer group, a club, a union or a music band.
- The need to find support from others is a reason why people join sport teams and why fans follow sporting idols from one game to another.

2. Essay 2

- The need to promote ideas, defend convictions, or advocate change is a reason why men join forces.
- Fear of isolation has prompted man to find solace in groups, be it going out to the cinema, going out for a beer or playing cards or bingo.
- Fear of ostracism—informal exclusion from a group through social rejection—as well as the fear of being singled out by others is a reason why people join organizations. Unemployment, homelessness and poverty are examples that have led men to be ostracized, thus losing their sense of identity and self-worth.
- Modern technology has reinforced people's feelings of belonging. They count their friends on Facebook, link in through professional networks, express their likes and dislikes and have the impression they are part of a large community.
- Belonging to a group provides a sense of identity (national identity, cultural identity, social identity, group identity)
- Belonging to a group or a clique offers people a sense of personal achievement and prove that they have managed to gain acceptance.

3. Possible answers

1. Essay 1

History has shown that seldom has man been able to live alone, nor has he ever expressed the desire to survive on his own. Robinson Crusoe, a castaway who spends 28 years on a remote tropical island near Trinidad, encountering cannibals, captives, and mutineers before being finally rescued, is one of those rare exceptions forced to live on his own. Another example is the hermit who chooses to remove himself from society. Both those extreme cases point to one direction: man is by nature a sociable animal. As Aristotle said, "an individual who is unsocial naturally and not accidentally is either beneath our notice or more than human. Society is something that precedes the individual. Anyone who either cannot lead the common life or is so self-sufficient as not to need to, and therefore does not partake of society, is either a beast or a god."

From time immemorial, man has always sought to regroup and live in a society. Be it the cavemen or the tribes, there has always been strength in numbers. Regrouping is necessary for survival, to defend oneself against the enemy and protect one's territory.

Family is obviously the pivotal and basic unit for a child. Nowhere else will you ever find the physical and emotional support from a group than the one you find in your family. Your family, extended or not, is part of you, and you are part of this tight-knit group. They will always be there for you inasmuch as 'blood is thicker than water'.

A group provides comfort and solace in times of trouble or stress. This is the case for religious organizations or churches, for example. When we are with people who partake of the same creed, we feel uplifted. We share the same prayer, we take communion together, we meet people from the same ilk at church. Our beliefs are based on tradition. These beliefs have been passed on from one generation to another. They have been tested over time. These beliefs tell us how to respond and how to act.

Support is also one major reason why people prefer group activities rather than standing alone. For example, in sport, being a team player is part of the game, part of the victory but also part of the defeat. When the team is off for an away game, fans will travel along, and on the day of the game root for their favorite players. Because he finds support in a group, man feels stronger.

Socialization is also one of the basic reasons why man craves to belong. Be it in his early age or his elderly years, man's need to belong can be seen all his life. At school, 12-year-old Johnnie will join a clique, associate with others and share activities. At college, he will join a student union, run for student government, be elected on the student board. He will also choose to sign up for student associations where he will find like-minded people with the same affinities. The need to be part of a group is therefore one of man's traits all his life long. Only in death will he pursue the journey alone.

2. Essay 2

The desire to be part of a group is deeply ingrained in man. Man cannot be a society unto himself. He's a cog in the vast social machine he contributes to as an individual.

The need to promote ideas has led man to enroll in clubs, join unions or political parties. When he is part of a political campaign, he will go out and hand out flyers, stick bills, man the phones, canvas door to door. He will find in those activities a common bond with people who think alike, share opinions and convictions he will fight for down to the wire. Once the campaign is over, he may even join the new government.

There are also negative reasons why people prefer being in a group. Fear of isolation is one. Too often, we read stories of people who have been left behind, by progress, forced retirement, idleness and therefore who have gradually dropped out of life. This is the case for the elderly, or senior citizens who are no longer visited by their families or who are too handicapped or too frail to venture outside. They join clubs to keep busy and find there the missing social link they crave for.

In the same way, the desire to belong can also be driven by the fear of being voluntarily left out. Ostracism, a procedure under the Athenian democracy in which any citizen could be expelled from the city-state of Athens for ten years, is still very present. Joblessness and deprivation are forms of exclusion in modern society. If we lose our job, it is not just the loss of income (affecting our sense of control) that hurts us, but also the loss of collegiality within a company with which we have identified ourselves. In such a situation, man loses his identity, his self-worth. He becomes invisible.

Modern technology has strengthened the sense of belonging. Social media have helped man build up new networks. They have friends (the more the merrier), they link in on the web, they post pictures and profiles to show and be seen, they boast of their experiences, skills and competencies. The time spent on those virtual sites gives man the illusion, however flinty it may be, that he is part of a large community and that his voice is heard across the city, the country or the world.

Thus, by being part of a group—the army's band of brothers, the drinking buddies—man recovers a sense of identity. We categorize ourselves in terms of other people and groups. When asked about yourself, you may well describe yourself in terms of your work and family relationships: 'I work for X Corporation.' or 'I am married to Steve and have three children'. Colors can identify your gang ties, blue for the Cripps, red for the Bloods; uniforms give you a sense of identity too, be it at school or in the Armed Forces. The sense of identity dovetails with the sense of achievement. It means that man has, at long last, been accepted into a group. His achievement at having breached the somewhat robust barriers of a group is, in that regard, one of the ways for him to move from the status of nobody to that of somebody.

04 WHY DO PEOPLE LISTEN TO MUSIC?

People listen to music for different reasons and at different times. Why is music important to many people? Use specific reasons and examples to support your choice.

1. Key words

to listen to music	écouter de la musique
classical / polyphonic music	la musique classique / polyphonique
pop music	la variété
rhythm / beat / tempo	le rythme / le tempo
the tone color / timbre	le timbre
sweet / mellifluous / harsh music	la musique douce / mélodieuse / dure
to play music / a musician	jouer de la musique / un musicien
to have musical ability	avoir un talent musical
to go to a concert	aller au concert
to attend a concert	assister à un concert
a concert-goer	un amateur de concert
to play in a band	jouer dans un orchestre
a symphony orchestra	un orchestre symphonique
a conductor	un chef d'orchestre
to sing in a church choir	chanter dans un chœur d'église
to compose / a composer	composer / un compositeur
(to share) musical tastes	(partager) des goûts musicaux
a communal experience	une expérience en commun
an expression of emotion	l'expression d'une émotion
the emotional power (of music)	le pouvoir émotionnel (de la musique)
to channel emotions	canaliser les émotions
to feel connected	se sentir associé
to practice an instrument	jouer d'un instrument
a piano sonata / a symphony	une sonate de piano / une symphonie
a trio / a quartet	un trio / un quartet
an opera / an oratorio	un opéra / un oratorio
an online music service	un service de musique en ligne
a music blog	un blog musical
to burn a CD	enregistrer / ripper un CD
music file swapping	l'échange de fichiers musicaux
to download a music file	télécharger un fichier musical

2. Talking points

1. Essay 1

- Listening to music makes people feel good about themselves and the world. Music can relieve man's sadness; it helps him to feel that he is not alone; on the other hand, music played in malls and supermarkets conveys the message that it is all right for the consumers to buy and indulge.
- Music is universal. People just can't do without music. We play music at all occasions: weddings, funerals, national holidays, the Olympic Games when medals are awarded, religious services, for example.
- Music channels or expresses man's emotions in ways no other medium can do. Music can manipulate, affect, induce emotions and stir sentiments. It can bring to depths of despair or lead to exaltation.
- Music soothes the soul and helps man to relax. Music takes man away from this world and transports him into a different one where he can imagine the impossible.

2. Essay 2

- Thanks to the communal nature of music, it is an experience enjoyed collectively. It defines the community we want to belong to and the friendships that we develop.
- Music as a cultural indicator helps connect man to place and time. It is no coincidence if musical tastes seem to cluster geographically and historically. Music helps man feel connected to one another. It is a form of identification with time and place beyond being a mere component of a local culture.
- Music, is a messenger or sometimes a harbinger of peace. Miguel Angel Estrella, an Argentine pianist and ambassador to UNESCO, founded *Musique Esperance*, a group that promotes peace and justice through music. He has formed Orchestra for Peace, made of young Israeli and Arab musicians from Israel, Morocco, Tunisia, Egypt, Jordan, Iraq, Syria and Palestine. He states, "If we are able to create a new humanism, we will be more credible to our children and the youth of today".
- Music can be blamed for violent but also good behavior. Parents believe the music kids listen to changes their perspective about life. They blame rap music for drugs, murders and sex and rock for melancholy, evil thoughts mixed with hate. Rappers are blamed constantly for crimes across America. Yet, kids involved in playing music enjoy a more harmonious development than those who are not. It is an amazing outlet for personal identity building and self-expression.

3. Possible answers

1. Essay 1

Music does not belong to one country, one culture, or one people. Music is universal and timeless. From the origin of the world to this day, man has played and listened to music. There are several reasons for that.

The primary reason we all listen to music is that it makes us feel good. For example, when someone is sad, they choose to listen to soft and soothing tunes that may reflect their mood and help them to feel better. They enjoy the flow and creativity of the sounds. Similarly, one of the reasons why they play music in shopping malls or shops is to help people feel good about themselves and encourage them to buy. Sweet and mellifluous music is relaxing; it eases the shoppers' worried minds or guilty conscience at spending, and thus has a positive impact on business.

Pondering whether there exists a universal language, most people would answer negatively. The Babel of tongues and the wide range of vernaculars, are proof enough that there is not one single universal language. Except if we take into account the language of music. Indeed, it is a human and universal language that has existed since times immemorial. Whatever the circumstances, music is pre-ordained and played: be it on national holidays, in the car while traveling, on a plane before taking off, in the elevator whisking you up to the 102nd floor, in church or on national holidays, it is the single common denominator to man's activity. We play music at funerals, but we also play it at weddings. Oratorios or Masses are sung at Christmas, while lighter music is performed at the Proms in June. A world without music is actually hard to conceive.

"If music is the food of love, play on". Shakespeare had it right. Most people listen to music to channel or express emotions like no other media can. Indeed, music is first and foremost a token of and an outlet for the love or the despair one may feel inside, but that we are incapable of translating into words. Listening to a Beethoven quartet, a Schubert piano sonata or a Wagner opera inspires higher thoughts or exalted emotions. Music thus is a universal translator of feelings, be it sadness, grief, happiness, similar to the feelings experienced by the composers who wrote the pieces. Music is in many ways the soundtrack of our lives: playing or listening to music can bring back memories and feelings that are long gone.

Music is soothing to man. It is like a balm and ointment for the troubled soul. In that respect, it is far more valuable than any medicine or drugs that doctors may prescribe over the counter. After a hard day's work, people relax by listening to music. It takes their mind off things and helps them unwind away from the frantic work pace at the office. At the same time, music transports you to dreamland where you can imagine what could be and not what is.

2. Essay 2

Music, halfway through sound and silence, is a universal medium. Even though the creation, performance, significance, and even the definition of music vary according to culture and social context, man has always composed, played and listened to it. There are several reasons for that.

Music is something that we share with others. One of the most profound features of music as an art form is its inherently communal nature. In many cases we rely on others to create music (be it the performer or the composer) and as a result it helps build community. We also tend to listen to music collectively. While recording technology has changed this to a certain extent, concert going is still a communal activity. And so, music helps define who our friends are—those with whom we have a connection and those with whom we do not.

As an art form that exists as part of a historical trajectory, music connects people to both past and future. Rock n' roll is typical of the 1950s and 1960s while electronic music belongs to the 21st century. Music is also what differentiates one culture from another, one country from another. It also connects us to place. It is the symbol of a region or a generation. The result can be a form of musical nationalism or identity. Bruckner and Mozart are Austria, Beethoven and Wagner are Germany, Rameau and Debussy are France. In Ireland, in Mali or in Thailand, music and songs help perpetuate traditions. Finally, music glues a country or a generation together. People raised on Elvis Presley rhythm and blues think and act different from people who have been fed a teenage regimen of Tokio Hotel pop, Celine Dion mushy singing or Snoop Dogg rap.

Music can be a universal messenger for and a harbinger of peace. It has played a crucial role in bridging or mending relations between countries. Orchestras and artists have performed in the name of peace and reconciliation. As Shakespeare wrote in *The Merchant of Venice* "The man that hath no music in himself, / Nor is not mov'd with concord of sweet sounds, / Is fit for treasons, stratagems, and spoils." An orchestra can be a model for cooperation among people and promote tolerance.

Music is sometimes blamed for aggressiveness. Contrarian lyrics, coupled with a harsh tempo may play a negative role in people's attitudes. Yet, teens that are involved in music—those who play on the school band, for example—have a lower risk of getting into trouble. For teens, music is an outlet for personal identity development. It helps them manage their moods and provides ways to connect with peers.

"Music to our ears" is an expression that every event in our lives has validated. Whatever our emotions, there is music to match. Unique in its form and content, it has nevertheless gathered people together and been there, not only as a prop to our lives but an outlet for man's thirst for creativity and self-expression. It is man's bread and water, his flesh and blood, his mortise and tenon, his heart and soul.

05 WHY DO PEOPLE VISIT MUSEUMS?

Many people visit museums when they travel to new places. Why do you think people visit museums? Use specific reasons and examples to support your answer.

1. Key words

to visit / to attend a museum	fréquenter un musée
a museum visitor / museum-goer	un habitué des musées
a museum visit / trip	une visite de musée
an art lover	un amoureux de l'art
to wander around a museum	se promener dans un musée
appreciation for the arts	la compréhension artistique
a fine arts museum	un musée des beaux-arts
a science / history museum	un musée des sciences / d'histoire
a natural history museum	un musée d'histoire naturelle
an archeology museum	un musée archéologique
an art gallery	une galerie d'art
a must-see place	un endroit à ne pas manquer
a permanent collection	une collection permanente
an (art) exhibition / a show	une exposition (artistique)
a temporary / interactive exhibit	une exposition temporaire / interactive
a display case	une vitrine
memorabilia	des souvenirs
cultural resources	des ressources culturelles
a repository of knowledge	un trésor de connaissances
a work of art / an artwork	une œuvre d'art
a painting / a painter	un tableau / un peintre
a watercolor (artist)	une aquarelle (un aquarelliste)
sculpture / a sculpture / a sculptor	la sculpture / une sculpture / un sculpteur
a photographer / a photograph	un photographe / une photo
to house / to donate a collection	abriter / faire don d'une collection
to build up a collection	monter une collection
a curator	un conservateur de musée
patronage / a patron (of the arts)	le mécénat / un mécène
a masterpiece	une toile de maître, un chef-d'œuvre
a guided tour / an audio guide	une visite guidée / un guide audio
attendance figures	les chiffres de fréquentation

2. Talking points

1. Essay 1

- A museum is a repository of history and forms a bridge between past and present. It preserves and displays a country's artistic, social, scientific or political heritage; a museum is a trove of knowledge; a place where we learn about a country's history (past and present) and culture from the inside.
- Visiting a museum is like traveling into the past. Artifacts are arranged chronologically and help you navigate in a country's past.
- Museums fulfill an educational mission. One of the primary roles of museums is to engage and educate the community. They provide an opportunity for visitors, especially the young, to understand how a nation was built.
- Museums promote feelings of national unity and identity. For example, the Beijing Custom Museum shows the real life, the traditions and customs of typical Beijingnese. The Forbidden City Museums contains a large variety of historical treasures and art works typical of Chinese history and Chinese ancient architecture at its finest.

2. Essay 2

- Museums promote greater understanding and acceptance of foreign cultures. By getting insights into a foreign culture, you understand better what was constitutive of its history.
- Museums help us explore and discover important aspects of our humanness. Museums allow us to reach beyond ourselves, to feel the connection to many others before us who experienced the same feelings, encountered similar revelations, endeavored to know their place and purpose, and struggled to express themselves through the arts.
- Museums offer a unique aesthetic experience, thus helping man by stretching the imagination and crossing mental boundaries. Looking at works of art helps us forget about the ugliness of life.
- Museums offer a communal experience: visiting museums fosters discussions about works of art. Indeed, touching the works of art with the eyes at Washington's National Gallery is much more exciting than going on a shopping trip to London's Harrods'.
- A museum is a place where we can meet artists (through their works) and understand a world remote from us. Preview events allow you to meet the artist and learn more about his or her aestheticism and technique.
- Some people go to museums to complete school assignments, others because they think culture will rub off on them by gazing at the Old Masters. Experience seekers may even go just to show off to their friends when they return from their world tour.

3. Possible answers

1. Essay 1

Visiting museums has become a signature stop on a journey abroad. Indeed, it is hardly conceivable to go to Paris and not see the Louvre, to fly to New York City and not pay a visit to the MOMA, to drive down to Madrid and bypass the Prado, or visit London and not the Tate Gallery. Record attendances show that museums have become part and parcel of traveling. Many reasons can be put forward to explain why museums are top of the list of package tour operators or high on the traveler's must-do list.

First, a museum represents a link between past and present. A museum is the best way for visitors to connect with the arts and traditions of a country's heritage. In a museum, a country's artistic, social, scientific and political heritage is being preserved. It is on display for all to see; indeed, there is no better place where you can learn about the past, where the past can explain the present, or where the present meets the past. In a museum, we can get first-hand information about the history and the culture of the land. For instance, the Egyptian museum in Cairo, exhibits over 12,0000 ancient objects including artifacts from palaces and tombs of kings and members of royal families.

Visiting a museum is similar to travelling into the past. Ellis Island, for example, is part of the immigrant experience to the U.S. during the first half of the 20th century. Through exhibits, you understand why so many people were attracted to that beacon of hope, Lady Liberty, which stands a stone's throw away: it was the first glimpse that immigrants caught of the New World, and it symbolized their dreams and aspirations.

A museum fulfills an educational mission, that of enlightening the masses, expanding the cultural horizon, explaining how a country's identity was shaped, and how original it is. Schools rely heavily on such informal learning environments to enhance their curricula. That is why they organize field trips to museums: to explain to the children of today the way their ancestors used to live and why today is different from yesterday. Museums thus provide an opportunity to understand how a nation was built.

Museums represent a bond, that of pulling together the threads which have been woven into the fabric of society. As such, museums promote feelings of national unity and identity, gathering together the arts and crafts that do a country proud. The Tower of London, home to royal armor, offers an insight into the personalities, power and physical size of England's kings. The Crown Jewels are the priceless symbols of British monarchy. They are still used today in coronation ceremonies and are a reminder that history is alive and well: King John is said to have lost the Crown Jewels in 1216; Edward III used them as collateral to pay his troops and Cromwell ordered the Jewels to be broken up, symbolizing the destruction of the monarchy. Visiting a country, but not its museums, would actually be tantamount to ignoring its past.

2. Essay 2

To understand a country, fail not to visit its museums. It is not conceivable to travel and not see the local culture and art, hence the reason why we all go to museums.

Museums provide an understanding and acceptance of foreign cultures. Past events take another dimension when they are explained in their context. That is why exhibitions of the Chinese terracotta warriors attract millions of visitors eager to understand what the armies of Qin Shi Huang, the first Emperor of China, were like. A King Tutankhamun exhibition draws crowds because it sheds light on the life of an Egyptian pharaoh of the 18th dynasty. By displaying the riches of one country, exhibitions foster mutual understanding between people.

Museums are also great places to understand who we are as human beings. Indeed, museums help us explore and discover significant aspects of our humanness. By visiting a prehistoric museum or department—such as the one in the British Museum—we get a sense of who we were and what we have become: the earliest human tools that were used in Africa and Asia two million years ago or the art and archaeology of Europe from the earliest times to the present day.

Museums offer an aesthetic, uplifting experience, that of seeing a great object of art. The beauty of the artwork makes life worth living despite all the troubles the world is faced with. In a museum, you are in a world apart, a world where beauty is first and foremost. It is a world where the work of art can make you forget the ugliness of life. Such feelings can be experienced when looking at world famous art such as Rembrandt's self-portrait, da Vinci's *Mona Lisa*, Van Eyck's *The Virgin and Child with Canon van der Paele*, Monet's *Impression, Sunrise,* or Hopper's *Nighthawks*.

Visiting museums is a communal experience, the sharing of feelings and memories about art. There are exhibitions that should not be missed, not because they are the talk of the town but because visiting a museum will enhance the knowledge about an artist, give a chance of seeing paintings that hardly ever leave their own country and above all experience that aesthetic emotion that only art can confer.

Finally, visiting museums is also a way of meeting the artists through their works that will help you understand their art better; you will also set foot into a different world. You'll begin to make out some recurring details that define a particular style. You'll get a feel for what a particular culture or time period considered important and valuable.

Museum visiting is also a leisure experience, something we choose to do outside of work and an activity that we take part in outside our domestic essentials. Above all, it is an exploration into the past that you undertake in order to understand the present. It is an initiation into the world of aesthetics that will make you more sensitive to the beauty of the world and the work of man. Going to museums is an unparalleled voyage into a world far remote from us, yet that is inside all of us.

06 WHY STUDY ABROAD?

Many students choose to attend schools or universities outside their home countries. Why do some students study abroad? Use specific reasons and details to explain your answer.

1. Key words

to travel / to study abroad / overseas	voyager / étudier à l'étranger
an international / border crossing student	un étudiant international
a diverse student body	des étudiants de diverse origine
to spend (one year) studying abroad	étudier un an à l'étranger
an exchange program	un programme d'échange
a study abroad program	un programme d'études à l'étranger
to study in a foreign country	étudier dans un pays étranger
to be encouraged / urged to leave	être encouragé / incité à partir
to apply to a university (for)	postuler à une université (pour)
to enroll in a foreign university	s'inscrire dans une université étrangère
to do graduate studies (at / in)	faire des études de 3e cycle (à / dans)
to pursue graduate work (in)	faire des études de 3e cycle
to carry out an internship abroad	faire un stage à l'étranger
to round off one's education (in)	compléter sa formation (en)
to practice a language	pratiquer une langue
to speak several languages	être polyglotte
to be proficient (in)	être capable de s'exprimer (dans / en)
to develop language skills	développer des qualités linguistiques
to be culturally aware	connaître une autre culture
a cross-cultural experience	une expérience interculturelle
a formative experience	une expérience formatrice
to broaden one's intellectual horizon	élargir son horizon intellectuel
to step out of one's comfort zone	quitter son petit confort personnel
to blend in	se mélanger
to overcome a challenge	surmonter un défi
to pack one's bags	faire ses valises
a life-enhancing / -defining experience	une expérience marquante
enriching / rewarding (a)	enrichissant / gratifiant
to help fight against prejudices / biases	contribuer à lutter contre les préjugés
a once-in-a-lifetime opportunity	une occasion unique dans sa vie

2. Talking points

1. Essay 1

- Many students choose to study abroad for the cultural experience. For them it is a cultural initiation to be immersed into and discover a new culture from the inside, to experience a different lifestyle, and to enrich themselves from a human point of view.
- Studying abroad is the best way to learn a new language and develop the cross-cultural skills that go with it. Being proficient in more than one language is a must in our globalized world. At the same time, it helps students broaden their vision of the world.
- Going abroad offers the opportunity to study in a world class university or attend a prestigious college. Some institutions are well known for the quality of their academic staff and research at the forefront of science.
- Such academic experience abroad is a way of discovering new ways of thinking and working, interacting and team working with students the world over, thus expanding one's outlook on reasoning and problem-solving.
- Studying abroad allows students to acquire the ability to think more originally, to discover areas of research they are not familiar with or that their college does not offer on its course catalog.

2. Essay 2

- Studying abroad is a life enhancing experience that changes students for the better. It is a human adventure during which you meet students from all over the world, expand your network, and acquire a greater tolerance of others' points of view and ideas.
- Studying abroad enriches students and helps them blossom, developing greater resilience, reliance and self-confidence which will be precious assets in their professional and personal lives. Having to overcome culture shock, homesickness and the language barrier contributes to personal self-development and growth. It serves as a catalyst for increased maturity.
- Studying abroad is a nice boost to resume building. It will catch the attention of a prospective employer. It says you are capable of adjusting to cross cultural environments. Studying abroad identifies you as informed, confident, self-sufficient, and able to learn quickly and adapt to changing conditions.

3. Possible answers

1. Essay 1

Pursuing higher education abroad has become a privileged way for students to gain a larger perspective. Such a life-changing experience is based on the premise that education is an investment in one's future. Multiple benefits, cultural, linguistic, academic accrue to those who spend time in another country.

Being on one's own, away from one's comfort zone offers a unique opportunity to discover the world. You are immersed into a wholly different culture that you gradually discover from the inside by talking to and exchanging with people from varied backgrounds. Studying abroad is a form of initiation to another world. Exploring cultures and civilizations outside of one's own, which happens when studying abroad, is intellectually refreshing and spiritually stimulating. By living abroad, you develop cross-cultural skills, a new lifestyle and new habits. Ultimately you develop an all round vision and therefore a different outlook of and on life's problems.

One of the main advantages to studying abroad is to become proficient in another language. There is no better way to become fluent in a language than by spending several months in a foreign country and gaining exposure to its culture. By staying abroad, students develop many of the cross-cultural skills that are necessary to work across borders in a globalized world. At the same time, they acquire a fairer and broader vision of geopolitics and the world.

Studying abroad is also a rewarding experience from the academic point of view. Forward-looking students leave their home country and seek to reap the benefits associated with attending a world-class institution abroad. Gaining admission to a prestigious college or university is often regarded as an achievement in itself. The quality of the academic programs, the opportunity to work at the cutting edge of research, the level of specialized instruction and the availability of professional resources are indisputable. It is no wonder that students vie to get admission to well-known schools in the U.S. or Britain, such as Harvard or Oxford.

Going abroad is a way of discovering different approaches to problems. For example, in my country, teaching is mainly theoretical: students sit in large lecture halls and listen to the professor. In America, for example, teaching is conducted through seminars and the case studies method. Teaching is on-hands and more practical-oriented. It gives a different perspective on the way to tackle and solve problems.

Studying abroad may also allow you to study subjects that aren't available at your home university. For example, if you study international relations in France, it will be from a European perspective. Alternatively, studying U.S. history from the American point of view can be complementary to your outlook and quite gratifying.

2. Essay 2

Each year, young people spend thousands of dollars to travel, live and study in universities, colleges and schools overseas. Studying abroad offers undoubtedly some invaluable benefits students can profit much from.

Studying abroad is a personal experience. You'll come back a new person. By studying overseas, you have a chance of meeting people who are not like you. They have different experiences, come from all walks of life, and will help you develop an international network of friends while broadening your vision of the world. A foreign university is a crucible of nationalities. You acquire a greater tolerance for the others' opinion and you develop the ability to think originally and see an issue from various angles.

Studying abroad helps young people to mature quickly and develop independence. Joining a foreign academic institution is often the first experience students have of living away from family and friends. They must overcome the initial homesickness and culture shock, conform to a different teaching style, adapt to unfamiliar social and cultural expectations and develop proficiency in a new language. These challenging and sometimes daunting tasks enable youngsters to emerge with greater maturity and self-confidence.

Finally, there are many professional advantages associated with pursuing a foreign degree. Studying abroad is a gateway to a successful career. First, it gives your resume a boost and improves your post-graduate employment prospects. Employers are looking for graduates who can communicate well with others. They know the importance of cross-cultural understanding and having an appreciation for different points of view. Second, when you graduate from a foreign university, it says much about you, your capacity to adjust to a cosmopolitan environment, not to mention your linguistic skills. So, prospective employers are likely to look more favorably at someone who has a foreign degree than a student whose academic career took place in the same alma mater. International graduates have therefore an added advantage over their peers in a highly competitive job market. Potential employers, when seeing that the candidate has undertaken a period of studying abroad, will see the applicant as somebody who is not risk adverse—somebody with a sense of adventure, unafraid of stepping out of their comfort zone and broadening their horizons. Chances of being employable are therefore greater when you go abroad to study than when you just stay home.

Studying abroad offers several concrete benefits for students in terms of the present and the future. That is why most students avidly seize on the opportunity when it is offered and work diligently to turn this opportunity into success. The student who has gone abroad knows that he/she will return home a more enlightened and mature person.

07 HOW TO HELP REDUCE THE AMOUNT OF RUBBISH?

Nowadays we are producing more and more rubbish. Why do you think this is happening? What can governments do to help reduce the amount of rubbish produced? Use specific reasons and details to explain your answer.

1. Key words

a consumer society	une société de consommation
a lifestyle / based on growth	un style de vie / fondé sur la croissance
to consume / to use (up)	consommer
to dispose of/to discard/to throw away	jeter
a throw away society	une société du gaspillage
rubbish / trash / garbage / litter	les ordures
a rubbish heap / waste products	un tas d'ordures / les déchets
waste (materials / matters)	les déchets
to be flooded with trash	être envahi par les déchets
a trashcan / a dustbin	une poubelle
to waste / wasteful	gaspiller / gaspilleur
a great amount of rubbish	une grande quantité d'ordures
hazardous / toxic waste	les déchets dangereux / toxiques
nuclear / household waste	les déchets nucléaires / ménagers
e-waste / chemical waste	les déchets électroniques / chimiques
waste disposal / management	le traitement / la gestion des déchets
to produce rubbish	produire des déchets
to bury waste	enterrer les déchets
to cut down on / to reduce waste	réduire les déchets
to contaminate / to pollute	contaminer / polluer
waste collection / burial	le ramassage / l'enfouissement des ordures
to break down / biodegradable	se dissoudre / biodégradable
to incinerate / incineration	incinérer / l'incinération
to recycle / to process	recycler / traiter
waste recycling / processing	le recyclage des déchets
a rubbish tip, a dump	une décharge
a landfill site	un site d'enfouissement des déchets
a plastic bag / a polybag / a pouch	un sac plastique
to package / packaging	emballer / le conditionnement
an awareness campaign	une campagne de sensibilisation

2. Talking points

1. Essay 1

- There are many ways of generating rubbish. The main culprit is the consumer society that encourages people to buy the latest product and follow the trendiest fashion, which is beneficial for growth and business activity.
- Planned obsolescence is part of the business wars. It leads to an increase in output as products are only good until a certain date. Competition among firms is another incentive for companies and brands to release new products.
- Waste disposal is one way of dealing with rubbish. Yet landfills are eyesores and cause environmental problems. They are only stopgap measures in a world growing more eco-friendly.
- Consumption reduction is the best option. People should be encouraged to consume less, to buy only what is essential and to re-use or recycle.
- It is a government's responsibility to encourage eco-friendly ways of cutting on rubbish through awareness campaigns. Other policies include individual rubbish weight and limiting packaging.
- Stringent fines ought to be imposed on polluters. Too often, polluters get off scot-free. They dump junk at night in forests or at street corners leaving it to others to discard the old items in a proper way. The polluter-pays-principle should be enforced to make the party responsible for producing pollution pay for the damage done to the natural environment.

2. Essay 2

- The consumer culture is based on the somewhat irrational desires of people to buy. The downside is the manufacturing of alluring products with nice wrappings, and over packaging… and the generation of rubbish.
- Recycling is an option to deal with waste generation; it saves energy and raw materials.
- Composting—organic matter that has been decomposed and recycled as a fertilizer and soil amendment—saves landfill space and helps to recover energy and fight against global warming.
- Energy recovery from rubbish is a practical option that has been little explored so far but that looks promising.
- Waste reduction or minimization should be encouraged. Repairing or reusing items means that they will last longer and won't need replacing with new items so quickly.

3. Possible answers

1. Essay 1

On average, a western household throws away about a ton of rubbish every year. In Britain, for example, they produce enough rubbish every day to fill Trafalgar Square right to the top of Nelson's Column. Where does this rubbish come from and how can man deal with the problem?

The consumer society, based on advertising, has been the prime suspect in increasing the quantity of rubbish we are being flooded with. Whenever we switch on the television, we are swamped by commercials that recommend that we should buy the latest car, the greenest detergent or the trendiest smart phone. Buying is good for business and bad for rubbish. Another technique that has been a source of waste generation is planned obsolescence or built-in obsolescence. Nothing is built to last. Planned obsolescence stimulates demand by encouraging consumers to buy sooner if they still want a functioning product.

There are many ways of dealing with waste. Waste disposal often involves burying rubbish in landfills and may not be the best option. Yet, it is one that is quite widespread nowadays. Sometimes the rubbish is exported far away to be stored. Those tips, or dumps where rubbish is buried are the oldest form of waste processing; yet many adverse impacts arise from landfill operations such as road damage, contamination of groundwater, off gassing of methane amongst other nuisances that also include the presence of pests, rats and flies.

Consumption reduction is by far a sure cure, as it focuses on mitigating waste production in the first place. The greatest proportion of household waste ends up as landfill and so people ought to be encouraged to cut down on the rubbish they produce. The best way of doing this is simply using less. People ought to ask themselves if they need a product before buying it. Taking their own bags when they go shopping is also a way of curbing the number of plastic bags that have flooded our communities. You can also be careful about what you buy. Choose items that will last longer and try to buy products you can use again instead of disposable items.

One of the ways to make sure that waste is better controlled is to inform people of the choices available to them to dispose of their garbage. To that end, government should launch awareness campaigns to sharpen people's attention to the problem of the ubiquitous plastic bag, the oceans that have become dumping grounds for all sorts of junk. Similarly, governments should impose certain restrictions on packaging, which should be made biodegradable. Dustbins should be weighed during collection time and consumers whose rubbish exceeds a certain number of kilos should be fined heavily. Rubbish generation is a problem we can deal with. All it takes is the effort of all.

2. Essay 2

Each year food shops give away enough carrier bags to cover the whole of London with a layer of bags. Each bag that goes to landfill will take 500 years to decay. How can this staggering amount be explained? And above all, how to deal with the billions of tons produced each year and which are hardly ever processed?

Rubbish comes in all forms. The consumer culture, or market culture—based on people's irrational desire to outspend their neighbors in that tug-of-war for the most fashionable products—is to be blamed. Packaging—layers of cardboard, foam and film—gives a product an appearance that is belied by the product itself. What matters is not so much the product itself but the way it is wrapped and presented. Plastic bags, handed out freely, are another bane of the war against rubbish generation. What are the options to wage and win the war against rubbish?

Recycling is one. You can recycle a wide range of rubbish, from paper and glass to batteries, televisions and clothes. Recycling saves energy and raw materials, and reduces the amount of waste sent to landfill sites. Most local councils run recycling collections from your doorstep, while waste and recycling centers (the local tip) can also accept many other materials for recycling.

You can also help to reduce waste at home by composting the household organic (garden and food) waste collected by local authorities. If organic waste is sent to landfill, it produces methane, which has strong climate change effects. Composting waste like tea bags, vegetable peelings, shredded paper and egg boxes reduces these climate change effects and saves valuable space in landfill sites.

Energy recovery, creating energy from waste by burning it to produce electricity, is a practical option that has been little explored so far. The energy content of waste products can be harnessed directly by using them as a direct combustion fuel, or indirectly by processing them into another type of fuel.

Another method of waste management is the prevention of waste material being created, also known as waste reduction or minimization. It consists in reusing old food containers as lunch boxes or old plastic bags as bin liners. Even when you have finished with something, someone else will often be able to use it. Secondhand furniture, clothes and electrical items like mobiles are especially popular: why not pass them onto friends and family? Another possibility is to sell them, donate them to charity or pass them on to associations via sharing schemes.

As long as zero growth is not a target of government, man will keep on generating rubbish. Free-market societies thrive on the production of goods and services as being the powerhouse of business. A few solutions have been implemented to help deal with the waste crisis, such as recycling, re-using, minimization but rubbish is here to stay, at least as long as no other social model has been put forward.

08 REVISITING THE PAST

If you could go back to some time and place in the past, when and where would you go? Why? Use specific reasons and details to support your choice.

1. Key words

history / in history	l'histoire / au cours de l'histoire
timeline	la chronologie
a time machine	une machine à remonter le temps
to go back in time	remonter le temps
time travel	les voyages dans le temps
a journey through the past	un voyage dans le passé
a time traveler	un voyageur dans le temps
backward time travel	les voyages dans le passé
to revisit the past	revisiter le passé
a past event	un événement passé
a lost era	une époque / une période révolue
the good old days	le bon vieux temps
to be transported back	être transporté en arrière
care-free / problem free	sans souci, insouciant / sans problème
stress-free	décontracté
to miss (out on an opportunity)	manquer (une occasion)
an unforgettable memory	un souvenir inoubliable
to be homesick	avoir le mal du pays
homesickness	la nostalgie
childhood years	les années d'enfance
to attend college	aller à l'université
university days / college time	la vie d'étudiant
summer vacation	les grandes vacances
to make new friends	se faire de nouveaux amis
to hang out with friends	traîner avec des amis
a sense of independence	un sentiment d'indépendance
a sense of responsibility	un sentiment de responsabilité
to do sth on one's own responsibility	assumer la responsabilité de ses choix
to pick and choose one's activities	choisir ses activités
to transition (to) / a rite of passage	devenir / un rite de passage
to grow up / to mature	grandir / mûrir

2. Talking points

1. College days

- Going off to college is possibly one of the momentous events a young person will remember all his/her life long. It is a first step in transitioning towards adulthood.
- College days are memorable because they are a time a discovery: discovery of a new environment, of new friends, a new program, checking out courses to expand people's knowledge base and develop an active and dynamic social life.
- College days are memorable because people discover a new sense of freedom, in particular, the freedom to choose their study hours or their own extra-curricular activities such as dancing or playing music.
- College days are a fond time to revisit because of the sense of responsibility people developed way back then. Living on their own, being accountable to no one but themselves, taking the first steps towards gaining a university degree, making useful connections before embracing a career provides a certain thrill and a sense of awe. Also, people's choices are theirs, and theirs only. College days are a good preparation for life.

2. A childhood spent in the mountains

- The childhood I spent in a little village in the Alps stands out as the best time of my life. The environment was gorgeous and life was lived according to the rhythm of seasons: biking in the summer, skiing in the winter. School squeezed in between.
- Childhood was carefree and problem-free. Life was spent remote from the world's concerns, in harmony with nature. Nothing could disturb the orderly pace of life.
- It was a time when I could enjoy a unique and privileged relationship with my grandparents. It was a learning experience: I did all sorts of activities which were uncommon to the city boy I was before: cabinetmaking, woodcarving, farm work, hunting, gardening.
- Childhood in the mountains was unique for the sense of independence I was able (and allowed) to enjoy. I learned to manage my time, take initiatives, develop my autonomy and later in my life embrace a career with confidence and a positive outlook on the world.

3. Possible answers

1. College days

Most people that went into higher education will remember their college days as one of the best periods in their lives. Indeed, there are many reasons why that period stands out in a person's life.

To begin with, going off to college is a momentous event for someone who's just fresh from high school and who has lived all his life at home. It is a major step forward for young people to transition towards adulthood and become themselves. This first step, away from the comfort zone is naturally filled with apprehension and questions, yet, we all remember when we proudly told our parents that we had been admitted to college and had made our final choice to live on the other side of the country.

College days are memorable because it is a time of discovery. You arrive in an unknown environment—usually after traveling several hours on the bus or the train. You are assigned a room, usually a roommate as well, and you meet people from all over the country and even beyond. You discover the school program and the many subjects you can pick and choose, taught by professors that you do not know yet. And, all of a sudden, you realize that college life has a more vibrant tempo than home life.

Second, college days are a time when you gain your independence. You have the freedom to room with a person that shares the same tastes and, hopefully, work habits as you. You have the freedom to choose the courses from the catalog and develop your worldviews. The freedom to keep your own hours too: if you want to stay up late and study in the library until midnight, or use the computer room into the wee hours, no one is going to stop you. Freedom to do as many extracurricular activities as you like, provided they do not interfere with your personal study plan. For example, I remember picking up lacrosse and tennis, but also taking part in student associations such as oenology or the junior enterprise, thus broadening my experience beyond the curriculum in a helpful way. The sense of independence you experience at college cannot be compared with anything you have done before.

In college, you develop a sense of responsibility that you have never experienced before. I remember moving off campus after my first two years and actually learning to live on my own in a flat I had rented in a big house. There was no dorm supervisor to help me, no roommate to share discussions with, yet, I was fully contented because I could organize my life as I wished, I could go out as late as I wanted to, organize parties for a few selected friends and, of course, see my boyfriend as often as I wished. Living on my own meant I learnt to manage my time and my budget, do the shopping or the housecleaning. Yet, I enjoyed the privacy of an apartment where I could work undisturbed by my classmates, away from the hustle and bustle of campus life.

2. A childhood spent in the mountains

If there is one time and place I would like to revisit, it is my childhood, which I spent in a little village in the mountains until I turned 12 and had to move to the city. There are many reasons why I would like to re-live that experience.

First off, the setting: picture a postcard-like view of the Alps' highest summit in the background. You can see the everlasting snow all year round and imagine the trekking of those alpinists on their way to the top of the mountains. Summer was spent frolicking in the fields or riding my bike up and down the mountain trails while in winter I would go deep powder skiing on the pristine slopes around the farm.

That time was blessed. Primary school was taught by an avuncular schoolteacher who was kind and patient with his young charges. Homework was unheard of and as soon as school let out the children would scatter and go home to help their parents with the farm work or play outside. Life was carefree then. We were remote from the rest of the world in that neck of the woods, untouched by what was happening out there. We lived according to the rhythm of the seasons and in harmony with nature. When I compare my life back then with today's rat race, it felt like living in a time warp.

Another reason why I believe that time was blessed was the relationship I forged with my grandparents to whose care I had been entrusted. My parents had been sent abroad for their jobs and they had decided that I should pursue my education in France. I remember how well I got along with my grandfather. He taught me cabinetmaking and how to carve out wooden toys. There was no TV back then and the computer had not even been invented. The toys we had we made them ourselves, keeping busy during the long winter evenings. We would do the farm chores too: feeding the poultry, milking the cows; in autumn we would go gathering the apples in the orchard that grandma would then can or turn into applesauce. I worked in the vegetable patch with my grandmother, picking up the tomatoes, peas, cucumber, zucchini and salad that would be the evening meal. My grandpa took me hunting too, and I learnt how to handle a rifle.

The feeling of belonging that I felt then was complemented by the sense of independence I enjoyed. Even though my grandparents kept a watchful eye on me, I was basically free to occupy my time as I saw fit. Whether it was going on hikes in the local mountain forests, spending the day outdoors, or reading in my room, my grandparents would give me much free rein in managing my own time, outside the chores I was assigned every now and then and which I enjoyed doing anyway. That sense of independence, that capacity to take initiatives and be autonomous served me well when I was admitted to college a few years later and still today in my professional life. There are lessons from the past that are not learnt at school and living in the mountains was an eye-opener. Those blessed days have remained with me and serve as a reminder that the past is a familiar country that we sometimes enjoy revisiting.

09 ON THE IMPORTANCE OF READING AND WRITING

Is the ability to read and write more important today than in the past? Why or why not? Use specific reasons and examples to support your answer.

1. Key words

to read / to write	lire / écrire
a reader / a writer	un lecteur / un écrivain
to publish / a publisher	publier / un éditeur
the publishing industry	l'édition
literacy	le taux d'alphabétisation
to be literate	savoir lire et écrire
to learn one's ABC	apprendre l'alphabet
to have a large vocabulary	avoir un vocabulaire riche
to build one's vocabulary	bâtir son vocabulaire
to express oneself	s'exprimer
numeracy	l'aptitude au calcul
to be numerate	savoir compter
reading / writing abilities	l'aptitude à lire / écrire
reading / writing skills	les capacités à lire / écrire
a life-long skill	une compétence utile toute la vie
the Middle Ages	le Moyen Âge
the Renaissance	la Renaissance
the Age of Enlightenment	l'Âge des Lumières
to enlighten	éclairer
the invention of the printing press	l'invention de la presse (typographique)
the written press	la presse écrite
the radio / television	la radio / la télévision
the Internet / the world wide web	Internet / la Toile
oral tradition	la tradition orale
to feed the imagination	nourrir l'imagination
to develop the mind	ouvrir l'esprit
to overflow with information	déborder d'informations
to be knowledgeable (about)	s'y connaître (au sujet de)
well-read (a)	savant
erudite / ignorant	érudit / ignorant

2. Talking points

1. The ability to read and write is more important today than in the past.

- Reading and writing are fundamental assets in today's society and in man's daily activities. The nature of society has shifted from a rural type of society to the high tech society thus requiring fundamental skills without which you cannot function properly.
- Day-to-day activities and the complexity of society require that we all learn and know how to read and write.
- Reading and writing are vital to land a job. Can we imagine a salesclerk that cannot read the price of a pair of shoes, or a contractor that cannot write a bill? Poor reading skills increase the amount of time it takes to absorb and react in the workplace. A person is limited in what they can accomplish without solid reading skills.
- Reading and writing are essential skills for fast communication in a globalized world, be it through snail mail, over the Internet, email, e-chatting, writing SMS (or just sending postcards). Whereas society used to be limited to the village, it has today expanded to include the country, the continent, and the world.
- Reading and writing are vital skills for getting and providing information. Dealing with new data, understanding the world, explaining it to others, has led to the development of all sorts of media. We need reading and writing skills to read newspapers, magazines, the Stock Exchange, the current events, and to understand the crises in the world.

2. The ability to read and write is no more important today than it used to be.

- The existence of alphabets in Europe and the rest of the world, including India, Africa and Asia, speaks volumes about man's necessity to codify language and therefore to learn to read and write.
- Reading and writing were the privilege of a few (the clergy). With the help of inventions and the development of education, reading and writing are now an essential goal of educators and education.
- Reading and writing are means of relaxation and escape. Reading is like taking a flight to great heights in pursuit of knowledge. It is also escaping into a different world (through novels) and gaining access to sources of information. Reading and writing have consequently accompanied the development of the world. In the past as today, those skills have been the core engines on the road to development.

3. Possible answers

1. The ability to read and write is more important today than in the past.

Reading and writing have become fundamental to function in today's society. Several explanations can be put forward to account for the heightened importance of mastering those skills, the first of which is the nature of society itself. We have evolved from a mainly rural society to an industrialized one and, today, to a high tech society. As society has become more complex, so have the skills that new jobs require. Whereas operating a yoke and a pair of oxen did not require reading or writing skills, today's engineer and scientist need to decipher and master complex data.

As society has become ever more advanced, it is hard to imagine performing day-to-day activities without reading or writing. Reading is necessary to understand the instructions on a medicine bottle, to fill out applications, read road or warning signs, train schedules, a subway map or even a road map. Can you imagine filling up your car tank, a bank form or writing a check if you can neither read nor write? How would you manage putting together DIY furniture without reading the manual? And what about learning how to use a computer or your cellphone if you are illiterate?

Reading and writing are vital skills in finding a job. A farmer's job was simple—keeping sheep, milking cows, seeding or harvesting—and no book was necessary as people relied on oral traditions. Today, virtually all jobs require reading. There are reports and memos that need to be read and responded to. Lawyers have to write briefs, doctors have to know how to read X-rays, and researchers must analyze and interpret data in order to process the overflow of information.

Transitioning to the hi-tech society has altered communication too. As trade barriers were lowered and the world opened up, reading and writing became more than tools, the very conditions for survival in a world going global. Reading and writing emails, text messages, chatting with your friends online, swapping files, are basic tasks that no one could even imagine without possessing those two fundamental skills. The change in the nature of communication at the local level was mainly oral, based on simple messages or errands. It now rests on sophisticated tools that require a solid command not only of the technology but the use of the technology, not of one language but of many.

As people's tastes and activities have become more varied, we have witnessed the development of newspapers and magazines catering to each and all of our needs. We live in an instant society in which we feed on news updates: a natural disaster, the death of a rock star icon, the looming crash on Wall Street, the results of the presidential elections, the winner in a sports competition, all this has resulted in the unprecedented development of the media and with them the development of reading and writing. That is why those skills are way more essential than they were in the past, recent or not.

2. The ability to read and write is no more important today than it used to be.

Education has always laid stress on the acquisition of the three skills: reading, writing and reckoning. Of course, we can always argue that the past means the cave men and that writing and reading were not essential thousands of years ago. Yet, throughout history, alphabets have been invented for man to read and write with. The history of the alphabet started in ancient Egypt where, by the 27th century BC, Egyptian writing already possessed a set of some 24 hieroglyphs. The Greek alphabet was carried over by Greek colonists to the Italian peninsula, where it gave rise to a variety of alphabets used to write the Italic languages. One of these became the Latin alphabet, which was spread across Europe as the Romans expanded their empire. India and Asia have alphabets as well, all descended from the Brahmi script, which is often believed to be a descendant of Aramaic. The point of alphabets such as Hangul (the Korean alphabet), Zhuyin in China, or more broadly Cyrillic, was to learn how to write and read, which was as essential in the past as it is in the present for society to develop and for man to communicate with one another.

Reading and writing have expanded owing to some inventions, for example Gutenberg's printing press, but above all the development of and the need for education. While reading and writing used to be the privilege of the Church, the clergy and the monks, transitioning from a regular to a secular society has gone hand in hand with the development of basic skills. Since the mid-19th century and the establishment of compulsory education, mastering the three Rs (reading, writing, reckoning) has been the intangible goal of educators. No child must be left behind who cannot read and write.

The development of the media, the publishing industry bear evidence to the necessity for man to know how to read and write. Thus, we have developed genres for everyone. Suffice it to browse in a bookstore and you will see that the sections devoted to self-help vie with the history corner, gender studies or the fiction floor. Books are meant for all audiences, the students of course but also the gardener thirsty for information on tulips or the holidaymaker eager to make the most of his vacation time to read. To read is to fly: it is to soar to a point of vantage which gives a view over wide terrains of history, human variety, ideas, shared experience and the fruits of many inquiries. Reading informs, entertains and nourishes the mind. As W. Somerset Maugham once wrote, "To acquire the habit of reading is to construct for yourself a refuge from almost all the miseries of life." Those needs are not recent. They show that reading and writing have always been indispensable to open up new worlds to man and help him on the road to progress and self-development.

10 THE PROBLEMS OF MOVING TO A NEW SCHOOL

When students move to a new school, they sometimes face problems. How can schools help these students with their problems? Use specific reasons and examples to explain your answer.

1. Key words

to move in / out / to relocate	emménager / déménager
to move overseas / abroad	déménager à l'étranger
to leave behind (friends)	abandonner (des amis)
to miss home / to be homesick	avoir le mal du pays
to adjust (to) / adjustment	s'adapter (à) / l'adaptation
to transition / a transition	être en transition / une transition
to struggle (to)	lutter (pour)
to get used (to)	s'accoutumer (à)
to make new friends	se faire de nouveaux amis
to feel isolated	se sentir isolé
a new kid on the block	un petit nouveau
a newcomer (to)	un nouvel arrivant (à / dans)
to discover a new curriculum	découvrir un nouveau programme
a new rhythm / pace of work	un nouveau rythme de travail
the work discipline	la discipline au travail
to overcome the language barrier	surmonter la barrière de la langue
linguistic skills	les compétences linguistiques
to experience anxiety / stress	se sentir nerveux / stressé
to be afraid not to fit in	avoir peur de ne pas s'intégrer
to blend in	se mélanger
orientation week / fresher's week	une semaine d'intégration
a freshman / a frosh	un étudiant de première année
a welcome week	une semaine d'accueil
to welcome the new students	accueillir les nouveaux élèves
to acclimate to student life	s'habituer à la vie d'étudiant
to introduce oneself (to)	se présenter (à)
to engage in group activities	s'inscrire à des activités
to join a student association	s'inscrire dans une association étudiante
hazing / harassment / bullying	le bizuthage / le harcèlement
to feel at home	se sentir chez soi

2. Talking points

1. Essay 1

- School authorities should organize an orientation week to help the newcomers find their way around, explore the campus, be given information on the labs, the library, the gym and so on.
- School authorities should help new students get used to new rules and policies: how to read the schedule, to adapt to an irregular daily routine or how to use their free time.
- They should point out to the staff members' requirements and policies regarding class attendance, dress code and expected behaviors.
- Senior students should be on hand to help the newcomers understand the school life, the extra curricular activities, or enroll in student associations. A mentoring system might be welcome, at least in the first months.
- Junior or seniors should encourage the new students to engage in communal activities.

2. Essay 2

- Transferring to a new school may have a psychological impact, a problem that school should not fail to address. The newcomers may be missing their old friends and feel disoriented by their new environment. Having a supportive senior on hand can go a long way towards helping a teen make the adjustment to a new school in mid-year.
- A school should ensure that they have academic advisors to address academic or personal problems, often linked to loneliness. A counseling service may help the students break the isolation barrier and forestall the risks that children play truant and drop out at the end of their schooling period.
- Many personal and psychological problems can be associated with transitioning (lower self-esteem, apprehensions, time management or behavioral issues, etc.). Having counselors at hand may give transferring and clueless kids a shot in the arm and put them back on the right academic track.

3. Possible answers

1. Essay 1

Moving to a new school is often a life changing experience for students, be they relocating students, transferring students, moving up from high school to college or even students moving in from another country. Actually there are many steps that can be taken to ease the difficulties of moving to a new school.

First, efforts to welcome and involve new students and families require institutional commitment, organization, and ongoing dedication. A school should organize an orientation week or day, or an open house. This event might take place one week ahead of the start of the school year so as to allow students to find their way around the new school and the campus. Students should be given guided tours of the campus, so as to get to know what and where the different buildings are, the opening hours of the library, of the computer lab or of the cafeteria. They might also meet with some of the school administrators during seminars and conferences to explain how the system works. If a student is transferring mid-year, a visit to the school prior to enrolling may help as well as introducing the student to potentially new friends who may share common interests. This can be useful to smooth the transition and reduce potential anxiety.

Second, the school authorities must do their utmost to explain the schedule along with the official rules and policies. Coming from high school, or transferring represents a cultural shock for students who have been accustomed to the more restricted and sheltered environment in a backwater, for example. Thus, it is much better if sound habits regarding discipline are instilled right from the start. This includes attendance rules, expected behavior on and off campus, traffic regulations, school bus schedules, for example; so students quickly get the hang of how the school functions.

Welcoming the newcomers should not be the privilege of the school authorities only. Indeed, when freshmen arrive to a new campus, they are usually welcomed by their seniors. It is essential that experienced students be on hand to present the extra curricular activities or explain campus life. Newcomers will be shown how to sign up for student associations, or how they can engage in a whole range of activities, be they social or physical. A BBQ party is usually set up for the new students, which helps generations break the ice, meet and mingle, and thus foster a congenial spirit that should reassure the newcomers and make them feel at home. Therefore, young people will not be left out; they will feel like they 'fit in' and they will tend to adjust more easily.

Having people on hand to present and explain the school to newcomers is to my mind a major step towards integrating the students and making them feel at home. In addition, it will help break the ice between the classes and give the impression that the new students already belong to their new school.

2. Essay 2

Changing schools can be an exciting and frustrating period. Youngsters entering a new school are confronted with multiple transition challenges. Those challenges are compounded when the transition also involves recent arrival to a new country and immersion into an unknown culture. In the short run, failure to cope with these challenges can result in major learning and behavior problems; in the long run, the psychological and social fallout may be devastating. There are several ways a school might be able to smooth the transition.

Transitioning, a process that is associated with entering a new school, may have a personal and psychological impact on a student. One of the most common effects is that you start missing your old friends. There are many reasons why people start splitting apart and going off to study in different cities, and feeling sad because you miss them is inevitable. Young people are in the phase of life when they are trying to establish their identity separate from their parents or family. A teen's friendship group often defines for them a big portion of their identity. So, for teens entering a new school, losing their prior social groups can be a genuine loss. Having to establish a new social circle and, in many ways, a new identity can be an anxiety-provoking, and potentially tough problem for a teen entering a new school.

A school should therefore ensure that it has a counseling service on hand to address the problems of loneliness. A counselor should set up a teen that is transferring in mid-year with a 'big brother' or 'big sister', an older, well established student who is kind and generous enough to show the new student around the school, introduce her or him to new friends. Of course, if the transition to a new school is not going smoothly, the guidance counselor or social worker should be available to meet privately with the teen to help troubleshoot difficulties with the transition to the new school.

Young people may encounter more personal difficulties, including lower self-esteem, fears about new social situations or the difficulty in managing their time. They may face problems coping with increased academic stress, or the disruption of previous peer relationships. These stressors may appear as anxiety and frustration and result in negative or disruptive behaviors. In cases where transitioning to a new school environment has been difficult, many young people display higher rates of truancy and school drop out at the end of their compulsory schooling period. A counseling service would be the appropriate answer to such problems.

Moving to a new school is often a sea change in perspectives, the passage from innocence to experience. It is a time when you become responsible for your own destiny and an experience you wouldn't want to miss out on or ruin. In that respect, school authorities or prospective friends cannot solve all the problems. It is also useful to have the parents on board.

11 CHANGES OF THE 21ST CENTURY

The 21st century has begun. What changes do you think this new century will bring? Use examples and details in your answer.

1. Key words

to bring major changes	apporter des changements majeurs
to turn the world upside down	révolutionner le monde
to usher in / to enter an age, era	inaugurer / entrer dans une ère
the advent (of) / to peer into the future	l'avènement (de) / interroger l'avenir
to outthink humans	dépasser la pensée humaine
the digital revolution	la révolution numérique
access to information / knowledge	l'accès à l'information / la connaissance
technological know how	le savoir-faire technologique
family structure / a blended family	la structure familiale / une famille recomposée
a single-parent family	une famille monoparentale
single parenthood	la monoparentalité
same-sex marriage	le mariage homosexuel
a gay family / gay parenting	une famille homosexuelle / l'homo-parentalité
a Chinese / Korean Spring	un Printemps chinois / coréen
the struggle for human rights	le combat pour les droits de l'homme
international relations	les relations internationales
globalization / to go global	la mondialisation / se mondialiser
to form new alliances	nouer de nouvelles alliances
the rise of a new empire	la montée d'un nouvel empire
oil peak / to harness solar energy	le pic de pétrole / apprivoiser le solaire
a renewable source of energy	une source d'énergie renouvelable
a water war	une guerre de l'eau
the world population	la population mondiale
to exceed 7 billion	dépasser les 7 milliards
a food crisis / food security	une crise alimentaire / la sécurité alimentaire
to out-run food supply	être à court de nourriture
to keep pace with population growth	suivre la courbe démographique
GMOs (genetically modified organisms)	les OGM (organismes génétiquement modifiés)
to eliminate sickness	éradiquer la maladie
a space settlement	une colonie dans l'espace
human travel to Mars	les voyages habités sur Mars

2. Talking points

1. Essay 1

- The structure of the family is bound to keep evolving: there will be more blended families, same-sex marriages, single-headed families and children born out of wedlock. The traditional family structure will be a thing of the past. The means of reproduction will change too with the development of surrogate motherhood.
- There will be more women in the labor pool as they are gaining access to the job market in greater numbers. Not only will they join the labor force in large numbers, but they will also break through the glass ceiling and achieve positions of responsibility within the corporate world.
- Children will leave the nest much later (around the age of 30) owing to the weight of student loans, rising property prices, and the need for extended studies, for example.
- The ageing of population the world over—and its attendant financial issues—is bound to raise acute problems of funding for governments. Women especially will be more vulnerable in a society where they will live longer than men and will often find themselves isolated.

2. Essay 2

- No one will be able to escape the prying eyes of the state. Individual freedom and privacy will be out, creeping authoritarianism will be in the name of the common good. The freedom of the individual will have to be carefully weighed against the intrusion into our daily lives by the state.
- Cheap technology will mean ubiquitous connectivity to networks, wherever we are and whatever devices we are using. Sensors will inform on everyday aspects of our lives, be they in the kitchen, the management of the household, our freedom of movement from one place to another, and above all the medical field, thus making our lives much easier.
- Technology will come to the rescue where care deficit is concerned. There will be moves to further extend the role of technology in providing help. Old people's homes will be linked up to their children's homes by webcam. More and more communication within the family is likely to be mediated by technology, facilitating the family life of people who have migrated from their home country.

3. Possible answers

1. Essay 1

Looking beyond the present times, it is hard to fathom what our planet will look like by the end of the century. There are bound to be startling trend changes to the way we live through the discoveries and innovations the next generation will come up with. What are the inventions that are most likely to shape the next century?

The past 30 years has been a generation of dramatic change in the structure of the family. The stigma that used to surround divorce and illegitimacy will be a subject for the history books. Gay and lesbian partnerships, surrogate motherhood, assisted reproductive technology (ART), with rights enshrined in law, will no longer prompt comment. Family life will have adjusted to a pattern of serial monogamy, with a much larger number of stepfamilies or blended families. Lone parenthood will be a common phenomenon, but not necessarily a long-lasting one. Children living with both their biological parents in the same household will be in the minority. There will be dozens of different types of co-parenting arrangements, with combinations of stepfamilies, or adults with children from previous relationships entering long-term relationships with others in the same position but choosing not to live together.

With more women gaining access to education, they will able to negotiate more equal relationships—already one in five women earns more than her partner. That proportion is likely to increase over the next decades as a generation of high-achieving schoolgirls arrives in the labor market. They will eventually breach the glass ceiling and achieve positions of responsibility in greater numbers than men. Woman will be the primary breadwinner. Even though earning power will be redistributed within the couple, caring responsibilities might prove more resistant to change. But this too is bound to evolve as fathers take on more childcare chores.

What is bound to increase too is cocooning, children leaving the nest at an older age. Kids used to be off their parents' hands by 18, but the combination of student loans, university fees and rising property prices has already reversed that, and the trend is likely to deepen. Parenthood is well on its way to becoming a minimum 25-year deal.

The ageing of population, including in emerging countries where the comfort of life has already started to bring major changes, will be a major political and social issue. We will work and live longer. Yet, the big unknown is how the medical treatment and care we need in our old age will be financed. Will taxes rise to pay for the number of heart surgery needed for octogenarians? Alongside financing the huge costs of medical treatment will be the enormous challenge of funding the much more prosaic matter of caring for the frail elderly, dressing them, cooking their meals, doing their housework and helping them to wash.

2. Essay 2

Predictions of technological advance have always emphasized the headline-grabbing pipedreams—robot housemaids to lift us out of domestic drudgery, cars being self-driven, a time traveler able to transport us back into the past, or even fast forward into the future. Even though stem cell technology and quantum computers remain alluring promises, what will the future look like? What inventions will shape it?

By the end of the century, no aspect of your life will be safe from the prying eyes of the state. Technology will be at the service of Big Brother: your personal data, shopping, drinking and driving habits will be shared across computer systems. Toilets—targeted for use in large companies—will analyze whether an employee has recently used illegal recreational drugs. Number plate recognition cameras will be positioned in motorways, enabling police to track stolen or suspect vehicles. Facial recognition for CCTV will be generalized. As for gene surveillance, experts will only need a tiny piece of hair or other cells from our bodies to draw all sorts of conclusions about our genetic inheritance, our parentage, the diseases we are prone to and what is likely to cause our eventual death. All that technology will be at the service of the government, and its use will force us to consider the delicate balance between individual freedom and privacy.

Information technology will transform our day-to-day lives. Cheap sensors, inexpensive computing power and ubiquitous connectivity will be the rule of the land. Everything large enough to carry a microchip will be automated. Fridges will read the use-by date on the milk carton and order another pint before the current one goes off. We will be sent gas bills that include an electronic reminder to pay them. We will do our laundry in washing machines that contact service engineers when their bearings wear down, and that automatically arrange a visit after finding a window in your electronic organizer. Even the medicine jar will know when it was last opened and how much its weight went down. Other electronic boxes of tricks will be able to monitor our health. We will have earrings able to read our pulse rates and bracelet monitors that analyze the composition of your sweat. Medical information will be sent through the skin to a central chip, which will be able to transmit all the necessary information to your doctor, back through the skin, when you shake hands with them at your appointment. Your updated medical history will be on the doctor's computer before you have even sat down. A whole range of technologies will be on stream to make our daily lives simpler.

On every aspect of the care deficit, people will turn to technology for help. Remote, web-based technology will administer health checks such as taking a pulse rate and measuring blood pressure. Webcams might be playing the role the telephone did in the 20th century, a vital communication link for families who live hundreds of miles apart. The changes brought on by technology will therefore serve man, fostering an environment in which the machine has become man's friend.

12 WHY DO PEOPLE ATTEND COLLEGE?

People attend college for many different reasons (for example, new experiences, career preparation, increased knowledge). Why do you think people attend college or university? Use specific reasons and examples to support your answer.

1. Key words

a school, a college / a university	une faculté / une université
to attend school	fréquenter la fac
to be a student / to study	être étudiant / étudier
a college graduate	un diplômé de l'université
to get / to receive an education	acquérir une formation
a rigorous educational environment	un environnement rigoureux
to obtain a college degree	obtenir un diplôme universitaire
the value of a college degree	la valeur d'un diplôme universitaire
to prepare for a career	se préparer à une carrière
career preparedness	la préparation à une carrière
a competitive job market	un marché de l'emploi compétitif
to upgrade / to enhance one's skills	améliorer ses compétences
to learn new skills	acquérir des compétences
qualified / unskilled	qualifié / non qualifié
a level / a standard of competence	un niveau de compétence
to expand one's knowledge base	développer ses connaissances
to deepen one's knowledge (in)	approfondir ses connaissances (en)
to increase one's earning potential	améliorer sa capacité salariale
a ticket to a high-paying job	la garantie d'un emploi bien payé
to land a decent job	obtenir un emploi convenable
to broaden one's interests	élargir ses intérêts
to become a more rounded person	devenir un honnête homme
to specialize / to major (in)	se spécialiser (en / dans)
to leave the nest	quitter le cocon
to be away from home	être loin de chez soi
a classmate / a roommate	un camarade de promo / un cothurne
an alumnus / alumna / alumni	un(e) ancien élève / des anciens élèves
personal growth	le développement personnel
self-development	l'épanouissement
to transition to adulthood	passer à l'âge adulte

2. Talking points

1. Essay 1

- Students choose to go to college or university to prepare for a career in a world becoming more and more competitive for jobs.
- College is a way of attaining a marketable degree and developing earning potential.
- A renowned college is likely to give you a leg up in the race for jobs. Status associated with a college name brand is a distinct asset.
- College offers a rigorous learning environment where people acquire new knowledge or broaden their knowledge base. College is an institution devoted to nourishing learning and intellectualism.
- College teaches intellectual abilities: critical reasoning, analytical skills, research skills, the crafting of rigorous arguments, how to plan and carry out independent projects. College is supposed to be about learning how to think clearly and be creative rather than the more rote learning style of high school.
- College is a place for socializing and developing a network of friends and building a set of contacts.
- People go to college to have new experiences. College is a step forward into adulthood. It helps a student grow and leads to personal discovery.

2. Essay 2

- A college education is a passport to the job market, especially in technology driven societies such as Germany, South Korea or the United States.
- A college degree offers a specialization in one particular domain, which is all the more necessary today in a world that has gone more complex and intricate than it used to be.
- Going to university can be the accomplishment of a lifelong dream or the American dream. It is a way of building a better life and improving one's career track record.
- College can also be a test to man's abilities. People who attend college want to put themselves to the test, see whether their knowledge can stand the trials of time or needs updating. It may be a question of pride and self-fulfillment, or an example to follow for the children.
- College or university is fertile ground for the birth of ideas and the concretization of ideas. Very often, man has been able to build a firm from the ground up only because he stumbled upon the idea while doing a project at university.

3. Possible answers

1. Essay 1

There are many reasons why people choose to attend college, one of the main being that college provides an entrance ticket to life. Actually, in a competitive work environment, low skilled workers have trouble landing a job, let alone keeping it. It is essential therefore to acquire the skill set necessary to survive and adapt in a technology-driven market and in that regard, a college experience cannot be done without. The knowledge is tested through exams and validated thanks to a degree that says much to a prospective employer about the quality of an applicant. All the more so as a name brand university is usually associated with status, which is a plus on the job market.

College is a way of attaining a marketable degree and developing earning potential. Statistics show that college graduation correlates positively with economic factors like lower rates of unemployment and higher earnings. The best jobs require a college degree, which is used by employers as an easy and cost-free screening device. You might be the greatest computer programmer in the world, but without an MSc in CS, the best jobs will be closed to you, unless you start your own company and become successful on your own terms, a high-risk path for which most people are ill-suited.

College offers a rigorous education environment where people can acquire or deepen their knowledge. College provides structure and resources for learning, doing research, and carrying out internships. Lab facilities, libraries, and access to scholars who have spent a lifetime in their fields are some of the services offered by universities. This is the place where students actually update their knowledge. The right college will provide the opportunity to acquire skills that are difficult for most to develop without the scaffolding of an in-tuned and quality teacher.

College is where you make new friends. It is a place for socializing and developing a network of contacts. The diverse demographics of a campus allows you to meet people who have traveled different walks in life and therefore to enrich yourself in the process through group work and discussions. Later in life, the connections you make in college will enable you to nurture a professional network of alumni.

People go to college to gain new experiences. A college is a new world for students, away from home and the coddling of parents. It is a place where students can experience freedom, try new things, and just grow up because of the new responsibilities they have to assume for themselves, not only education—the need to get that diploma—but financial as well. A college experience is a step forward into adulthood. It helps students discover who they are in their years on campus. For others, college might not be so much finding themselves as creating themselves.

2. Essay 2

The reasons why people attend college or university are plain to see in a society that requires that skills and knowledge be at the cutting edge, on the one hand, and constantly updated, on the other.

First, a college education is a passport that will open wide the doors of the job market. In South Korea, for example, the state's authorities have mandated that all students go into higher education and obtain at least a bachelor's degree that will help them boost the country's hi-tech industry. The American president has urged to lift the level of education too so as to guarantee that educated kids fit in with the requirements of a job market that is growing more complex. To land a job in a competitive firm, you need competitive students. A competitive spirit goes with a college education.

Even though education should prepare well-rounded students, college helps the students to specialize in a branch of science. It is essential to acquire competencies to perform at the top level: if you want to become an oncologist, in-depth knowledge of science, and thus long years of study, are necessary. A software developer needs to master programming. Only at university can students enhance their knowledge and skills in order to fill in the technical positions that are so much in demand today.

Going to university is the accomplishment of a lifelong dream: that of climbing up the corporate ladder that will propel a graduate towards positions of responsibility. If you wish to ask for a better salary, there is no better voucher than a university degree. Thus, people opt to sign up for distance learning programs or evening classes to enhance their curriculum and acquire the indispensable competencies that will give them a leg up in their career track. A higher diploma commands a higher salary.

People go to college to test their intellectual abilities. After a few years stuck in a routine job, they feel it necessary to have a breath of fresh air and check whether their abilities can withstand the trial of a demanding education. Even though no financial rewards may welcome them back once they have re-entered the workforce, at least they will have proved to themselves and their families that they can do it, thus acquiring a modicum of self-esteem that is bound to make them feel better about themselves.

Finally, people go to university to discover and meet new people. At college, they will live independently and develop life skills in addition to buying an education for life. They will integrate a new network and interact with people brimming with ambition. Creative ideas spring up after long hours of brainstorming and there are countless success stories of students who have met their intellectual match at college and boldly set out to start a company or a business. The founders of Google are a case in point.

College is the indispensable rite of passage if you wish to acquire knowledge, hone your skills, improve your life conditions or make new friends. Above all, a college opens many doors and broadens the intellectual horizons of people thirsty for knowledge.

13 WHY DO PEOPLE WORK?

People work because they need money to live. What are some other reasons that people work? Discuss one or more of these reasons. Use specific examples and details to support your answer.

1. Key words

to work / to have a job	travailler / avoir un emploi
to go to work / an affliction	aller au travail / un malheur, une détresse
to motivate / motivation	motiver / la motivation
to complain about work	se plaindre du travail
to hold a job / a low-paid job	conserver un emploi / un emploi sous-payé
to provide a living wage	offrir de quoi vivre
to make / to earn a living / money	gagner sa vie / de l'argent
to provide for one's family	faire vivre sa famille
to be financially independent	avoir l'indépendance financière
the pursuit of happiness	la poursuite du bonheur (matériel)
to gain experience	acquérir de l'expérience
to promote / promotion	promouvoir / la promotion
to climb up the corporate ladder	grimper dans l'échelle de l'entreprise
a selfless pursuit	une entreprise altruiste / désintéressée
to be driven by the profit motive	être motivé par l'appât du gain
to contribute to society	contribuer à la société
to seek knowledge	acquérir des connaissances
to sharpen / to hone one's skills	affûter ses compétences
to give sb an identity	donner à qn une identité
to give a meaning (to)	donner un sens (à)
meaningful / purposeful (a)	qui a un sens / un but
a sense of accomplishment	un sentiment d'accomplissement
personal fulfillment	l'accomplissement personnel
to interact with one's co-workers	interagir avec ses pairs
to socialize / socialization	fréquenter des gens / la socialisation
to do volunteer work	faire du bénévolat
to acquire / to gain / to achieve fame	acquérir la gloire
a workaholic	un bourreau de travail
to be proud of one's work	être fier de son travail
to have a passion for one's work	être passionné par son travail

2. Talking points

1. Essay 1

- Work is what gives your personality an identity. Work defines who you are and how competent you are.
- Working is a way of being useful, to the family, to the firm, to the country. Volunteer work, free by definition, lures people into helping others.
- Working helps improve society: a biologist hopes to find the wonder cure, the surgeon alleviates a patient's sufferings, an artist brings happiness in people's lives.
- People go to work because the workplace is a way to interact with people. It is a place to exchange, communicate, but also to share.
- People work to acquire knowledge, develop expertise and become proficient in what they're doing. They develop a sense of accomplishment and personal fulfillment.
- People work to gain recognition from their peers and to acquire fame. Reaching the top is what motivates people to push themselves at work.
- Work is a passion and a form of addiction for the workaholic.
- People work to enjoy the benefits of life; work is not an end but a means that helps them take advantage of life's comforts.

2. Essay 2

- People go out to work to gain practical experience. It is the case for the student, the apprentice, or the intern eager to start off in their careers.
- Personal satisfaction explains why people go out to work (outside the financial rewards). Some feel they are on a mission too: work gives a meaning to their lives.
- Being recognized by the work you do makes people tick. Work gives them an identity. Conversely, the lack of work deprives the jobless of their identity.
- People enjoy interacting with others: be it with workmates, the customers, the clients, the patients, people love the socialization aspect that work confers.
- People love the challenge their work offers: problem solving, task management and fulfillment at the edge of a worker's capabilities justify why they go out to work.
- Some people work for the fun and the thrill that the jobs brings.
- Some jobs—like some computer games—are great at engaging people's curiosity and creativity.
- Glory may be another incentive for people to work. For example, many of the contributors to Wikipedia or to the Linux open source software system, for instance, are motivated by the chance to be recognized by their peers for their technical achievements.

3. Possible answers

1. Essay 1

People are always complaining about the woes of work: they have to get up at the crack of dawn, suffer the hardships of a long commute before they finally reach their destination, only to endure the pressure of a job they are not fit for but have to keep so as to make a living. They say they have to work to live but would financial gain and material comfort be the only reasons why people have a job? I believe not.

Work is first and foremost what gives your personality an identity. Work defines who you are and how competent you can be. Work helps shape your self, your qualities or the weaknesses you need to work on to be a better person. Challenge and risk-taking define the entrepreneur; selflessness and commitment define the soldier; a passion for knowledge and how to transmit it defines the teacher.

Working is a way of living a meaningful life and being useful: to the family, to the firm, to the country. This feeling of purposefulness brings about joy and happiness as people realize they are actually being helpful. For example, the machine tool operator knows that his job is as essential as that of the HR manager for the functioning of the firm. A primary school teacher's job is as significant as a university professor's one. A private is aware that his superiors rely on him to carry out a military operation. Work therefore brings a feeling of satisfaction and self-fulfillment.

Work is an engine of change. People expect their work to improve society: the researcher hopes to find a new cure thanks to groundbreaking research, the surgeon seeks to hone his skills and alleviate suffering, the artist to bring happiness in people's lives, the actress to make people dream. Work, not money, can foster change in society. A society of idle people would soon sink into chaos and would be doomed to oblivion. Contributing to something larger than oneself is what makes people want to work.

Other people—especially lonely people—also go to work because the workplace is a way to interact with others. It is a place to exchange, communicate, and share. It is a place away from the solitude and isolation of the home. Work has an impact that may extend beyond the frontiers of the workplace when co-workers become friends.

There are plenty of other reasons why people work, be it to acquire knowledge, develop expertise and become proficient in what they're doing. The quest for excellence goes through work experience and often leads one to the pinnacle of power and glory, hence providing a sense of accomplishment. To wit the artist who, by dint of hard work gains international fame, the entrepreneur who has pushed back the frontiers of technology, the physicist chasing the elusive boson. Through their efforts and work, all gain the worldwide recognition of their peers and therefore inspire many to follow in their footsteps.

2. Essay 2

There are many reasons why people work—apart from the necessity to sustain one's family or gain financial independence—among them dedication, self worth, love for challenge or curiosity.

One of the first reasons that prompt people to go out to work is to gain some experience and build up their knowledge base. The student who takes on a part time job, the apprentice, the intern are all looking for a leg up in their lives and work is the prerequisite to advancing their careers. In that respect, money is not the prime factor to work.

Another inspirational factor why people go out to work is personal satisfaction. A job worth doing is worth doing well, so the saying goes. People enjoy going out to work because they feel they are contributing to society and something that is larger than themselves. When the doctor, the nurse, the researcher or the teacher are at work, they feel that they are working for the welfare of mankind, saving lives, alleviating pain, looking for solutions to problems, advancing science, transmitting knowledge. These people have a distinct feeling they are on a mission, that they are accomplishing meaningful and purposeful tasks.

Another motivation that drives people to work is the recognition by others of their performance for the organization. Some people are thirsty for recognition and long for their work to be valued in the eyes of others. For them, working is a way of saying 'I exist'. This is all the more true as people assume responsibilities within an organization that may impact high-level decisions.

Other people who go out to work enjoy the interaction with their co-workers. They love the atmosphere in the workplace, or going out to the local pub for a drink and enjoying some quiet time for relaxation and socialization once the workday is over. They also like the camaraderie and interaction with co-workers, patients, and managers. They truly love the clients or customers they have committed to serving.

Finally, some workers enjoy change, challenge, and diverse problems to solve. For them a job is like a mountain to climb: once they have reached the summit, they see other mountains and relish the challenge of scaling them. A job is like an intellectual game, a puzzle to solve. It is stimulating to the brain.

All in all, the reasons why people work are various, at least as various as the jobs themselves. Be it the entrepreneur eager to find the killer app, the researcher looking for the wonder cure or the teacher proud of his/her students' achievements, money is by no means the prime underlying factor. Quite the opposite indeed: the best reward for a job well done is not money but pride, fulfillment, all things that are worth much more than a pay slip.

14 THE INFLUENCE OF TV AND MOVIES

How do movies or television influence people's behavior? Use reasons and specific examples to support your answer.

1. Key words

to watch television	regarder la télévision
to turn on / to switch on TV	allumer la télévision
to turn off / to switch off TV	éteindre la télévision
to go to the movies	aller au cinéma
a cinema buff / cinema goer	un mordu de cinéma
a film / a movie / a soap opera	un film / un feuilleton télévisé
a documentary	un documentaire
to rerun / a rerun (of)	rediffuser / une rediffusion
a blockbuster	un film à grand succès
to be influenced (by)	être influencé (par)
to exercise influence (on)	exercer une influence (sur)
to escape the influence (of)	échapper à l'influence (de)
to have a far-reaching impact (on)	avoir un fort impact (sur)
to spend hours (+ ING)	passer des heures (devant / à)
to affect people's behavior	affecter le comportement des gens
to turn people (into)	transformer les gens (en)
a passive consumer	un consommateur passif
a couch potato / to entertain oneself	un téléphage / se distraire
to be addictive / to be hooked (on)	encourager la dépendance / être accro (à)
channel hopping / zapping	le zapping
a remote control / to channel-hop	une télécommande / zapper
to be addicted to TV / films	être accro de télévision / films
to be desensitized to violence	être insensibilisé à la violence
to be packed (with)	être bourré (de)
to play / to practice a sport	pratiquer un sport
inactive / unimaginative (a)	inactif / manquant d'imagination
critical thinking	l'esprit critique
man's perception of the truth	la perception humaine de la vérité
to extol a virtue	louer / vanter une vertu
to denounce / denunciation	dénoncer / la dénonciation
to condition / to brainwash	faire un lavage de cerveau

2. Talking points

1. The positive influence of TV and movies

- TV is an educational tool. TV opens up our horizons, widens our scopes and shows pictures of countries we cannot visit or events we cannot attend.
- TV and movies raise people's awareness on issues such as war and terror, justice, freedom of speech, the environment or capital punishment.
- TV and movies are sources of information that not only shed light on past and present events but also help man form his own opinion.
- TV and movies are great sources of entertainment. They cater to all audiences: the sports person can watch games, the musician can attend a concert in his/her armchair, the kids can watch cartoons, the student can have access to science, literature, arts or history programs.

2. The negative influence of TV and movies

- TV and movies, especially western movies, exercise a negative influence on the young generation. The youth copy their heroes' hairstyle or dress code (see, for example, the influence of Gothic or horror movies).
- TV and movies depict violence as if it were normal. Violence-packed movies lead the vulnerable minds to act in the same way, which desensitizes them to the harm that violence—seen as a cure-all for all the ills of society—inflicts.
- TV makes people more inactive. Hooked on the idiot box, unable to tear their eyes away from the screen, kids snack on unhealthy food, fail to get physical exercise and therefore develop obesity. The lack of physical exercise means the negation of interaction between young people and the loss of commonality.
- Children are bombarded with imagery that they can neither respond to nor be given time to think about and assimilate. TV confronts them with a reality that is not responsive to them. It is a world they cannot enter, and where their action and initiative make no difference.
- TV makes people less imaginative. Watching TV is a passive activity, a state of mind where stimuli are served to them and choices are being made for them. By watching, they do not exercise their imagination as everything is given to them, hook, line and sinker.
- Modern parents have lost their natural authority over children, so we have to resort to bribery to get them to do what we want. Modern parents do not have to work at parenting, because they rely on TV to keep their children busy and out of their way.

3. Possible answers

1. The positive influence of TV and movies

The use of TV and the cinema is more often decried than praised. Yet, I believe that TV and movies can influence man in a positive way. There are several reasons for that.

First off, TV and the cinema are educational tools. They open up man's horizons. Historical films enlighten him on some periods that he can only imagine in his mind. By watching *Saving Private Ryan* or *Band of Brothers*, man can feel what soldiers experienced on the battlefield. Movies or documentaries about the fauna and the flora show animal life in the raw. No visit to a zoo compares with watching lions and tigers roaming free the savannah or chasing antelopes. TV and films open windows on other countries' customs, landscapes, people and traditions; they replace the journeys man cannot undertake and whet our appetites by suggesting destinations he might want to travel to for his next holiday. TV and movies therefore play a useful role, that of enlightening man, of showing him the remote corners of the world he has not visited.

TV and movies are great means of awakening man's conscience. Through fiction or reality, the power of image frames today's social, environmental or health care issues, such as violence, discrimination, poverty, global warming, extreme weather phenomena or obesity and malnutrition. Movies expose problems. They denounce the abuses and lay bare the scandals that at times plague the management of some government. Soderbergh's *Erin Brockovich*—a 2000 biopic—is a dramatization of the fight of Erin Brockovich against the US Pacific Gas and Electric Company (PG&E) which has been contaminating the groundwater and trying to cover up the life threatening illness of many residents. In the same way, Michael Moore has raised concerns about globalization, assault weapons ownership, the American health care system and the war in Iraq. *An Inconvenient Truth* (2006) is about Al Gore's fight to warn people against the dangers of global warming.

Three, TV and movies are meaningful ways to shape opinions. First, TV and movies are sources of information. They show what happened and shed light on why those events took place. Second, they are forums on which experts and scholars are invited to share knowledge, exchange ideas and explain phenomena. Finally, they let you make up your own mind without imposing or commanding.

Last, movies and TV are sources of entertainment. For the harried employee who wants to relax after a hard day's work, the bed-ridden person, the disabled elderly stuck at home or the people living in a remote area, TV and the cinema offer ways to unwind without having to go through any hassle. Besides, be it the sports people, the young kids or the intellectuals, Disney movies, ESPN or the History Channel, TV and movies offer all kinds of way to enrich oneself without leaving home.

2. The negative influence of TV and movies

Television and movies exercise a significant influence on people's ways and minds, especially the young people's. Be it the content, the subject or the characters' actions, movies and TV act as a form of conditioning of our ways of thinking and living. I believe their influence is heavily biased against our humanness and therefore is quite negative.

First off, the influence of TV and movies is visible in man's everyday behavior. Be it the way we dress and look, the habits we get into, the addictions we develop, TV and movies play a negative role. Today's youth is more concerned with appearing than being. It is not the true values of the soul and heart but the fake images of how we look that matter. Boys are fond of earrings, piercings, and pendants. Girls are keen on smoking Marlboros; they have strange hairdos and use swear words.

Second, it will come as no surprise that in a gun-loving country such as the U.S.A., all forms of violence and fantasy have taken over the film makers' imagination. Movies and TV series extol the virtues of violence, gore, suffering and death. The one way to justice is with a gun. Zapping an enemy is as easy as pie. The daily fare of violence and brutality that is being served feeds man's appetite for more of the same to such an extent that life, real life, has now come to imitate "art" (the cinema genre). Thus, man is no longer in a position to make a difference between good and evil or between right and wrong. Episodes of school or workplace massacres are cases in point. Desensitized to the sight of blood, man has turned into the animal that he sees on the screen.

Three, TV has replaced the communal activities of yore. Kids lock themselves up in their bedrooms to enjoy gory shows, lying on their beds and snacking. The consequence is that we now have whole generations of kids fed on a daily regimen of violence and unhealthy food, which has led to grave concerns regarding obesity and other related diseases. Whereas kids used to go out and play, or do sports, they prefer to stay glued to the screen. Instead of interacting with real people, they take shelter in a fantasy world.

Finally, TV and movies have turned the viewer into a passive absorber of pictures. Man spends hours soaking up images, waiting breathlessly for the next episode, hooked on his *TV Guide* timetable. Man depends on TV so much that he can no longer exercise his critical thinking or his imagination. TV, movies have become the ultimate dispensers of truth. What you see is what is true.

TV and movies have many ways of influencing man. Yet, it is the negative side that is being emphasized, not the positive, such as informing in the name of democracy, denouncing abuses, exposing scandals, for example. TV can be a valuable educational tool as well if it is not used by parents to keep the children quiet and out of their way. Yet, those benefits are heavily outweighed by the negative impact TV and the cinema exert on our daily life.

15 A TRANSPORTATION VEHICLE

Choose one of the following transportation vehicles and explain why you think it has changed people's lives (automobiles, bicycles, airplanes). Use specific reasons and examples to support your answer.

1. Key words

a means of transportation	un moyen de transport
the car / the plane / the bicycle	la voiture / l'avion / la bicyclette
to drive (a car) / a driver, a motorist	conduire (une voiture) / un conducteur
to fly (to) / to ride (a bicycle)	voler, aller en avion (à) / aller à vélo
to travel by car / plane	voyager en voiture / en avion
flight / air travel	les voyages en avion
to book a flight	réserver un vol
to board / to get off a plane	monter à bord d'un / descendre d'un avion
to fly to the four corners	voyager aux quatre coins de la planète
comfort / comfortable	le confort / confortable
speed / fast / convenient	la vitesse / rapide / pratique
safe / accident prone	sûr / sujet aux accidents
to expand man's horizon	élargir l'horizon
the range	le rayon d'action
to reach one's destination	atteindre sa destination
travel time	le temps de déplacement
to cover huge distances	couvrir de grandes distances
a long-haul / long-distance flight	un vol long-courrier
to shorten distances	raccourcir les distances
cheap fares / a low cost carrier	des tarifs bas / une compagnie à bas coût
to rescue people	sauver des gens
relief work / to ferry	le travail de sauvetage / transporter
ground transportation	le transport par voie terrestre
a taxicab / a personal vehicle	un taxi / une voiture particulière
an off-road vehicle	un véhicule tout terrain
a highway / a motorway	une autoroute
a turnpike / a toll road	une autoroute à péage
to give the economy a boost	relancer l'économie
to spark the creation of a new industry	donner naissance à une nouvelle industrie
to do without a car	se passer de voiture

2. Talking points

1. How the airplane has changed people's lives.

- The airplane has changed the speed at which people travel or goods are transported. What used to take weeks can now be done in a matter of hours.
- Remote locations, which were barred to visitors in the past, have been made accessible to man. The airplane offers access to distant markets. Now it is possible to consume tropical fruits and exotic vegetables all year round, which was unthinkable before.
- The airplane is convenient: it carries loads of people and tons of freight in a short amount of time compared to other means of conveyance. Thanks to the airplane, travelling is no longer the privilege of a happy few.
- The airplane is a safe means of transportation. There are far fewer air crashes than car or bike accidents.
- The airplane has given rise to a whole new industry, providing employment to millions of people, be it the aircraft industry or airport and airline management.
- The airplane is used in times of emergencies. When a disaster occurs, planes are rounded up to send relief and rescue workers to the stricken areas. Air tankers combat wildfires, helicopters rescue stranded mountaineers or flood-stricken people.
- The plane has made it possible to travel in a relaxed and pleasant environment where cocktail and meals are served to the passengers.

2. How the automobile has changed people's lives.

- The car has freed man from the constraints of immobility. We use the car to go to work, to go shopping, to go on holiday.
- The car is a wonderful invention, allowing people to travel together whenever and wherever they want. Man is no longer the slave of schedules and timetables.
- The car has given rise to a new industry that has in turn provided jobs for millions of people: the car manufacturing sector but also the tourist industry, the road infrastructures, national parks, etc.
- The car has changed the way people have designed and built cities. The car has made for the expansion and extension of the city to the far suburbs.
- The car is a convenient way for transporting people or goods. Taxicabs, vans, trucks, semi-trailers are evidence of how useful an invention of the car has been.
- Groundbreaking inventions in the automotive industry have allowed the car to go farther and reach places that used to be hard to get to in the past.
- The car has become a safe means of transportation due to advances in automotive science and stricter traffic regulations.

3. Possible answers

1. How the airplane has changed people's lives.

The advent of the airplane has changed the way we travel and the places we travel to, making it faster and more convenient for people to go from here to there. There are several reasons why the aircraft has become one of the most popular means of transportation today.

The first reason is speed. Savvy travelers favor air travel because it is the fastest method of transport around. It can cut hours or days off of a trip. Transoceanic travel used to take months; traveling to the far corners of a country as wide as China, the U.S. or a continent such as Africa or Asia meant traveling weeks on horseback on cramped ships or using impassable roads. The speed of air travel also allows the transport of critical materials like organs and necessary medications to patients in urgent need. Without the airplane, the pace of both business and pleasure would slow down considerably all the more so as air travel is no longer the privilege of a happy few. Any destination is now within the reach of the average man thanks to low cost companies.

Another advantage of air travel is efficiency. An airplane can transport a large group of individuals or freight in a relatively short amount of time compared to ground travel. A car may hit traffic several times on a long-distance trip, costing passengers hours in lost time, as well as engine wear and mileage. There are also no stops for bathroom breaks, fuel top-ups, or leg stretching during a flight.

Air travel is much safer than any other means of transportation. The airplane is less accident prone than other methods of travel. Car traffic has grown heavy in some countries, thus leading to more fatalities on the road. In other countries, car traffic looks like the Wild West with drivers refusing to comply with local rules and regulations, and which are thus seldom enforced for lack of highway police.

The airplane has benefited the economy as well. The air travel industry has created employment for millions of mechanics, pilots, stewards, customer service representatives, and designers. There are also indirect jobs like airport retail services, airline catering, rental car facility staffing, and security. These jobs often offer free or discounted travel, health care coverage and pensions for those who qualify, making a positive contribution to the lives of both employees and their families.

Finally, by shrinking distances, the airplane has made the world a smaller and more accessible place. Since far travel only takes a matter of hours by jet, it's feasible and practical for a young person to pursue college in the U.S., even if he/she's from Australia. It is also a boon to business, because it allows qualified specialists to take employment where they're needed most. Air travel also brings tourists to parts of the world that can greatly benefit from traveler dollars.

2. How the automobile has changed people's lives.

Although the car was invented in the late 19th century, its impact on civilization has been significant on how people travel and work. The car has changed the way people live and move, pushing back the city limits and making it possible to dwell in remote suburbs, to visit relatives, to discover amazing landscapes, to enjoy paid leave, to spend a weekend in the countryside, or simply go shopping.

First off, the car is a wonderful means of traveling for man and his family. The car means freedom for many people, freedom to travel where and when they want. The car has freed man from the timetable and schedules that are attached to train or plane travel, for example. It enables man to explore the byways or travel far and wide along crisscrossing highways.

The car has fostered a whole industry, which has catered to man according to his means. Henry Ford's dream to put a car in every garage has exceeded the carmaker's expectations. Motels have sprung up along motorways, fast food joints have been conveniently built to answer every need and whim of America's mobile people. Thus, millions of jobs have been created thanks to the car.

The car has also changed the way people have designed and built cities. Whereas people would congregate around stations to hop on city bound trains that would carry them to their work, the car has helped them to travel in comfortable conditions to their workplace, and not worry about missing the first or the last train. While suburbs were being built beyond the city limits, whole areas within the city were pedestrianized and humanized.

Naturally, the car has always been a convenient way of transporting people or goods. For example, taxicabs, vans, trucks, semi-trailers are evidence of how useful the invention of the car has been.

Depending on the availability of public transportation, the car is also a convenient means to travel from one place to another. Naturally, the car can go wherever buses or trains do not go. In the same way, recent types of off-road vehicles such as 4-wheels or SUVs offer the possibility for people to reach places which otherwise remain inaccessible to common forms of transport, due to impassable or dirt roads. With the development of safety features such as air bags, safety belts, collision warning devices, the car has also become much safer. Road enhancement, stricter regulations have added to the feeling of security, turning the car into a useful transportation tool but also a vehicle to experience freedom.

16 THE ARTIST AND THE SCIENTIST

It is generally agreed that society benefits from the work of its members. Compare the contributions of artists to society with the contributions of scientists to society. Which type of contribution do you think is more valued by your society? Give specific reasons to support your answer.

1. Key words

to value / valuable	attacher de l'importance à / de valeur
to make a contribution (to)	contribuer (à)
a scientist / to be indebted (to)	un savant / être redevable (à)
a figure / an equation / a theorem	un chiffre / une équation / un théorème
a science textbook	un manuel de science
a researcher / a research worker	un chercheur
scientific research	la recherche scientifique
to do research (on)	faire des recherches (sur)
to invent / an invention	inventer / une invention
to discover / a discovery	découvrir / une découverte
to pave the way (to / for)	ouvrir la voie (à)
the progress of science / medicine	les progrès de la science / médecine
to raise the standard of living	élever le niveau de vie
to increase life expectancy	augmenter l'espérance de vie
to take one's minds off troubles	faire oublier les tracas
to cure / a cure	soigner / un remède
to save lives / life-saving	sauver des vies / qui sauve des vies
to deserve recognition	mériter la reconnaissance
to lift one's spirits	élever l'esprit de qn
to entertain (an audience)	distraire (un public)
a means of expression	un moyen d'expression
a painter / an actor / a musician	un peintre / un acteur / un musicien
a writer / a poet / a playwright	un écrivan / un poète / un dramaturge
to do photography / a photographer	faire de la photo / un photographe
a museum / an exhibition	un musée / une exposition
a performing artist / a masterpiece	un interprète / un chef d'œuvre
to be witness (to)	être témoin (de)
to pass on a legacy	transmettre un héritage
to nourish the soul / to feed the mind	nourrir l'âme / l'esprit

2. Talking points

1. The scientist

- Scientists have made marked contributions in all domains: physics, astronomy, medicine, engineering, biology, applied math, energy, communications, technology.
- Scientists have helped save lives: Fritz Haber's synthesis of nitrogen has helped the world grow nutritious food for billions; Norman Borlaug's engineering of disease-resistant wheat has helped stave off mass starvation. Alexander Fleming discovered penicillin, the first antibiotic. Christian Zoeller did research on the tetanus vaccine. One of the most significant medical devices ever invented, the implantable cardiac pacemaker, is the work of Wilson Greatbatch.
- Scientists have helped society advance on the road to progress, raising our standard of living and ushering in revolutions in technology (the invention of modern appliances), transportation (the car, the plane), computer science or technology (Charles Babbage, and more recently Henry Ford, Bill Gates, Steve Jobs, are examples of scientists and inventors).
- Those inventions or discoveries (Faraday's electricity) have helped man live more comfortably, freeing him from drudgery work to enjoy leisure time, allowing to travel long distance, eat more varied and healthy food and improve his wellbeing.

2. The artist

- The scientist addresses the rational side of man, and appeals to his reason, whereas the artist—painter, photographer, musician, architect, film maker, actor and actress—is more concerned with the emotional aspect of his personality.
- Artists are capable of soothing the minds of the people. In the hustle and bustle of life, artists help man relax by transporting him into a different world.
- Artists reflect their times and their culture. A painter or a writer shows us in pictures and words what we're like as a people. Art is actually a form of communication.
- Actors and other performers, such as singers and dancers, entertain us. They take our minds off our troubles, and remind us of the power of imagination.
- Artists help keep their societies mentally and emotionally healthy. They are an outlet for man's emotions and feelings.
- Artists appeal to man's creativity and imagination. A great scientist can also be a great artist. Leonardo da Vinci and Pascal are cogent cases in point.
- Painters, photographers and writers, play a crucial role in denouncing the horrors of dictatorship, war or the injuries of existence. Science fiction writers point out to the evil of technology. Art makes us look closer at issues. It may be a form of meditation but more often than not it is a call to action.

3. Possible answers

1. The scientist

No contribution has been more significant that that of scientists to advance mankind's progress. What scientists bring to the world outweighs what artists can do for society.

Be it in the medical, biological, technological or energy field, scientists have made distinct contributions that can be measured every day. Thanks to breakthroughs in medicine, epidemics have been controlled and vaccines have been found. Cloning and GMOs have increased agricultural output in order to feed a more crowded and hungrier world. Although nuclear fission is still some way off, progress in offshore oil exploration or fracking has slaked man's thirst for energy. The advent of revolutions in technology, such as the Internet, web-enabled communications, and satellites have shrunk the world, making it easier to get and keep in touch with our loved ones.

Scientists' dedication has helped preserve lives. Be it Marie Curie's discovery to prolong or save millions of lives, Edward Jenner's discovery of smallpox inoculation, Robert Koch who discovered the bacterium that causes TB, Luc Montagnier who developed the blood test to isolate the HIV, the list is endless of scientists who have saved or prolonged life. Linn Enslow's chlorination of water was hailed as a major public health advance of his time. By discovering that different people's blood had different characteristics, Karl Landsteiner turned blood transfusions into a routine procedure, paving the way for other medical procedures that we don't even think twice about today, such as surgery, blood banks, and transplants.

Scientists have served man by helping him to raise his standard of living. Many countries have been lifted out of poverty, following the industrial revolution (and science progress), thus moving Europe from the Middle Ages to the digital age. Thanks to the computer revolution, America, and then Europe and Asia have stepped into the 21st century. A rising tide lifts all boats, as the saying goes, and in that respect scientific progress in one country has had knockoff effects in others.

Furthermore, scientists have helped man live more comfortably. Machines and robots have taken over the drudgery of the work he used to carry out in the past, thus freeing him for leisure time or more rewarding occupations with family or friends. The airplane and the car have allowed man to travel effortlessly. Trucks bring fresh food to our tables overnight. Aircraft have put exotic countries within reach of budget travelers as well, thus expanding not only man's horizons but also raising cultural awareness. Obviously, the hand and mind of the scientist have been instrumental in fostering a revolution in our way of living and traveling. No artist, however worthy, can claim such a legacy.

2. The artist

Artists and scientist both contribute to society yet the impact they have is quite different. Whereas the scientist addresses the rational side of man, and appeals to his reason, the artist—painter, photographer, musician, architect—is more concerned with the emotional aspect of the personality.

Artists have the capability of soothing the minds of the people. Art enables people to unwind and calm down, especially given the hectic pace of life they lead. Listening to a piano concerto or an aria by Schubert is relaxing after long and strenuous hours spent in the office. In the same way, visiting a museum, looking at Dutch old masters takes the mind off worries and transports man into another time and world, offering a form of escapism.

Artists reflect their times and their culture. A painter or a writer shows us in pictures and words what we're like as a people. They record our culture for future generations. They are witness to time and as such are part of the history of a nation. Impressionism, Cubism, Surrealism all are evidence of the changes the world has gone through, in the same way as Zola's realism or Chateaubriand's romanticism did.

Actors and other performers, such as singers and dancers, entertain us. They take our minds off our troubles, and remind us of how beautiful and exciting our imagination can be. During a concert, not only can we reconnect with the beauty and purity of Bach or Beethoven's music, but we can also enjoy the rhythm and beat of creative music by more contemporary artists performing live on stage.

Artists also help keep society mentally and emotionally sound. It has been proved that children who participate in the arts at school, such as painting or music, do better in their other studies. Art of all types is oxygen to the human spirit.

Artists such as painters, photographers and writers, play a crucial role in denouncing the horrors of war or the hardships of poverty. *Guernica*, a painting by Picasso, was created in response to the bombing of a Basque Country village in northern Spain by German and Italian warplanes at the behest of the Spanish Nationalist forces, during the Spanish Civil War. *Guernica* shows the tragedies of war and is a reminder of the suffering it inflicts upon innocent civilians. In *J'Accuse*, Émile Zola took the highest levels of the French Army to task for obstruction of justice and anti-Semitism by having wrongfully convicted Alfred Dreyfus to life imprisonment on Devil's Island. Photographers such as Mathew Brady's pictures of the American Civil War, Jacob Riis's images of New York squalor in the 1880s, Dorothea Lange's prints of the Great Depression stand as the eyes of time in the same way as Ansel Adams, Atget, Brassai, Cartier-Bresson, Man Ray, Nadar, Stieglitz chronicled the shabbiness of life, the ruthlessness of man or the injuries of existence. Artists indeed play an indispensable role in society.

17 VISITING A FOREIGN COUNTRY

You have the opportunity to visit a foreign country for two weeks. Which country would you like to visit? Use specific reasons and details to explain your choice.

1. Key words

to tour a country	visiter un pays
to make / to go on a trip	faire un / partir en voyage
to go on a journey (to)	partir en voyage (à)
to travel (to / in)	voyager (à / en, dans)
to draw people / to be drawn (to)	attirer les gens / être attiré (par)
to be (well) worth visiting	valoir (tout à fait) le détour
a dream destination	une destination de rêve
a learning experience	une aventure enrichissante
a life-changing experience	une expérience marquante
the Seven Wonders of the World	les Sept Merveilles du monde
a historic landmark	un monument historique
a tourist attraction	un site touristique
an unforgettable experience	une aventure inoubliable
to enrich sb's life	enrichir la vie de qn
to learn / to practice a foreign language	apprendre / pratiquer une langue étrangère
to go sightseeing	faire du tourisme
exotic / remote / distant	exotique / reculé / lointain
to be like / unlike	être semblable à / différent de
a gorgeous scenery	un beau paysage
breathtaking	à vous couper le souffle
ever-changing / varied	changeant / varié
to admire / to enjoy / to take in	admirer (un paysage)
the beauty of the scenery	la beauté du paysage
a variety of scenery	une variété de paysages
a rich cultural life	une vie culturelle riche
a cosmopolitan city	une ville cosmopolite
cultural diversity	la diversité culturelle
futuristic / vibrant / bustling	futuriste / dynamique / animé
freedom of speech	la liberté de parole
a history buff	un mordu d'histoire
a warm / inviting climate	un climat chaud / accueillant

2. Talking points

1. The United States of America

- The United States is where history was made and is being made. It is where the first written constitution was drafted and modern democracy was born. This is also where slavery has left the most profound scars and where Martin L. King spearheaded the fight for equality amongst people.
- The United States has a rich cultural history that has left its imprint on every child's mind in the world. Be it the Westward Movement, Walt Disney's movies, Hollywood's dream factory, Western movies, the cultural mix is part and parcel of a child's psyche, feeding the imagination and providing inspirational role models.
- The human factor is another reason to visit the United States: it is a unique blend, called the melting pot, a country where people from all over the world have flocked to start a new life and make their dreams possible. The people are actually one of the strengths of the country, as evidenced by their resilience and capacity to overcome and conquer challenges.

2. South Africa

- South Africa offers a unique mix of wildlife and beautiful landscapes. Its outdoor attractions, and untamed wildlife are unique in the world.
- Africa's biodiversity is another reason to visit. Kruger is one of the oldest established game reserves in Africa and provides people with the opportunity to see animals in their natural habitat.
- South Africa is a place where history happened. It is the home of Nelson Mandela, the hero of the fight against apartheid and a beacon to the world.
- South Africa possesses a unique mix of cultures, owing to the motley and varied origins of its people from African, Asian and European groups. The diverse cultural blend is present in South Africa's artistic and culinary traditions.
- South Africa has some of the most pristine and protected coastlines and beaches in thc world.
- There are no language barriers in South Africa since nearly everybody speaks English. Even though there are 11 official languages, English is spoken by nearly everybody so one won't have problems to communicate.
- South Africa's vineyards are world-famous, dating back to the mid-1600s and, later, developed by the Huguenots who settled in the Cape region. Napoleon Bonaparte, King Louis Philippe of France, Frederick the Great of Prussia, the Lords Seventeen of the Dutch East India Company, and many other powerful figures coveted the wine from Groot Constantia for its quality and exclusivity.

3. Possible answers

1. The United States of America

Some people wonder whether travelling is worth the costs and challenges. I believe visiting another country can reward you in many ways: even though you'll definitely encounter issues you would not face at home, going abroad is well worth the time and effort. As for me, the country I would like to visit most is the United States of America.

There's something special about standing where history happened. Whether you visit the Statue of Liberty in New York harbor, stand on the steps of Independence Hall in Philadelphia, see Washington's home in Mount Vernon, or walk across the killing fields of the Shenandoah Valley, you feel a certain, unmistakable thrill. For this is where American history was made. The backwaters of Louisiana are still ringing with the songs of slaves toiling on the cotton plantations whereas the Yukon still bears the scars of the gold frenzy that took place in the 19th century. American history is all the more present as our childhood has been filled with myths: Indians and cowboys, trail-blazing pioneers, the Westward Movement, Lewis and Clark, David Crockett, Kit Carson, and John Wayne stand as tall as the rocks in Monument Valley. They're all part of our psyche.

A second reason why I would like to visit the United States is its culture. Even though it is anchored in the past, it is forward looking and visionary. Americans may be attached to their roots, yet they know when it is necessary to move forward and be bold. Being a passionate cinemagoer, I would love to visit where films actually are made, Hollywood, the studios. Yet, I also believe the spirit of enterprise is alive and kicking, so, detouring to Silicon Valley is a must. More particularly, America is said to be a rainbow society in which all cultures can blend in and yet keep their distinctive features.

Even though Americans are independent thinkers, they bring together the wisdom of many different cultures and background. Be it Chinatown, Harlem, Little Italy, large cities have witnessed the waves of immigrants who came over and changed the one culture into a varied one. I don't know of any other place in the world where you can get the same cultural mix that you have in the United States.

A last reason I would love to visit America is that I have heard that Americans are a friendly people: making contact is quite easy; people there are open-minded, ready to have a drink or lend a hand, with a smile on their faces and an easy-going manner. They call you by your first name. Yet, nothing pulls together the strength of the American people better than a disaster-scale event, as we recently saw with the Katrina disaster. The Americans jumped into the fray and went down to help the stranded people of New Orleans. This is the hallmark of a tight knit community of people that know that active solidarity is not a shallow word. For its history, its culture and its people, there's nothing that compares to the United States.

2. South Africa

Of all countries worth visiting, South Africa stands out for several reasons. South Africa offers a unique mix of culture, wildlife, and beautiful landscapes. Despite being the most modern African country, South Africa is infused with vibrant culture and has the wild bush at its back door. It has a rare mix of modern development, African culture, outdoor attractions, and untamed wildlife that you will find nowhere else in the world.

Kruger National Park is the place to visit to view African wildlife. It is one of the oldest established game reserves in Africa; it provides people with the rare opportunity to immerse themselves in the bushveld with the lion, elephant, and all the other animals, birds, and reptiles for which Africa is famous. Kruger's incredible array of species is sure to leave people in awe. Yet, despite the phenomenal wildlife, one of the things about Kruger I look forward to is the sunsets. Until you have watched the sun slowly descend in the Western sky, with the sounds of Africa in the air, you have missed out on one of life's great moments. Yet, South Africa's natural offerings are far larger than just what is located in Kruger. Though South Africa has less than 1% of the world's land surface, it has 6% of the world's known mammal and reptile species and 10% of the world's plant, fish, and bird species.

I would also love to learn more about the history of South Africa. It is home to Nelson Mandela, a man the whole world admires. He and other remarkable ANC leaders of the mid-1900s led a bloodless revolution that resulted in the overturn of apartheid and the freedom for millions of colored people. I would certainly love to walk the streets of South Africa where a young democracy is in the midst of blooming.

South Africa's culture is a unique blend of many people descending from African, Asian, and European groups. It has been described as the "Rainbow Nation". Some of the predominant groups are the Venda, Sotho, Nguni and the Shangaan-Tsonga. Other predominant groups are the Afrikaners of Dutch descent, whites of British ancestry, and large groups with Indian roots. Major urban areas are melting pots of culture where you will find shops selling food of all different types. On the streets of Cape Town, for example, you will find shops selling samosas and curries, corner stores with racks of slowly cured biltong which was perfected by the Dutch, tea shops where locals eat fresh scones with their hot tea, and many vendors peddling hand-made African art, paintings, and wood-carvings. The rural areas of South Africa are where you can still experience true African culture. There are entire communities and regions where locals still live in huts, in a manner similar to the way in which past generations lived. There you will find a country in where cattle is a central status of wealth, traditional artwork flourishes, and best of all, dancing and singing are an important part of life. The fantastic thing about South Africans, no matter their ethnicity or where they live, is that they are, for the most part, very accepting of others and optimistic about the future.

18 A GIFT TO REMEMBER

People remember special gifts or presents they have received. Why? Use specific reasons and examples to support your answer.

1. Key words

to make / to give (out) a gift	faire un cadeau
to pick / to choose a gift	choisir un cadeau
a gift giving occasion	une occasion de faire des cadeaux
a giver / a recipient	un donateur / un destinataire
to receive a gift / a regift	recevoir un cadeau / un cadeau recyclé
a gift idea / a gift box	une idée de / une boîte cadeau
to be showered with gifts	crouler sous les cadeaux
to wrap (in) / to gift wrap	emballer (dans) / du papier cadeau
wrapping paper	le papier d'emballage
a gift certificate / voucher	un bon d'achat
a gift token / a token gift	un chèque cadeau / un cadeau symbolique
a pet / a puppy / a budgerigar	un animal familier / un chiot / une perruche
a hand-made gift	un cadeau fait main
a stuffed teddy bear	un ours en peluche
to make sb happy / to please sb	rendre qn heureux / plaire à qn
an expression of love / friendship	une marque d'amour / d'amitié
gratitude / to be grateful	la reconnaissance / être reconnaissant
a travel souvenir / a Christmas gift	un souvenir de voyage / un cadeau de Noël
an engagement / wedding gift	un cadeau de fiançailles / de mariage
to celebrate a special day	célébrer un jour spécial
to commemorate an event	célébrer un événement
to show that one cares	montrer que l'on aime
thoughtfulness	la gentillesse, la prévenance
to bring joy / pleasure	apporter de la joie / du plaisir
to be ecstatic / overjoyed	être fou de joie
to affirm a personal bond (with)	affirmer un lien personnel (avec)
to strengthen a bond (with)	renforcer un lien (avec)
a token of appreciation	une marque de reconnaissance
to mark a milestone	marquer un événement
to reward / a reward (for)	récompenser / une récompense (pour)
to go to the trouble (to)	faire l'effort (de)

2. Talking points

1. Essay 1

- Gift giving is a tradition in most societies. There are many occasions for gift giving: birthdays, Christmas, graduation, engagement, wedding... yet few gifts stand out.
- Gift giving is a way to celebrate or commemorate a special event. It is a way of turning a page, marking an event and remembering that event.
- What matters is not so much the nature of the gift as the gift giver. Some expensive gifts given by people you hardly know are worth much less in emotional terms than the gift given by someone you care for and you love. A gift worthy of the name has an emotional meaning more than an economic value.
- A gift reminds people of the good times they spend together. A game console, for example, will help someone share happy moments with their friends. A bike that a child will be able to ride with friends will be more precious for the opportunities it offers than the object itself.
- A gift is a token of friendship or love. When you look at it, it reminds you of the person that gave it to you. A gift is all the more valuable as it comes from someone you love.
- What matters is not the economic value of a gift but its emotional impact on the recipient.

2. Essay 2

- The gifts we remember usually withstand the test of time. The value of a gift is measured by how long it has stayed with you, not its material value.
- A gift has a strong emotional value: it is a token of love and affection. What matters is not so much the gift itself but the person that gave it to you.
- A gift is like a symbol of belonging. It can play a symbolic role, that of asserting membership in a family or club. A family ring presented to a daughter is a way of pointing at the responsibilities she is bound to assume. It can also be the symbol of a bond between generations as well as the passage into adulthood.
- Gifts are all the more valuable as people have been waiting before being able to receive them. The longer you wait before receiving a long sought-after present, the more valuable the gift can be, and the happier you are.

3. Possible answers

1. Essay 1

Gift giving is a tradition in most societies. Yet, some gifts stand out in people's minds while others have left little or no memory. What are the reasons why people should remember the gifts they have received?

First off, we give gifts to celebrate or commemorate a special event. When I was admitted to college, my parents gave me a rare edition of a novel by Hemingway with a note 'We are proud of you'. I still look at it with fondness. Other special occasions are when you get engaged or married and showered with gifts from friends and family. There are other opportunities to celebrate events and milestones among which school graduation, birthdays and Christmas are the most common. Remembering the gift is as precious as the event is special.

Another reason why people remember the presents they have received is not so much the event as the giver. My grandmother once gave me a camera. She had noticed that I was fond of photography and praised the black and white pics I had taken with my Kodak. Detecting I was more talented than even I suspected, she presented me with a Leica which I still have today and that has never left me on my trips as a photojournalist. Whenever I look at my camera, I remember my grandmother with fondness. It was a meaningful gift that showed she cared, a gift all the more valuable as it was to decide of my choice of a career.

Another reason why people remember the gifts they have received is because they remind them of the happy moments they used to spend together. I remember with crystal clarity receiving a red bicycle for Christmas and the many trips I undertook riding it with friends. First, it would be short trips around my hometown but soon those trips extended into week-long journeys that allowed us to travel across regions and countries.

A gift can be a token of friendship or love and therefore it has a special meaning we remember it for. When he left home to go to college, my brother gave me his wristwatch advising me to study hard and fulfill my dreams. I was only 12 then, but it left a distinct memory. Similarly, every small gift given by my closest friend is symbolical of our enduring friendship. They are reminders of the bonds that year after year have strengthened our friendship.

We are eager to receive gifts from our beloved ones. Their emotional meaning is the main reason why people bear in mind the intimate feelings they have received from others through time. Not only does a special gift help us relive our beautiful memories in the past, but it also reminds us of our former significant emotional states. Gifts play a pivotal role in keeping people close together in life and in memory.

2. Essay 2

What are gifts if not remembrances of things past, small objects that allow us to peer into the past and recall the happy times? Not all presents play that role. Only a few withstand the test of time and that is why we remember them fondly.

We usually receive various types of gifts for different occasions. Irrespective of their cost and quality, all the gifts I have received underscore one thing: there are a few people who love me, think of me and care for my wellbeing. When I grow older, I am sure these gifts will be my best companions: through them I will be able to remember the good times we had together.

A gift has an emotional value: it is a token of love and affection. It is not so much the gift that you receive that makes it special as the person who gave it to you. Presenting a gift is the best way to let the others know how much you care for them. A gift you have received from others shows the affection and love they have for you. The thought that 'someone else is thinking of you' not only makes you happy but also boosts your self-confidence and raises your energy level. A gift is like a driving force, a motivator to fight against all odds because it says you are not alone and you can achieve success. A gift is a reminder that there is someone who loves you more than you love yourself.

Three, a gift is a symbol of belonging. When my elder sister turned 18, my mother gave her a ring that had been in the family for several generations. That ring, adorned with gemstones, was valuable—in an economic sense—but above all in a historical way. It marked a significant milestone in my big sister's life—transitioning into adulthood—but above all it was the evidence of the bond between generations. It was a way for my mother to pass her generation's responsibilities and duties on to the younger generation. When my sister looks at it, she thinks of her family and feels they are at her side, but more significantly it is a reminder of the goals she needs to reach to fulfill the expectations that the family have held for her.

Finally, a reason why people remember presents and gifts is because they have been waiting for so long before receiving them. Hardships and financial problems can at times prevent a family from giving their children the things they have been longing for because they just cannot afford them. When I was younger, I looked green with envy at my friend who had been given a bicycle for her birthday. My mother could not afford to buy one, what with being a single mom and scraping an existence on the brink of poverty. So, when my grandfather bought me my first bicycle, it was the happiest moment in my life. Moreover, he personally taught me how to ride and I spent all my spare time cycling after that event. I have kept the bicycle in my garage and when I look at it (with a smile on my face), it says that things are all the more precious as they are rare, and this includes not only the happy memories I had of riding it but above all my grandfather's love and care.

19 IMPROVING YOUR COMMUNITY

You have decided to give several hours of your time each month to improve the community where you live. What is one thing you will do to improve your community? Why? Use specific reasons and details to explain your choice.

1. Key words

community service / work	les travaux d'intérêt général
volunteer work / volunteering	le bénévolat
to do volunteer work	faire du bénévolat
selfless / altruistic	altruiste, désintéressé
a moral duty / to invest (in)	un devoir moral / s'investir (dans)
to dedicate one's time (to)	donner de son temps (pour)
a non-profit organization	un organisme à but non lucratif
a non-governmental organization (NGO)	une organisation non-gouvernementale (ONG)
environmental volunteering	l'écovolontariat
ecological restoration / re-vegetation	le replantage
weed removal	l'arrachage des mauvaises herbes
to teach prisoners / inmates	enseigner dans les prisons
to teach immigrants remedial French	enseigner le français aux immigrés
an action priority zone	un zone d'éducation prioritaire (ZEP)
a low income district	un quartier défavorisé
an underprivileged / disadvantaged kid	un enfant issu de milieux défavorisés
an at-risk / handicapped kid	un enfant à risque / handicapé
remedial work / mentoring	le travail de remédiation / le mentorat
to coach a youth sports team	entraîner une équipe de jeunes
to serve soup kitchen	servir des repas à la soupe populaire
to visit homeless people	aider les sans-abri
a homeless outreach program	un programme d'aide aux sans-abri
to sleep rough / on the streets	dormir à la dure
to volunteer at a senior center	être bénévole dans une maison de retraite
to organize a food drive	organiser une collecte d'aliments
a charity organization / a charity	une association caritative
home help	l'assistance à domicile
the Red Cross / the Salvation Army	la Croix rouge / l'Armée du salut
to visit sick children	rendre visite aux enfants malades
a volunteer fire department	une brigade de pompiers volontaires

2. Talking points

1. Teaching underprivileged kids

- Getting involved in the community means serving it by being an active participant.
- Doing good does not necessarily mean saving the world or dealing with mass starvation. It is not about money either. Selfless local action does matter.
- Working with deprived kids in an inner-city school or an underserved district is a way of capitalizing on one's skills and returning in-kind some of the gifts one has been blessed with.
- Helping children from low-income families with their schoolwork and homework means making a positive contribution to the future of a country. Actually, without a high school education, chances are that those kids will be doomed to a life of deprivation. The country will be the poorer for it.
- Helping struggling and disenchanted children is a way of boosting their confidence while showing them they can overcome the difficulties they have in class. There are values such as determination and perseverance that one can teach through remedial schoolwork in addition to the schoolwork.
- Children should be aware that there's no such thing as a free lunch in this world and therefore that they should try their best to rise to their teachers' expectations.

2. Helping the elderly

- Volunteering at the local senior center and helping the elderly citizens is a rewarding activity.
- More often than not, elderly people are isolated: they may be far away from their family, they may have few friends left to rely on, or they may just be widowed. Yet, the tasks they face are the same as when they were young and able-bodied. Therefore an extra pair of hands and eyes can do no harm.
- Senior citizens have memories to share, stories to tell. They are the repositories of knowledge; they have a trove of wisdom at their disposal. Listening and talking to the elderly is a way of connecting with the past as well as for them to stay connected with the present.
- There are many things I can do to help the elderly beyond listening to and talking with them: doing the gardening, the shopping, taking them for a stroll, setting up a game of Bingo, reading them stories are ways of keeping them connected and active in society, which is good for the brain as well as the motor skills.
- As the elderly are the necessary link between generations, I believe that helping them will contribute to strengthening the fabric of society and make it more cohesive.

3. Possible answers

1. Teaching underprivileged kids

There are many reasons why people engage in community service work, the central one being that they wish to be active participants in building up or improving the welfare of the community they live in. They realize that, at some point, they have to start walking the talk rather than just talking the walk, or as many a wise fisherman would say, "You gotta fish or cut bait."

Actually, creating positive change, making a difference need not be at the scale of solving mass hunger or alleviating world poverty. We can all of us take on some of the smaller-scale problems or opportunities that might be lurking outside our front door. Similarly, helping out is not about making money, as most organizations value the time, talent and willingness to roll up our sleeves more than anything else.

I, for one, would choose to do remedial work with the deprived kids of the neighborhood high school. There are several reasons for that. The first is that I believe I have a gift for sciences that might as well be put to good use. I would enjoy teaching those kids that have fallen behind in their math and are struggling to keep pace with schoolwork. Helping them cope with the physics or biology problems after school would be a way for me to return in kind the gifts I have been endowed with.

I also believe that working hard in school is a way for stragglers to get out of the rut they are in. If they do not succeed at school, they will be sentenced to a life of menial work, with little hope of climbing out of the poverty trap their parents find themselves locked in. So, while I am teaching math, physics and even a smattering of earth sciences, I will also be helping the pupils to catch up and, hopefully, succeed.

Second, many of those kids have lost all hope of making it. Actually, some may have become disenchanted with an education system that offers dim hope for those who are lagging behind. As there is no one to help them in their homework or do remedial work with them, this is where I can make a difference: by bolstering their confidence and showing them that, by dint of hard work and perseverance, there is a way out.

Three, by teaching them basic science skills, in addition to showing them how to organize their work load, I will be preparing them for a life with a future. If they can be convinced that hard work pays off at some point, it is half the battle won. If those efforts lead to graduation, then they will be able to move on on their own and, who knows, be admitted to the local community college and carry on with their studies.

Teaching is at the core of a child's future. It is never too late to start helping the underachievers at school. Yet, students should be aware that this is a team effort; should they wish to pass the exams with flying colors, they have to meet me half way. Yet this is a challenge worth taking up. You can try and fail, but you cannot fail to try.

2. Helping the elderly

While many people are concerned about the direction in which our country is heading, it sometimes seems like one person can't make a difference. That is why I believe volunteering a few hours each week to some community activity is a fruitful way of investing in the future of our society. Actually, if there is one activity I would choose to get involved in, it would be helping our senior citizens at the local nursing home or providing elder care at home. It can be a positive and rewarding feeling.

Some people may think that helping the elderly people is time wasted. After all, those people are a burden on society and cost much more than they bring in. I happen to think that elderly people play a key role and that extra hands can do no harm in smoothing out the final years of their lives. More often than not, nursing home patients are often alone. They may spend days on end without seeing any visitors. The friends of their age are on the wane, the family are far away or just too busy to bother. If I visit them I will bring a bit of company, a smile and lend an ear and listen to their stories.

Second, most elderly people have played a useful role in society. Yet, when they reach the twilight of their lives, they are pushed aside to make way for the younger generation. Elderly people carry with them the memory of the past. They have borne witness to major events of the century; they have stories to tell. As a consequence, their experience is valuable if not because they are storehouses of knowledge but also of wisdom. They are treasure troves for the generations to come.

By visiting the elderly, I will also be able to help with simple tasks. Often, the homes are understaffed or just overwhelmed by the demands of more senior citizens. I will be able to help at lunch or dinner time or going out for a walk so they can enjoy a bit of sunshine instead of being parked all day long in front of the TV set. Walking them out will be an opportunity to interact and share, an activity that is essential for the brain functions and the motor skills.

If the senior citizens are at home, I will be able to help them with basic tasks like going shopping with them, raking the leaves, clearing the snow in the driveway or doing yard work, depending on the seasons. Senior citizens love gardening and often require sturdy hands for the job. Even though I do not have a green thumb and flowers are not my cup of tea, a pair of strong hands can definitely be great when gardening. There is a lot of kneeling, back bending, or picking that an older person might have trouble with. I will also be able to use my skills to help set up a game of Scrabble or Bingo or, if I go to the pool, take an elderly person with me to enjoy the sun or paddle along.

Elderly people are crucial links in mankind history. Beyond experience, they have values to pass along; interacting with them is a way of bringing generations closer. Even though it takes selfless dedication to maintain the intergenerational links, it is worth it.

20 STAYING IN GOOD HEALTH

People do many different things to stay healthy. What do you do for good health? Use specific reasons and examples to support your answer.

1. Key words

to keep / to stay fit	se maintenir en forme
health / healthy / a healthy lifestyle	la santé / sain / un style de vie sain
to prevent / to ward off disease	éviter la maladie
to be in good shape / good form	être en bonne forme
fitness / a fitness coach	la forme / un préparateur physique
to exercise / to work out	faire de l'exercice
to go jogging / running outdoors	faire de la course à pied en plein air
to ride one's bicycle	faire du vélo
sedentary / inactive / desk-bound	sédentaire / inactif
to go to the doctor's	aller chez le médecin
to visit a doctor	avoir un rendez-vous médical
to do a physical / medical check-up	passer un examen médical
to keep one's weight in check	surveiller son poids
to lose / to gain weight	perdre / prendre du poids
to be overweight	être en surcharge pondérale
weight gain / to slim down	la prise de poids / maigrir
to eat a healthy diet	avoir un régime sain
to eat healthily / to eat right	manger sainement
to avoid foods high in fat	éviter les aliments à base de graisse
to be full of vitamins	être plein de vitamines
wholesome / unwholesome (food)	sain / malsain (aliments)
a diet / to snack	un régime / grignoter
to cut out unhealthy snacks	supprimer les casse-croûtes malsains
(organic) produce / a nutrient	des produits (bio) / une substance nutritive
carbohydrates	les hydrates de carbone
to give up alcohol	renoncer à l'alcool
to get enough sleep	avoir son content de sommeil
to have a social life	avoir une vie sociale
to connect with people	fréquenter des gens
to form bonds (with)	se lier (avec)
to express one's emotions	exprimer ses émotions

2. Talking points

1. Essay 1

- Health is a precious asset that one ought to hold on to carefully. Exercising is a way of maintaining our health: jogging, walking, bicycling, rollerblading, playing Frisbee, being active, especially if one has a desk-bound job. Going to the local gym is another option as well in addition to practicing yoga, going to tai chi classes or dancing.
- To practice sports is mandatory. To spend active holidays, in the mountains, for example, in contact with nature, is a way of recharging the batteries.
- Following a healthy diet helps keep disease at bay. Fat-laden foodstuffs ought to be avoided and the consumption of fruits and vegetables encouraged. Fish and chicken should be preferred to red meat. If going out to eat can be an option, we should prefer home cooking and never skip a meal.
- Going to one's doctor's regularly is a must. Medical checkups, cardiovascular, diabetes or eyes tests are ways of monitoring one's health. One should never procrastinate in case one falls ill. One should visit one's care provider immediately.

2. Essay 2

- The greatest wealth is health, mental as well as physical health. One option is to pursue one's passion and indulge in one's hobbies (playing an instrument, building models, collecting stamps). One can learn a new skill or take on a challenge to meet a goal.
- Combining physical activity with a balanced diet nourishes the body and the mind and keeps man feeling good, inside and out. It is essential to keep one's brain active: going out to evening classes, visiting museums, joining a choir, doing crosswords or jigsaw puzzles keep one's mind sharp.
- Having an active social life is also conducive to a healthy life. Connecting with other people, forging bonds with friends is essential. Joining a club or group of people who share your interests provides a sense of belonging and is good for your mental health.
- Should one want to keep one's mind and body healthy, one must find an activity that de-stresses. If could be watching a movie, going for a swim, or just spending some quality time with your kids or grand-kids.
- A healthy life is a life without excess. Avoid all risky behaviors such as extreme sports, drinking, smoking, doing drugs which are habit forming and harmful to the body. One ought to do everything in moderation even though it does not mean forgoing all pleasures that can derive from drinking a glass of wine, for example.

3. Possible answers

1. Essay 1

Our health is possibly one of the most precious assets we have and that is why it is worth preserving it. I personally have several recipes to stay in good form and ward off disease.

The first (and foremost) thing I do to stay in good health is exercising. I refuse to spend hours on end watching television, sprawled out on the couch and snacking on junk food while sipping sugary soda. A healthy person is an active one. That is why I go out—whatever the weather—to exercise: walking 15' a day, jogging, rollerblading, riding my bicycle, doing the housework. I have also signed up for a gym. I go there twice a week to walk the treadmill, do aerobics and stretching and swim. I have also scheduled yoga as well as tai chi classes and I'm on the softball team. I go dancing once a week.

Another way of staying healthy is to practice sports at a higher level. For example, I love tennis. I am a member of the local tennis club and I go and play there at week-ends, weather permitting. In the Summer time, instead of visiting exotic beaches and lying down on the sand to soak up the sun, I go to the mountains. There, I spend the day outdoors, hiking, walking up and down trails. I believe contact with nature is a way of recharging one's batteries after a long and exhausting year in the office or in the lab. It is always healthy to get away from it all provided one keeps up some form of activity.

Naturally, eating healthily is a must if one seeks to thwart disease. An apple a day keeps the doctor away, so goes the proverb. A well-balanced diet is essential to maintain health. So, I avoid fat diets like the plague. I hardly ever eat meat and prefer fish, chicken and beans. Vegetables and fruits are on my menu: they are full of the vitamins, oils, enzymes and minerals the body craves to build a fully functional immune system. In that respect, I would rather do the cooking than go to the restaurant. When I cook, I prepare my food so as to preserve all the nutrients. I do not skip meals and believe a healthy breakfast is the cornerstone of a good diet. Even though water is the drink of the wise man, one glass of red wine a day does no harm to health.

Going to the doctor's and the dentist's regularly and preventively is also indispensable for those who want to keep healthy. I go for a physical once a year. I have a cardio and an eye test, and my blood pressure checked. Even if I have only mild symptoms (like a sore throat or a slight fever) I do not think twice and rush to the doctor's surgery. Screening tests find diseases early, when they are most treatable, and can actually help keep a disease from developing in the first place. Of course, I make sure I have full health coverage but even though I have to pay more out of pocket, consulting a doctor is a form of life insurance worth taking.

2. Essay 2

The greatest wealth is health, mental as well as physical health. Health is like money: we never have a true idea of its value until we lose it and that is why it is a necessity to keep fit.

The first thing to keep healthy is to pursue one's passions. Of course, not everyone can make a living playing Bach or Beethoven to sold out audiences, or jet around the world trying new foods or even churn out bestselling fantasy novels. But that is no reason to give up on one's dreams. To keep healthy, I set time aside to practice the piano. When I go out I take photos and if I have to stay indoors, I build model trains. All those creative activities enrich my free time and nourish my imagination. In the same way, when I want to learn something new, I take evening classes, or visit museums. I am always busy doing things and indulging in my hobbies. I am one to believe that there isn't enough time in the day to pursue all my activities and therefore I avoid channel surfing, or gawping at Facebook for hours on end.

I also believe that social activities are necessary to a healthy life. I have a few but trustful friends whom I see on a regular basis. I value developing meaningful relationships with them. We visit each other's homes, organize dinner parties or day trips. We share things that are unique among us, be they thoughts, apprehensions, favorite movies, pet peeves, musical tastes and... laughs. My friends make me laugh, and laughing is an important part of health. As an Irish proverb goes, 'A good laugh and a long sleep are the best cures in the doctor's book'. Forging deeper interpersonal connections contributes to the expression of my feelings, which, in turn leads to a healthy life. Of course, if I think I am in a controlling, manipulative relationship, I back out immediately. It is better to stand strong on my own than be held back by someone else.

I believe a healthy life is a life without excess. I gave up smoking a long time ago and took to sports. I shun away from risky behaviors as well: no unsafe sex; I steer clear of the sun; when I drive, I refuse to speed and take my time to travel. No thrill-seeking either: I do not envy all those who go bungee or BASE-jumping for the rush of adrenaline they get from it. Whatever I do, I do it not for the instant gratification but for the long-term emotional and physical balance. A long and healthy life means a reasonable and well-balanced lifestyle.

Everything I do is in moderation. Instead of running ragged at the gym three days a week, I park farther away, walk the dog, take the stairs instead of the elevator and do the gardening myself. I set time aside for each meal instead of gawping at the idiot box, eating my veggies distractedly. Of course, I allow myself the occasional indulgence to blow off steam and have a glass of wine thus keeping me satisfied and in good spiritual form as well. There are other things worth doing to keep the mind healthy and sharp (reading is one) and have a positive outlook on things.

21 GENERATION DIVIDE

Every generation of people is different in important ways. How is your generation different from your parents' generation? Use specific reasons and examples to explain your answer.

1. Key words

a generation gap	un fossé des générations
the millennial generation	la génération Y
to grow wider	s'élargir
to bridge a gap	combler un fossé
to belong to a generation	appartenir à une génération
a lost generation	une génération perdue
the touch-screen generation	la génération écran tactile
to undergo changes	subir des changements
to grow up	grandir
to better / worse off	mieux / plus mal s'en sortir
a way of living / a lifestyle	une façon de vivre / un style de vie
to be born and bred	naître et grandir
to thirst for change	aspirer au changement
a hectic pace of life	un rythme de vie frénétique
the rat race	la course à l'argent
the progress of technology	les progrès de la technologie
to have (satellite) TV	avoir la télévision (par satellite)
a satellite dish	une parabole
a TV channel	une chaîne de télévision
to listen to the radio	écouter la radio
to get one's news off the Internet	lire les nouvelles sur Internet
an electronic gadget	un gadget électronique
to be computer based	s'appuyer sur l'informatique
to depend on computers	dépendre des ordinateurs
a globalized world	un monde globalisé
to be open / narrow-minded	être ouvert / étroit d'esprit
to go into higher education	faire des études supérieures
to be spoiled / spoilt rotten	être gâté / pourri
to remain taboo (to) / a taboo	rester tabou (pour) / un tabou
selfish / hedonistic / shallow	égoïste / hédoniste / superficiel

2. Talking points

1. The present generation compared to the past generation

- The present generation has many electronic gadgets at its disposal that has made life easier. Thanks to modern technology, the present generation works with computers while everything used to be done on paper.
- Communication (SMS, Skype, smart phones instead of landlines) has been made much easier for the present generation.
- The present generation lives in the information age. Information is available quickly and 24/7. It is obtained mostly from the Internet.
- There are more TV channels and videos. There used to be one TV channel only and no VCR. People used to go to the cinema whereas today the young download movies.
- The world is no longer your village. Thanks to affordable means of transportation, borders have opened up and travelling has been made easier; so have opportunities to study abroad.
- Societal barriers have been torn down. Homosexuality is no longer a taboo, abortion has become a right, same-sex marriage is gaining traction. Women have made strides in gaining equal rights. The world has become a more tolerant place to live in, at least in the West.
- For the present generation, education has become a right. Affirmative action has helped the minorities go into HE, for example.
- The world used to be a more dangerous place. Military duty was mandatory whereas today, except in a few countries, young people do not have to serve their country in the armed forces.

2. The past generation compared to the present generation

- The previous generation had strict standards of behavior whereas today's generation seems to have become more permissive and loose about ethics and morals.
- The village used to be the world for my parents. Now the young chat on the Internet, holding virtual conversations with friends and neighbors the world over.
- The past generation would gather around the fireplace and play parlor games; today's young are glued to their computers and play multiplayer online games with people they do not know.
- Life used to be quiet and slow-paced. It has become hectic and fast-paced. We would take time to discuss issues. Now we need to make instant decisions.
- The written word and education were sacred, whereas today the information we have is taken from the net and is not always safe and secure. Education was the privilege of a few. Now it has become a right for all.

3. Possible answers

1. The present generation compared to the past generation

Each generation possesses features that are typical of its times and progress. Many names have been coined to describe them, be it Baby Boomers, Gen X, the Millennials or the Homeland Generation. Each generation is different from the previous one.

The main difference between my parents' generation and mine lies in the development of technology. With the spread of electronic devices, the computer and the world wide web, people are now able to perform tasks that were unknown to my parents' generation. Whereas my parents put pen to paper, we now PDF our homework or school reports. Whereas we used sophisticated pocket calculators, my parents used old-fashioned machines that had only limited functionalities.

High technology has changed the way we communicate too. Young people today have smart phones, they chat on the web, exchange SMS or Skype. It is as easy as pie for them to talk to their keypals on the other side of the planet. Whereas my parents wrote letters that took days or weeks to reach their destination, today's young chat over the net in real time. Whereas the telephone was a precious and expensive commodity, cellphones are ubiquitous today.

Another feature of today's generation is the ease of access to information. We now live in the information age, where news is available live 24/7 online or from CNN. Whereas it would take days for information to reach my parents, we now have instant news—breaking news—thanks to satellite communication. The news my parents would read would look stale today in comparison. Young people are hungry for the latest and spiciest news. They need to know immediately what has happened to their favorite pop stars.

Unfettered access to information has extended to entertainment. Movies, cartoons, documentaries that can be accessed from the home have changed the way we consume our entertainment. Whereas my parents would make it a treat to go out to the cinema, we think nothing of downloading a film or buying a DVD online and watching it on the computer. There used to be one official TV channel, there are now many private ones, catering to everybody's tastes.

Whereas my parents lived in a tight-knit village, my generation now lives in the world. Borders have been pushed away, globalization has set in, bolstered by the revolution in transport and communication. Today's young people travel more extensively than the previous generation did. My parents used to stay in France for their holidays and their education, we now travel to the other side of the world and study abroad.

Much progress has been made in the way we live: my country is at peace whereas my parents knew war. Social and societal advances have granted more rights to the minorities. All in all, we live much better today than we used to.

2. The past generation compared to the present generation

Many old people rue the fact that the world has changed for the worse, that we do not live up to the same standards of probity and integrity that we used to. Today's generation has become much more tolerant, even permissive, in terms of what is acceptable and not. Thus, age-old values such as respect for elders and teachers, the sanctity of marriage are no longer in, whereas pot-smoking, same sex marriage or coming out are quite fashionable. It seems to me that our generation has lost its bearings; it has become unprincipled and clueless.

In the same way, I do not believe that the world we live in today is more tightly knit than the one we used to know. By expanding the frontiers, we may have gained some friends, or people we call so, but actually we have failed to notice that it is better to have a few real and trustful friends than have a large circle of people we only know virtually through social media or networks. It is better to meet people face-to-face and know you can count on them if need be than have lots of acquaintances we know little about.

In the same way, communal life has gradually disappeared at the expense of family and friends. There used to be a time when parents and children would gather around the fireplace to talk, read or play parlor games. Television then became the electronic hearth, soon to be replaced by the computer. Today, generation Me is hunched over the computer, engrossed in multiplayer online games or hooked on FB chatting with complete strangers. The spirit of togetherness has made room for that of individualism. Parents and friends used to help and support each other. Youth today look on the Internet for recipes. My parents used to have meaningful conversations. Now we just chat. Content is out, communication is in.

Whereas life in the village used to be slow-paced, now city life has become hectic and frantic. All we think of is beating the traffic, dropping the kids off at school and picking them up, rushing to work, expediting chores and trying to get some rest at week end. My parents used to live within walking distance of their workplace. Now young people have to spend hours commuting.

Finally, one of the great differences and the reason why I think my parents' generation was better off was that we had time to reflect because the world was not an instant one. For example, we had textbooks at school. My parents believed in hard work and a strict education. The written word was sacred and so was knowledge. Today, information is to be trusted only if it comes from the Internet. Youth have debunked school. Getting into higher education is no longer considered a challenge as university has opened its doors wide to virtually anyone with an underrated high school diploma.

There are huge differences between the previous generation and mine. Yet, even though technological progress is not to be shunned, I believe that life as my parents used to live it was much better than today.

22 A NEW INVENTION

If you could invent something new, what product would you develop? Use specific details to explain why this invention is needed.

1. Key words

to invent / an invention	inventer / une invention
to innovate / an innovation	innover / une innovation
technology / technological	la technologie / technologique
to come up with an idea	inventer / trouver une idée
to come across a problem	rencontrer un problème
to work out a possible solution	imaginer une solution possible
a brainwave / a Eureka moment	une idée de génie / un déclic
to take an idea from paper to market	mettre une idée sur le marché
to turn a concept into reality	réaliser un concept
to market an invention	lancer une invention
to identify a need / a want	identifier un besoin
to design / to develop a model	concevoir / développer un modèle
to build sth from the ground up	construire qch en partant de rien
a hi tech device / a prototype	un dispositif hi-tech / un prototype
hand held	qui tient dans la main
to be designed (to)	être conçu (pour)
a technological prowess	une prouesse technologique
to be useful (to)	être utile (à)
a treatment (for) / a drug	un traitement (contre) / un médicament
a wonder cure (for)	un remède miracle (à / pour)
a miracle drug / to suffer	un médicament miracle / souffrir
the pharmaceutical field	le domaine pharmaceutique
to benefit (from)	profiter (de)
to make life more comfortable	rendre la vie plus confortable
to perform a task	accomplir une tâche
an arduous / demanding task	une tâche difficile / exigeante
to outperform man / flawlessly (adv)	faire mieux que l'homme / sans erreur
a time machine	une machine à remonter le temps
automation / automated	l'automatisation / automatique
cost effective / automated	économique / à la pointe du progrès
to revolutionize / labor saving	révolutionner / qui économise le travail

2. Talking points

1. The self-driving vehicle

- There are plenty of famous and less so famous inventions that are being used every day. The driverless vehicle looks like it could be a useful one.
- A fully autonomous vehicle would make the roads safer thanks to an array of assisted-driving features that would drastically reduce the carnage of road accidents and the medical costs associated with them. As the car is self-driven, there would be fewer risks of the motorists falling asleep on the road, for example.
- Fully autonomous cars would contribute to significantly cutting gas and CO_2 emissions, by eliminating congestion.
- A robotic car would provide mobility for the growing number of older and disabled people in the rich world and in some emerging markets too.
- People who spend hours driving every day would get a chunk of their life back, to work, rest or play while they are on the road. Business travelers might be able to sleep in driverless cars that would hurtle down the motorways at night, delivering them to the next morning's meeting fresh as a daisy after a nap.
- Parents would welcome a car that does the school run for them. Teenagers would no longer be put off getting their first car by tough driving tests and steep insurance rates because they would need neither licenses nor personal insurance.
- There would be no need to spend hours on end behind the wheel, making sure to comply with the Highway Code or the speed limit and checking for speed traps.
- When people went shopping, a self-driving car would save the time they usually take looking for a parking spot.
- Auto theft would be deterred, as tracking devices would alert the owner or the police of a vehicle's whereabouts.

2. A treatment to cure disease

- Inventing the miracle pill or drug to tackle the scourge of cancer would eradicate a disease that strikes many people worldwide, whatever the country they live in or their social background.
- A magic pill would alleviate pain and cut the emotional toll killer diseases inflict on friends and family.
- Finding a magic pill would have an economic impact saving lives but also preventing from bringing ruin to families that can ill afford costly treatment.
- Some countries need a strong manpower to help move the country on its way to progress. A magic treatment would keep a young population in form and help steer scarce resources towards building much-needed infrastructures or schools.

3. Possible answers

1. The self-driving vehicle

Long the stuff of science fiction, the self-driving car is a necessary technology that has the potential to deliver huge environmental benefits. So, if I had the time, I would invent and develop the robotic car.

The first reason to build an autonomous car is enhanced safety. Assisted-driving features such as sensors and V-to-V (vehicle to vehicle) communication would reduce crashes by maintaining a safe distance between cars in steady traffic. As the driving is left to the machine and everything is fully automated, there would be no risk of drivers being distracted, of inattention or driver error. Gadgets, cameras and other technological wizardry would take over and make decisions on the driver's behalf and overrule him/her in an emergency, for instance, braking to avoid a crash.

Features like embedded control systems that automatically accelerate and brake with the flow of traffic could prevent accidents but also cut down the greenhouse gases emitted by vehicles. Roads would be used more efficiently. There would be fewer emissions because of less road construction. Gas emissions would be reduced by driving in convoys. Similarly, automated vehicles could be shared among people, thus driving down the manufacturing costs and waste generation.

Elderly and disabled people would be able to find some mobility as they could drive wherever they want, whenever they want. The visually impaired, for example, would just hop in and visit those places that public transportation does not get at.

As the driving would be fully automated, motorists would be able to use their time wisely when traveling long or short distances. People would be left with much more time to be productive and complete all the work in their commuting time, for example. No need to spend hours on end behind the wheel, making sure to comply with the Highway Code or checking for speed traps either. The driverless vehicle would read road signs and admonish the driver if he/she breaks the speed limit. Motorists could read, work on reports, play games online, chat with friends and family, in other words spend more cost-efficient time than if they were actually driving. In addition, they might also travel at night thus saving some useful rest time.

When people went shopping, a self-driving car would save the time they take looking for a parking spot. They would just let the car drive them to their destination and drop them off at some point before picking them up once they have done their errands.

And naturally, stealing such fully automated vehicles would be much more difficult. Car-tracking GPS devices would help find the vehicle, alerts would warn the owner of any invasive intrusion. All in all, there would be many advantages to inventing such a vehicle, the greatest of which would be making the road a safer place to travel.

2. A treatment to cure disease

Throughout history, inventions have helped people explore new worlds, build communities, develop resources, increase productivity, ease burdens, and enjoy life to the fullest. Every year, thousands of new inventions hit the shelves. Many will be flops, but some will become must-have items in every home. Why haven't we cured cancer yet is a question I often ask myself for if there's one thing that I would like to invent it is the miracle pill or drug to tackle that terrible disease once and for all. There are many reasons for that.

The first of them is, naturally, that cancer strikes many people worldwide. This modern day scourge spares no one, rich or poor. Cancer indeed varies from one continent to another, one century to the next but it is still there, changing, evolving depending on the environment, diet or climate. Coming up with a cure would benefit everyone, not only those privileged few that can pay for costly treatment.

Another, more basic reason to justify the invention is to alleviate suffering. People who undergo chemotherapy or are treated through transplants are usually under great pain. Terminal cancer is sheer agony. In addition to the physical pain experienced by the patients, there is the emotional toll that such a dreadful disease takes on family and relatives. Watching life ebb away and your beloved slowly die saps even the strongest and causes people to sink to the depths of despair.

The third reason is economic. A terrible disease, just like an epidemic, wreaks havoc on a family or a country. Aids, for example, has cost billions in useless treatment and lost income in addition to laying waste to entire generations. Breast, lung or colon cancer are killers that have brought ruin to families. Low-income households in particular, have been hard hit by disease. They lack proper medical coverage and have to mortgage their homes to be able to pay for health care. Quite often too, saddled with debt, they just cannot afford treatment or hospital care.

The situation in emerging countries is even worse where basic necessities are not addressed. African governments in particular, are ill prepared to deal with the continent's growing cancer burden. Rising pollution, adopting western dietary habits, high smoking rates, poor nutrition and aging populations are among the factors leading to an increase in African cancer cases. The WHO estimates that by 2020 Africa will account for more than one million new cases of cancer annually. But Africa is the continent least prepared to cope with this new pandemic even though many of the cancers found in Africa are preventable or treatable when detected early; yet, because of a lack of resources and basic infrastructure, people do not have access to cancer screening, early diagnosis, treatment and palliative care. A wonder drug would go a long way towards helping the continent blossom and thrive.

23 HONORING A FAMOUS PERSON

Your city has decided to build a statue or monument to honor a famous person in your country. Who would you choose? Use reasons and specific examples to support your choice.

1. Key words

the subject for a statue	l'objet d'une statue
to commission a statue	commander une statue
to erect a statue	ériger une statue
to build a memorial	construire un mémorial
to deserve the honor	mériter l'honneur
to be famous (for)	être célèbre (pour)
to make a contribution (to)	contribuer (à)
to pay attention (to)	faire attention (à)
to commemorate	commémorer
commemoration	la commémoration
to be remembered (for)	dont on se souvient (pour)
to cherish	chérir
to dedicate one's life (to) (+ING)	consacrer sa vie (à)
commitment to the work	le dévouement au travail
cultural heritage	l'héritage culturel
a durable symbol (of)	un symbole durable (de)
an act of heroism / heroic	un acte d'héroïsme / héroïque
to be hailed as a hero	être accueilli en héros
to make a hero	transformer en héros
to salute the heroism (of)	saluer l'héroïsme (de)
to risk one's life	risquer sa vie
to have grit / skill	avoir le cran / les compétences
to answer the call to action	répondre à l'appel
to look up to sb	admirer qn
to display courage	faire preuve de courage
to have a mind of one's own	être indépendant d'esprit
in the face of danger / adversity	devant le danger / l'adversité
self-sacrifice	le sacrifice de soi
a moral example / a role model	un exemple, un modèle
ethics / ethical	l'éthique / éthique

2. Talking points

1. The firefighter

- Firefighters are heroes for the simple reason that they save lives and, beyond, protect the community they serve. Their concern is for the people in need.
- Firefighters possess a sense of sacrifice and dedication. On call 24/7, they often sacrifice family or personal life to help others.
- Firefighters work for the common good. They are not concerned with the selfless pursuit of fame and glory. They put other people's lives before their own and thus are true examples of altruism. Serving is their motto.
- The firefighters' sense of ultimate sacrifice is exercised without expecting any rewards or gain for their action. What matters for them is to do their job as professionally as possible.
- Yet, firefighters are also human. Their actions are performed in full cognizance of the possible risks and costs those actions may entail. They are willing to accept sacrifice but up to a certain point. They know how to keep a cool head in all situations.
- We all look up to the firefighters for their actions. We have all dreamed—at some point—of becoming firefighters. They lead by example and that is reason enough to praise and honor their action.

2. Charles de Gaulle

- A true statesman, de Gaulle embodies all the qualities of a hero: determination, ambition, vision. He fought during two world wars with courage. He was made prisoner and was wounded in action several times. His courage was also at work when, at the end of WWII, he entered Paris though resistance from Vichy partisans had not been overcome yet.
- A man with a vision, he determined early on that a war could not be won without mobile armored divisions.
- A man 'with a certain idea of France', he refused to cave in to Petain's regime, in his country that was then under the sway of Nazi Germany. His idea of grandeur was also at play when France withdrew from NATO or when he endeavored to turn the country into a nuclear powerhouse.
- Not being one to seek fame and glory for himself, de Gaulle went through the wilderness after losing the 1946 elections and returned to power when asked to do so.
- A man with an ambition for France, he launched several industrial projects and led a country that had trouble putting war issues behind on the road of progress and expansion.

3. Possible answers

1. The firefighter

Should I want to build a monument to commemorate a famous person in my city, I would choose the firefighter. I live in a dry and wooded area where actually, for lack of maintenance by the land owners, wildfires often break out, endangering the lives of people and animals alike while threatening to destroy property.

The first and foremost reason why I would choose the firefighter is, of course, that firefighters risk their lives to protect the homes and livelihoods of farmers on the edge of wilderness. Many a times, they have been called to put out blazes; their heroic actions have saved many lives while preserving the farms and cattle. Such bravery is not typical of my region only. On 9/11, 2001, for example, Americans saluted the heroism of the first responders who died running up the twin towers' staircases as office workers sought to escape. In July 2013, the country once again had to mix admiration with grief as it mourned the deaths of 19 firefighters near Yarnell, Ariz., the greatest single loss to any fire department since 9/11. As residents ran from their burning homes, the firefighters rushed toward the flames that would soon overtake them, trying to subdue the blazing chaparral. Their only concern was for people in need.

Firefighters are heroes to my eyes. They commit to their job with selfless dedication, training hard all year long, often sacrificing family life and other activities to be ready when duty calls. Training in arid conditions and rugged terrain, while carrying 20-kilo packs on their backs, they never think twice when the question comes down to saving people or preventing a fire from spreading and plunge into action without hesitation.

Firefighters are a special breed of people who work for the common good. They are not after the selfless pursuit of glory. They never put their own interests before others. For me, rushing headlong and with a purpose to save people is a clear example of altruism: giving one's lives so that others can be saved.

The firefighters' heroic acts are performed with recognition of possible risks and costs. Firefighters are not daredevils courting death. They know the risks and prepare for them. They are true professionals, with a sharp awareness of the risks they run when battling the flames. That is why, after all, they may not be compared to the true heroes some of us may think they are. Firefighters do not rush headlong into action but know how to keep a cool head when assessing a situation and weighing the risks versus the stakes. This makes them human and that is another reason why I would like to have a monument built for them. They are not abstract actors in society but men and women with a keen knowledge and apprehension of the dangers that their profession entails, armed with a determination to apply those skills they train so hard to hone all year long.

2. Charles de Gaulle

Many people have played a key role in my country, yet none as great as Charles de Gaulle. A soldier and a statesman he embodies all the qualities that are required in order to get penciled into the hero category: determination, ambition, and vision.

De Gaulle was first a military hero. Educated in France's finest military academy, he fought in both world wars, was made prisoner in Germany during World War I and repeatedly wounded while fighting on the front lines. De Gaulle's courage was also evidenced when Paris was liberated and he returned to the French capital a hero, walking into Notre Dame cathedral undaunted and impervious to the hail of bullets fired by Vichy militia and fifth columnists.

De Gaulle also had a clear vision of how war ought to be conducted and how necessary it was to modernize the French army. In the 1920s and 1930s, he proposed to introduce mobile armored divisions, central to warfare, as proved by a successful armored counter attack he mounted during the 1940 Battle of France in Montcornet.

As he wrote in his *Memoirs*, de Gaulle had 'a certain idea of France'. In WWII, when his superior, Marshal Philippe Pétain, gave a radio address to convince the French people to give in to a German takeover, de Gaulle flew to London—almost being shot down by the German air force in the process—and responded to Pétain by giving a famous radio address, broadcast by the BBC on 18 June 1940, exhorting the French people to resist Nazi Germany. He organized the Free French Forces with exiled French officers in Britain and rejected the armistice with Nazi Germany right from the outset, an act of treason for the Vichy regime and for which he was sentenced to death in absentia.

Unlike many politicians today—de Gaulle had a selfless view of his own mission, a view he shared with the first U.S. President, George Washington. Not one to seek political glory, he retired from politics in the early 1950s. Yet, he was voted back to power as President of the Council of Ministers by the French Assembly during the May 1958 crisis, a mission he welcomed for a lofty ideal and the common good—saving his country. De Gaulle led the drafting of a new constitution founding the Fifth Republic, and was elected President of France in 1965.

Immensely patriotic, de Gaulle and his followers held the view, known as Gaullism, that France should continue to see itself as a major power and should not rely on other countries, such as the United States, for its national security and prosperity. During WWII he insisted that France should be considered as a full-fledged nation when dealing with his British allies and the United States, and that she should retain full freedom of action.

Above all, de Gaulle had an ambition for France whose industrial projects he encouraged to launch during what was called the Thirty Glorious Years. For being "a man of the day before yesterday and the day after tomorrow" (André Malraux), de Gaulle is the one I would choose to build a monument for.

24 MOVING TO A NEW CITY

A person you know is planning to move to your town or city. What do you think that person would like and dislike about living in your town or city? Why? Use specific reasons and details to develop your essay.

1. Key words

attractive / unattractive	attractif / peu attractif
a district / a neighborhood	un quartier
a residential area	un quartier résidentiel
poor housing / an inner city / a slum	l'habitat pauvre / un ghetto / un bidonville
posh / upscale / affluent	chic, cossu / haut de gamme / riche
dodgy / unsafe / an inner city	miteux / peu sûr / un ghetto
unaffordable real estate	des logements inabordables
to afford renting	avoir les moyens de louer
to be priced out of the housing market	être impossible de se loger
a museum / an art gallery	un musée / une galerie d'art
a movie theater / an opera house	un théâtre / un opéra
a historical landmark	un bâtiment historique
heavy traffic	une circulation dense
traffic congestion	les embarras de la circulation
a traffic jam / a congested street	un embouteillage / une rue embouteillée
a disused transit system	un réseau de transport à l'abandon
to enjoy peace and quiet	aimer le calme
peak hours / rush hours	les heures de pointe
a park / a green space	un parc / un espace vert
a biking lane	une piste cyclable
urban sprawl	l'étalement urbain
to get around (in)	se déplacer (dans)
to travel long distances	faire de longs déplacements
safe / reliable public transport	des transports en commun sûrs / fiables
crowded / packed with people	bondé
a shopping center	un centre commercial
educational facilities	des écoles / universités
night life	la vie nocturne
outdoor activities / a park	des activités de plein air / un parc
quaint / picturesque	au charme suranné, désuet / pittoresque

2. Talking points

1. Essay 1

- There are many disadvantages to living in my city, the first of which is the substandard housing conditions in a country that is expanding rapidly. There are several slum districts and few modern apartment buildings.
- Pollution is a major hindrance. Traffic congestion is an intractable problem. With factories spewing out noxious fumes, the city is not a healthy place to live in especially for vulnerable people like the young and the elderly. Smog shrouds the city most of the year, and sewage goes untreated. The city reeks. We hardly ever see the sun.
- Congestion is a nightmare in a city teeming with people and with little or non-existent public transportation. The ubiquitous car is clogging the streets, thus adding insult to injury to the air pollution problem.
- There are many social problems in our poor city, such as crime, alcoholism, drug abuse. Unemployment, especially youth unemployment, goes hand in hand with muggings and thefts. The city is not safe.
- Yet, the city is attractive to tourists because of its historic past and the many buildings or landmarks that are evidence of its past splendor. Some districts have retained their age-old traditions and are attractions for visitors.

2. Essay 2

- Living in the capital city has many advantages, especially educational opportunities for my friend's children and relatives. We have the best schools in the country and some of the top research facilities.
- The city student community is cosmopolitan and varied. The cultural life, sustained by young people, is quite vibrant. There are many cultural events all year long.
- Career-wise, the city offers unparalleled opportunities to build a fruitful and enriching career, be it on the national or international level.
- The city enjoys a reliable and affordable transit system. The subway and bus system works round the clock, without strikes or breakdowns. It is clean and safe too.
- The city is eco-friendly and encourages the use of bicycles. Bike lanes and a bike sharing scheme make it easy to commute to work, for example and spare the expenses associated with having a car.
- On the downside, the city is an expensive place to live in. Rents are high and buying a house is out of the reach of the average man.
- The climate may be a deterrent to those who have grown up or lived in sunny climes. We have four seasons and winter can be particularly harsh and punishing.

3. Possible answers

1. Essay 1

If a friend of mine was to move to my city, I would probably urge him to stay away. In the country I live in, cities have grown quite fast and urban life has become more a headache than a pleasure. There are few incentives to settle in my city.

First, living in my city is uncomfortable because of the poor housing conditions. Lured by job prospects, people have poured in seeking to start a new life; they cram in unsanitary lodgings that have no electricity or sanitation. Others have chosen to live in shacks and slums that have sprouted almost everywhere. Lack of funding has prevented the government from building modern apartment buildings.

Second, cars and industries have worsened air pollution. Smog hangs heavy most of the year and we hardly ever see the sun. Rivers are used to reject untreated sewage, which makes it hard for children and elderly people to breathe. Waste goes untreated or is burned up and ends up in noxious and reeking landfills. All of this makes the city an unhealthy place to live in.

In this city teeming with people, congestion is a recurrent problem, especially during morning and evening rush hours when streets are packed with vehicles. Daily traffic jams make it impossible for people to get to work in time. Because of the lack of adequate transportation, people use their private cars to commute to work. Even though city government has recently taken steps to address a problem that threatens to spin out of control, much remains to be done to curb the number of cars entering the city and parking everywhere.

Because of poverty in this part of the world, my city faces many intractable social problems. Crime, alcoholism, drug abuse are rampant. Many young people are on the dole and have turned to stealing and trafficking to make both ends meet. Assaults are frequent too and for that reason the tourists have been deterred from visiting the place.

Yet, my city is a historic one. As the first capital of the country, it has retained some of the splendors of the past. Ancient pagodas dot the city; the old district is a gem worth visiting, with its quaint, narrow alleys, lined up with old shops that give the visitor a taste of 18th century life. Many craftsmen are still there who sell artifacts and genuine items, far remote from the tourist trade of sleeker and more polished towns.

All over the world, cities are on the rise, and mine is no exception to the rule. Yet, I believe that local authorities should try to relieve cities of overpopulation. Traffic conditions will have to change drastically and more parks will have to be built. On the other hand, because it is an ancient capital, much remains to be done to preserve the quaintness of some districts and rehabilitate old buildings. This is, to my eyes, the prerequisite to attract more visitors and bolster local tourism.

2. Essay 2

Moving to a new city can be a daunting yet exhilarating experience. When a friend told me he would soon be moving to my city, which is my country's capital city, I found many advantages that he would find in his new home.

First, I pointed out to the education opportunities for his children. I live in a city that boasts the finest schools and universities. Be it the high school system or college life, I am confident that his children will find here all the opportunities to excel and follow the best academic paths possible. Not only are the schools staffed with the best professors, they also have the best research facilities in the country. The medical and biological colleges, in particular, are at the cutting edge of science.

Another advantage of my city is that, because of its cosmopolitan and varied student community, it is more youth-oriented than any other place I know. There are plenty of cinema and theater houses, two opera houses, and several museums that cater to the art lovers, from primitive sculpture to contemporary painting. There is an intense cultural life all year round, with exhibitions, music festivals, and events that promote the arts. As the city wants to attract young people, admission fees are kept to a minimum. The local nightlife is also quite exciting but this is not the main reason why people move in.

Career prospects are naturally quite exciting. In a city that is the seat of government and the hi-tech industry, I believe there are plenty of opportunities to climb the corporate ladder and carve out an interesting professional path. As the city is an international hub too, chances are that you will connect with people and industries from all over the world and have a stimulating career. For someone who wants to change jobs, living in a big city is the right move.

Even though my city is big, transportation is quite reliable. We have a safe transit system, with subway running on time and reaching out to every district. The city is also eco-friendly. The town authorities encourage riding your bicycle to work and if you do not own one, there is a bike-riding scheme that allows flexibility and convenience in your daily commutes. No need to add that a car would be incongruous in a city that prides itself on its green, pedestrian-friendly policies.

Even though living in my city has plenty of advantages, I still believe that it is not a cheap place. People need to have incomes in the top brackets to be able to afford to buy or even rent a place. Because of the powerful attraction of the city but also the limited space to build new high rises, you need to be well off to live here. Also, the climate is not always lenient. For people who live in sunny California or Florida, moving to a more continental climate may be a deterrent. We have four seasons, and winter can be harsh, spring long in coming and the summer hot and humid even though I believe a change of season is better for health than a one-climate place. Yet, high rental costs or weather conditions are far outweighed by the other advantages of living in my city.

25 A GOOD CHILD

What are the important qualities of a good son or daughter? Have these qualities changed or remained the same over time in your culture? Use specific reasons and examples to support your answer.

1. Key words

to expect (sth) (from)	attendre (qch) (de)
a blessing (to / for)	une bénédiction (pour)
to bring up, to raise / to educate	élever / éduquer
the offspring	les enfants, les rejetons
upbringing / education	l'éducation
to grow up	grandir
child-rearing / parenting	l'éducation des enfants
a generational difference / divide	une différence entre générations
to become an adult	devenir adulte
to demand / to require	exiger
to obey / to disobey (sb)	obéir / désobéir (à qn)
obedience / obedient / disobedient	l'obéissance / obéissant / désobéissant
to quarrel / a quarrel	se quereller / une querelle
to pick a fight (with)	se quereller (avec)
to support / supportive	soutenir / qui soutient
loyalty / loyal (to)	la loyauté / loyal (envers)
to respect / respect / respectful	respecter / le respect / respectueux
to honor / duty / dutiful	honorer / le devoir / respectueux
to gain / to lose respect	gagner / perdre le respect
disrespectful / contemptuous	qui manque de respect / méprisant
to rebel / rebellious / arrogant	se rebeller / rebelle / arrogant
to earn the respect (of)	mériter le respect (de)
politeness / polite / rude	la politesse / poli / grossier
to make one's own decisions	prendre ses propres décisions
to go against one's parents' wishes	aller à l'encontre des désirs de ses parents
to throw a tantrum / to dote (on)	faire un caprice / adorer, être gaga de
to use bad language	être grossier
to perform well in school	bien réussir à l'école
to care for one's parents	s'occuper de ses parents
to do one's parents proud	faire la fierté de ses parents

2. Talking points

1. Essay 1

- Children owe their parents respect. They should defer to their judgment and take their advice into account.
- Children owe their parents obedience. They should refrain from disobeying or breaking family rules. Parental authority is constantly defied by children eager to test the limits of their own freedom.
- Children ought to look after their parents when the parents reach old age. They should try to be there for them and not foist off the responsibility of caring for them to others, by parking them in a nursing home, for example. Too often today, parents are considered as a burden on the children. We used to live in a caring society, but we now live in an individualistic one.
- The nature of the family itself has changed. The standard model is being phased out. Divorces are on the rise, blended families have become acceptable, and the nature of marriage itself is evolving. The children's behavior, obligations and duties bear the brunt of such changes. Their education has changed too.

2. Essay 2

- The generation gap has widened over the past decades. Progress is changing the face of the world more quickly than in the past. What children believe in today does not necessarily echo what parents used to believe in.
- Children refuse to conform to age-old rules set up by their parents. They no longer wish to follow what their parents' square society model mandates and prefer the wayward and independent-minded spirit of the beat generation. Square is out, hip is in.
- Changes in society, such as social networks, online video games, mandatory schooling, sports activities have altered the makeup of a child's circle. Whereas work, especially fieldwork, was dictated by the seasons, with children working alongside their parents, now it is the school year, week-ends, study-abroad programs, breaks and vacations that pace the adolescence years. The parents used to be the role models, now it is classmates, cliques, gangs or even Internet heroes.
- The waning of parental influence and the shift in values extend far beyond the school. With modern means of communication, children are now opening up to new value sets, remote from their parents. Movies, videos, keypals, web resources, Skype have an impact on a child's education and upbringing.

3. Possible answers

1. Essay 1

The qualities of children have changed over time. Whereas kids used to follow more or less their parents' lifestyle—as is still the case today in some emerging countries—in contemporary society children have moved away from the standard model of the past. The qualities of a good son or daughter are no longer what they used to be.

Respect for one's elders was a precept, or commandment, that children formerly raised in the Christian faith used to follow. As church attendance was a duty-bound obligation, what was preached at church was applied in the home. Respecting one's parents meant deferring to their judgment and taking their advice to heart. Never would kids dare to stray from the strait and narrow the parents imposed on them. Things have changed today: children are brought up on a heavy regimen of television and/or role models that are remote from the parents' ones or do not conform to the Church's tenets. Kids have become much more independent-minded than they used to.

Quite often too, there is a crisis of authority, especially in single-parent homes where absentee fathers are a thing of the past and where the mother has trouble coping with her offspring all the more so as kids are influenced by their peers. Children no longer obey their parents or their elders. They want to lead their own lives. Whereas children used to do the chores, be helpful and comply with the home discipline, they now do their own thing. Rules are made to be broken as if children wished to test their own freedom and check how far they can dare parental authority.

In the past, children used to take care of their parents in their old age. That was especially true at a time when the state could not provide for senior citizens, when social security was unheard of and when communities were strong and families tight-knit. Today, young people care little about their parents. Whereas we used to live in a caring society, we now live in a selfish, individualistic and ego-centered world where it is every man for himself. Once they have left home children are so busy building a life for themselves or looking after their own children that they often forget to visit their parents. Yet, there was a time when it seemed logical for children to repay in kind the attention and the love lavished unto them by caring parents.

Whereas children owe their parents some loyalty, it looks like such allegiance is shifting, but not necessarily because of the children. A family used to be a rock solid unit. Parents would stick it out to the bitter end. They would weather marital storms, if only for the sake of children. Children were the very reason why a marriage lasted. Today, divorces are on the rise and the model of family no longer encourages loyalty. All in all, I believe the qualities of good children have changed according to changes in culture, whether parents like it or not.

2. Essay 2

Generational differences have existed throughout history. Yet, fast-paced cultural change, driven by technological progress, the rise of youth movements defying entrenched authority in some countries, the rebellion against social norms, the changes in such matters as musical tastes, fashion, culture and politics owing to the globalization of culture have helped to widen the gap between generations to such an extent that children and parents have now adopted a widely different set of values. 'The Times They are a-Changin' as Bob Dylan wrote in 1965. The way parents expected to behave in their youth no longer applies to what they can expect from their own children.

To begin with, children today tend to rebel at a younger age than in the past. Many figures such as Salinger's Holden Caulfield in *The Catcher in the Rye*, the hippies' counter culture and earlier on Elvis Presley's songs prompted widespread waves of soul and identity searching, the refusal to conform to a certain model or follow rules. The square society has given way to the beat society. Often, against their parents' wishes, kids leave home and travel the wide world. They start smoking at an early age, dabble in drugs and drink when they are not even 12 years old. Their attitude is as much one of defiance and rebellion as it is a way of asserting who they are in their struggling quest for an elusive identity.

Values have changed too, driven by mandatory schooling. In the past, children would leave school early and work alongside their parents on the farm. They would help with the chores, and, when they went to school, would listen to their parents' advice to work hard to have a chance of making it. Role models have changed today, as well as influences. As children spend longer days in school, friends have gradually replaced parents as models to look up to or emulate. Some kids today find a greater sense of belonging in the cliques or the gangs than in the family. They no longer look up to their parents but seek to impress friends and partners.

The growing influence of external forces coupled with the waning of parental clout extends beyond the school limits. Social networks, access to internet resources, the revolution in communications media expose children to influences outside the realm of the home. Even though children live at home, their world is outside the home. They hardly come down for dinner and prefer to stay in their room and chat with people they hardly know. Movies, videos, discussions show them that it is normal that their own values be questioned and challenged. What they see on the screen changes their values: for example, traditional parents will want to educate their children to live a virtuous life next to them whereas studying abroad makes children realize that life in the home village does not square with their ambition to climb the corporate ladder or create their own firms some 10,000 miles away. TV, the Internet, means of transportation may have shrunk distances, yet they have also widened the cultural gap.

II. Making an argument

01 MATCHING EDUCATION AND SKILLS

Educational institutions should actively encourage their students to choose fields of study in which jobs are plentiful. Use specific reasons and examples to support your opinion.

1. Key words

to look for / to land, to get a job	chercher / trouver un emploi
an education geared (towards)	une formation orientée (vers)
vocational training	la formation professionnelle
to enroll (in courses)	être inscrit (dans des cours)
to sign up (for)	s'inscrire (pour)
to be equipped (with)	être armé (pour)
to seize a job opportunity	saisir une occasion professionnelle
a fast-growing sector of employment	un secteur professionnel porteur
a growth area	un secteur en croissance
a declining career / a career on the wane	une carrière en perte de vitesse
a career choice / track	un choix / une voie professionnel(le)
a career trend	une tendance professionnelle
full employment	le plein emploi
the job market	le marché du travail
a job search	la recherche d'un emploi
to be unemployed / jobless	être au chômage / sans emploi
career information	des informations sur les carrières
to fill a vacancy	pourvoir un poste
a job related to one's education	un emploi à la hauteur de sa formation
to match supply and demand	faire correspondre l'offre à la demande
a job skills–education mismatch	la disparité entre la formation et les compétences
to qualify (for) / qualification	être qualifié (pour) / la qualification
to be stuck in a rut	être enlisé
a university degree	un diplôme universitaire
a job skill level	un niveau de compétence professionnel
a road to nowhere	une voie de garage
to be sidelined	être mis sur une voie de garage
a dead-end job / an odd job	un boulot sans avenir / un petit boulot
to acquire / to gain skills	acquérir des compétences
commoditization / a commodity	la marchandisation / une marchandise

2. Talking points

1. Choosing fields of study where jobs are plentiful

- Academic institutions should monitor which sectors are growing and which are on the wane before making decisions on their educational policies.
- Government funds schools and therefore should be allowed to dictate the curriculum. Education comes with a sticker price. Public monies should not be wasted on formations that lead to dead end jobs.
- Such a government hands-on policy would cut down unemployment and raise the hopes of a sometimes disillusioned youth.
- Government must take into account the general interest of the country, not the individual interest. It must be able to face problems such as demographic changes, especially the aging of the population and train the youth to useful jobs.

2. The choice of an education must remain an individual freedom.

- The choice of a career is a fundamental freedom that should be left to each student's initiative and not imposed by outside power or the diktat of policy makers.
- The choice of a career should depend primarily on the assessment of one's own skills, abilities, talent, qualities, interests, availability and geographical location.
- Unlike a refrigerator or an automobile, an academic degree should not be considered as a commodity. If that was the case, universities might be dependent on industry and researchers and academics would become the producers of products.
- In some fields where jobs are not plentiful, careers are doomed to disappear altogether (handicraft, craftsmen, for example). It would require huge investments in training the academic staff to teach some subjects that attract only a minority of students and which no longer meet the needs of a technocentric society. On the other hand, giving up on teaching those niche subjects would mean the loss of traditions and identity.
- The risk is to train specialists in one sector, thus paying lip service to what an education should be: to educate all-round people.

3. Possible answers

1. Choosing fields of study where jobs are plentiful

That educational institutions should encourage students to choose fields of study in which there are jobs available makes sense. Indeed, no institution would encourage people to embrace careers in declining sectors such as textile or woodworking, photo processing, or bookbinding, to give a few examples. Those jobs have been on the wane since the advent of the digital age and are only held by a small minority today. Training a majority of students in those jobs would be irrational, ludicrous and a waste of money. It stands to reason that learning basket weaving today has no economic sense in the western world. Education experts and officials should therefore take into account growing and struggling sectors before deciding on policy-making.

The second argument in favor of the proposition is plain enough. Public monies should not be wasted to make allowances for a declining job market. First, it is essential that a country be mindful of its economic development in a competitive world. Second, a policy that would listen to the market trends and forecasts would thwart unemployment and the attendant evils that go with the unsuccessful quest of a secure job. The youths would no longer be compelled to hop from one odd job to another, or from one placement to another, waiting in vain for an opening and a fixed position. On the other hand, it would provide a nation's youth with jobs that pay, not jobs that sideline people and sentence them to a life without a future. Taxpayer's money would benefit from such a policy into the bargain.

Indeed, institutions should take into account the general welfare of a nation, not the individual concerns of students more interested in becoming, say, gas station attendants than programmers, eye specialists or software developers. In the same way, institutions should be able to adjust to the changing reality of a nation. We have seen over the past decades the graying of the population. There are plenty of jobs to be had in home help, nursing and health care. Yet, there are not enough nursing schools to handle all the applicants. The career options related to computers are absolutely off the charts. There are some professions that are always in demand, no matter what. Doctors, surgeons, actuaries, lawyers will remain a growth sector.

All in all, it is a government's duty to ensure that the country develops harmoniously and in keeping with progress. On the other hand, it must make sure that the young people who are being trained should not be left on the wayside and actually contribute to the nation building. That is why government should exercise a modicum of authority to make sure the economy—the pillar of development—goes in the right direction.

2. The choice of an education must remain an individual freedom.

However attractive it may be, the proposition to actively encourage students to choose fields of study in which jobs are plentiful is illusory and fallacious. It flies in the face of long standing traditions of freedom. It is a complete disregard for students' tastes, motivations and abilities and the very definition of education.

Education, by tradition, should be free and open to all. Conversely, all students should be entitled to an education of their choosing. Can we imagine a country in which the only career tracks would be programming, engineering or teaching? Freedom to choose one's trade is as sacred as freedom to speak or to worship. It is a fundamental right that cannot be infringed upon. Therefore, the choice of a career should not be imposed by outside power. Thrusting a formation down the throats of students would be counterproductive and probably lead to fierce protest. A democracy worthy of its name should offer and not constrain, it should propose and not impose.

Second, the choice of a career depends primarily on an assessment of a person's skills, abilities, qualities, interests, availability and geographical location. Some students are more gifted for mathematics or computer science, others have a taste for the humanities or the arts. Some would rather choose the short track to a job, others are willing to stay in school and pursue higher education. Not taking such arguments into account would doom students to failure and the country to spiritual ruin.

Imposing a limited choice of education programs in the name of economics, would mean the commoditization of education. A university would be turned into a diploma mill, complying with the orders of industry to meet employment needs. A degree would likely be considered as a commodity, traded on the job market according to the laws of supply and demand. Education would become a product in the same sense as a car, a fridge or a house, bought, sold and traded in the same way. Worse, education would be at the mercy of government policy makers, ready to marshal expertise for the war effort—bomb making, cyberwarfare or other more sinister scenarios, for example. University presidents and chancellors would be invited to sit on the boards of directors of private industry, Fortune 500 companies and multinational corporations. The faculty would no longer be simply pursuing research as a contribution to human knowledge or as an aid to education. They would be essentially the producers of products.

By offering a limited choice of educational programs, a country would run the risk of losing out on traditions. Jobs that are not plentiful yet are necessary to ensure that arts and crafts live on—drawing, glass blowing, woodcarving would be off the map. Cooking traditions would likely go the way of the horse, so would fashion designing. Some careers would be doomed to disappear altogether. Above all, such a proposition would give the lie to what education is and should remain: the training of the spirit in the name of loftier ideals, i.e. educating men and women to become thinkers, not producers.

02 THE SAME CURRICULUM FOR ALL

A nation should require all of its students to study the same national curriculum until they enter college rather than allow schools in different parts of the nation to determine which academic courses to offer. Use specific reasons and examples to support your opinion.

1. Key words

a curriculum / [pl. curricula]	un programme
to impose / to set a core curriculum	imposer un tronc commun
on the curriculum	au programme
a uniform curriculum	un programme uniforme
mandatory / compulsory ÷ optional	obligatoire ÷ facultatif
to meet the needs (of)	satisfaire aux besoins (de)
to design / to develop a curriculum	concevoir / mettre au point un programme
to introduce / to change a curriculum	introduire / présenter un programme
to fashion a curriculum	élaborer un programme
curriculum content / subjects	le contenu / les sujets d'un programme
a broad-based curriculum	un vaste programme
to homogenize / homogenization	homogénéiser / l'homogénéisation
a strong knowledge base	un solide socle de connaissances
to acquire / to gain knowledge	acquérir des connaissances
a unique / common measurement system	un système d'évaluation unique
formative years	les années de formation
to maintain the same level	maintenir le même niveau
a criterion [pl. criteria]	un critère
to complete high school	terminer ses études secondaires
to lag behind / a laggard	être à la traîne / un traînard
to determine a standard level	déterminer un niveau homogène
to foster academic harmony	encourager l'harmonie scolaire
to ignore a student's personality	faire fi de la personnalité d'un élève
to allow a degree of flexibility	permettre une certaine flexibilité
to fall by the wayside	être laissé pour compte
to customize the teaching process	personnaliser l'enseignement
to switch schools	changer d'établissement scolaire
a gifted student	un élève doué
to dumb down education	niveler l'éducation par le bas

2. Talking points

1. Students should study a uniform curriculum.

- A uniform curriculum would provide a standard level for all. Students would have a solid knowledge base and therefore would be well rounded before entering college.
- A uniform curriculum would equalize the educational field between rural and urban areas and erase differences between high and low achievers. The same curriculum for all would help fill the knowledge gap and guarantee educational quality for all. No one would be left on the roadside.
- A same curriculum would make for a value centered education and a stronger nation. Kids would be taught the same values that form the hard core of a nation – and then develop a sense of unity and nationalism to boot.
- One single curriculum would mean equality of opportunity for college admissions. A uniform curriculum would put an end to the mad race for the top schools; it would ease the admission process to college, as there would be one single national exam, based on the same criteria.
- A uniform curriculum would ensure a stable and universal learning pattern with quality teachers teaching the same content to all.
- A uniform curriculum would encourage and not hamper the mobility of parents, students and teachers.

2. The curriculum should be diversified, not homogenized.

- A uniform curriculum would mean the end of diversity, at the local level. It would erase the specificities of each region / state / local or regional history / geography / language and ignore the regional identities; it would be an end to the freedom to augment a curriculum as local authorities see fit. A nation's educational system might then defeat its own purposes in the long term.
- A uniform curriculum would mean the end of personality diversity and talent. It would provide a single mold and undermine the originality and uniqueness of a personality, stifle creativity and innovation. It would ignore each student's qualities and gifts.
- A uniform curriculum would sap competition between schools and students and make the schools equal, dragging quality down instead of lifting it up in some cases.
- A uniform curriculum would suppress freedom to teach and the ways of teaching. What would matter in the short term would be teaching by the test so as to meet a country's obligations.

3. Possible answers

1. Students should study a uniform curriculum.

The proposition argues in favor of a unique nation-wide curriculum for all schools up to college rather than granting freedom to schools to decide upon their own curricula. Indeed, a unique, common curriculum would serve several purposes.

A national core curriculum would be beneficial to a nation in many respects. First of all, it would provide all children with fundamental knowledge and skills. A common core curriculum would ensure that the children grow up into reasonably informed, productive members of society equipped with the same background and able to stand up to the scrutiny of employers, supervisors or any managers whose companies they would apply for. A same diploma, sanctioning a core program, would pass the stress test of knowledge and therefore earn students solid-rock credibility.

Second, a common core curriculum would be the national equalizer when crunch time comes to apply to universities. No longer would there be a yawning gap between rural and urban communities, between the economically challenged and the affluent upper class district schools. The mad race to the most selective colleges might therefore come to an end. All students would run with the same chance of being admitted, at least academically. In addition, a core curriculum would provide a predictable foundation upon which college administrators and faculty could more easily build curricula and select course materials for freshmen that are neither below nor above their level of educational experience.

Third, a core curriculum would ensure that all school-children are taught the essential values upon which any democratic society depends to thrive, and even survive—values such as tolerance, freedom, respect, and so on.

Another argument in favor of a single core curriculum concerns the quality of teachers. Indeed, compelled to teach by the curriculum, so to speak, teachers would be accountable to demanding programs that are the same all over the country. Incidentally, the differences between schools would be erased as the same stringent standards would be applied across the board.

Last but not least, teaching by the curriculum would make easier the transfer of students from one region to another, according to their parents' professional mobility, for example a new posting or deployment for the military. Thus, by being able to move around the country without fearing any loss in educational quality, families would be in a position to meet the employers' demands and follow the employment trends much more easily. As the curriculum would be the same everywhere, they would run no risk of losing out on transferring to a new position. All those advantages would eventually benefit the students, the schools but also the country's educational level as a whole.

2. The curriculum should be diversified, not homogenized.

Designing a core curriculum would not be in the best interests of the students. Such a system flies in the face of individual freedom and initiative, barring which a nation's educational system might defeat its own purposes in the long term.

The first, and significant flaw to adopting a single curriculum would be the loss of diversity. The inflexible nature of a uniform national curriculum would preclude the inclusion of programs, courses, and materials that are primarily of regional or local significance. In such countries as India, China or the United States, which tend to take into account local disparities in their curricula, local or regional history would be put on the backburner to the benefit of a national curriculum. Local vernaculars would no longer be taught; in France, we can hardly imagine Corsican or Alsatian becoming the mainstream language in a revamped unique curriculum. Students would be worse off as a result of their ignorance of the traditions, values, and cultural contributions of the people whose citizenship they share. Freedom should therefore be left to each regional authority to augment and adapt the curriculum as they see fit.

The second flaw to the proposition has to do with the quality of the students themselves. Not all students wish to go to college and upping the standards to the benefits of a few regardless of the majority of students willing to pursue other avenues after high school is a blatant violation of an individual's right to choose their education.

And what should be said about the uniqueness of individuals? Such a system would cast in the same mold all students, independently of their talent, skills, taste or intelligence. Forcing the weak students to meet college-level education, for example, would be sure to sentence them to long years of study so that they could rise up to the demanding standards expected from college students.

On the other hand, such a system would ignore the originality and independence of each school system. Some schools cater to students willing to study law or medicine, or put the emphasis on the arts and humanities, dependent on the students' bends and personalities. There are also special ed schools, reserved to handicapped or disabled students. Should they be expected to meet the rigid national standards too?

Additionally, a single core curriculum would make light of the originality of some teachers. Indeed, some methods are better suited for high achievers, just like others are so for the low achievers. Therefore, adopting a common curriculum would doom to failure any creative approach, thus stifling pedagogical innovation.

In the final analysis, the standardization of pre-college level education is like a double-edged sword. While it could serve as an insurance policy against a nation of dunces and illiterates, at the same time it might serve to obliterate cultural diversity and tradition. The optimal national approach is a balanced one that sets a core curriculum yet leaves the rest up to each state or to each school district.

03 MAN'S OVER-RELIANCE ON TECHNOLOGY

As people rely more and more on technology to solve problems, the ability of humans to think for themselves will surely deteriorate. Use specific reasons and examples to support your opinion.

1. Key words

a game changer	un événement marquant
a game changing discovery	une découverte révolutionnaire
advances in technology	les progrès de la technologie
the progress of science	les progrès de la science
the advent (of a technology)	l'avènement (d'une technologie)
to usher in (an age of)	inaugurer (une ère de)
the horse-and-buggy generation	la génération d'antan
tech trends	les tendances de la technologie
the digital revolution	la révolution numérique
technological wizardry	le génie technologique
to be computer savvy	être calé en informatique
a breakthrough	une avancée décisive
state-of-the-art technology	le nec plus ultra de la technologie
to be a great boon (to)	apporter une aide précieuse (à)
to rely on / reliance (on)	compter sur / la dépendance (sur)
to help solve problems	contribuer à résoudre des problèmes
to free man (from)	libérer l'homme (de)
to ease man's life	faciliter l'existence
to free human imagination	libérer l'imagination
low-level, menial tasks	des tâches subalternes
repetitive / dull	répétitif / ennuyeux
to dull man's abilities (to)	émousser les capacités de l'homme (à)
to be subservient (to)	être soumis (à)
to make man lazier	rendre l'homme plus paresseux
man's ingenuity	l'ingénuité humaine
to think outside the box / creatively	réfléchir de façon originale
to preclude / to obviate creativity	empêcher / exclure la créativité
to undermine man's ability to think	saper la capacité de l'homme à réfléchir
to impair man's reasoning skills	diminuer la faculté de raisonnement
to impede the ability of man (to)	empêcher l'homme (de)

2. Talking points

1. Technology has not obviated man's ability to think for himself.

- Technology is dependent on the human ability to think and make choices (every implementation of and advance in technology is driven by human intelligence and decision making).
- Technology is a boon: it provides time for people to think creatively. Free time can be devoted to complex creative thinking; it helps man to understand hidden and complex phenomena and explore unchartered territories, from the outer space to the human body.
- Developing a new technology calls for man's ingenuity. It requires a creative mind and logical thinking.
- Technology has made man more knowledgeable and creative through the development of networks and connectivity. The digital revolution has allowed for an unprecedented exchange of ideas. Access to medical information permits patients to self-research symptoms for a more informed doctor visit. This exercise opens pathways of thinking that were previously closed off to the layman.
- Technology has freed man's imagination to come up with innovative solutions to world problems (pollution, nuclear safety, sustainable development, human rights, censorship in authoritarian regimes).
- Technology raises new issues that did not exist without technology, calling for more creative thinking and imagination.
- The development of new technologies calls for ever more complex thinking abilities. Technology has sharpened man's mind to come up with the killer app.

2. The reliance on technology has crippled man's ability to think.

- Man's over-dependence on technology has lessened his capacities to calculate, to argue logically, to write clearly, to articulate his thoughts.
- Man has lost his sense of orientation when deprived of the right technology. He can no longer navigate the streets in the city, or make a difference between north and south.
- Traditional cuisine has been lost to the benefit of microwave cooking and the inclination to cut time and money and thinking out elaborate meals.
- Because of technology, communication has been reduced to a minimum. Whereas he could exercise his imagination and share thoughts in writing, man is content with just communicating a few terse sentences in poor vocabulary.
- Deprived of his electronic devices, man is a crippled animal, unable to think and function independently in everyday life.

3. Possible answers

1. Technology has not obviated man's ability to think for himself.

The idea that technology has crippled man's capacity to think independently verges on the absurd. Technology is dependent on the human ability to think and make choices, not the other way round. Technology far from being an obstacle to independent thinking has been a boost encouraging people to advance bold ideas.

Technology has freed man from mundane problem solving and allowed him to engage in complex thinking. It has freed the mind from the tedious tasks of painstaking calculations and provided more time for creative thinking. While technology may diminish some mental skill sets, it has enabled other, more essential types of thinking to thrive, providing boundless opportunities to understand hidden phenomena.

Developing new technology calls for man's ingenuity. It requires a creative mind and logical thinking. Every day, new operating systems, mobiles, computers are coming to market. The advancement in computer indicates how it has improved our problem solving but also our thinking ability.

By providing access to information otherwise unavailable and connecting people at a distance, technology has helped man to share ideas and, together, come up with original and creative approaches to problem solving. For instance, data mining or grid computing have enabled man to speed up results through the use of state-of-the-art computers, thus allowing researchers to focus on exploring further hypotheses and testing untried theories. Technology has thus enhanced man's curiosity and knowledge.

Technology has itself created new issues that did not exist without technology. The proliferation of automobiles has introduced a need for fuel conservation on a global scale. With increasing energy demands, global warming has become a concern inconceivable to the horse-and-buggy generation. The problems that have developed alongside the growth of technology call for more creative thinking, not less. Solutions require the unfettered imagination of maverick scientists and politicians.

At the same time, globalization, competitiveness between firms and the race to patent filing have hastened progress and sharpened man's brainpower. Be it microprocessors, nanotechnology, tablets or computer performance, progress has demanded that man think fast to come up with the killer app that will reduce the competition to naught. Technology, in that case, has offered myriad challenges to the mind in a world where only the fittest or the most innovative survive.

Technology is part of human experience. Given the history of the human race, there will be no limit to the number of problems to tackle. There is no need to retreat to a Luddite attitude to technical advances, but rather the necessity to embrace a hopeful posture as to the possibilities that technology provides for human inventiveness.

2. The reliance on technology has crippled man's ability to think.

The impact of technology has been felt in all sectors and transformed the world we live in. Be it transportation, navigation, communication, medicine or the workplace, we have come to rely heavily on technology in our everyday life. If, on one hand, technology such as high speed train, satellite navigation systems, brain scanning techniques, stem cell research, mobile telephony, wireless networks or computer-assisted programs have made man's life less burdensome, on the other, technologies galore has obviated the ability of man to think for himself.

One may be tempted to put forward the hypothesis that man's reasoning and creative capacities have been greatly reduced by his overreliance on technology. For example, man cannot do without a pocket calculator to do simple math. Man's blind trust in cash registers or ATMs and the technology behind them has freed our mind from the tedious tasks of doing simple operations, yet deprived us of exercising our reasoning and math skills.

Man's sense of orientation has been greatly impaired by new technology. Without his satnav system, he gets lost in the maze of streets for the simple reason that he can no longer read the city map. When he drives to a destination, his GPS is like a leash on his guide dog, telling him where to turn, or when he has arrived. And when the signal from the satellites is weak, woe betide the unlucky traveler for he won't be able to read the road map and travel that byroad that is so much more picturesque because the GPS has indicated it is not the shortest way to his destination.

In the same way, the development of new technologies has blunted man's eagerness to prepare good meals. He's just as happy with microwaving supper these days, thus losing out on traditions and originality, not to mention the bland taste of the dishes that are being served to him. Food has become standardized thanks to those money and time saving devices. Recipes that were the spice of life have been replaced by a list of ingredients on the product's label.

Last but not least, new technologies such as text messaging, have reduced man's thinking process to a bare exchange of shortened words, impoverishing language and thought process, and curbing his ability to express and articulate deep ideas. Text messages are designed to be short, with a limited number of characters, thus eliminating all deep and elaborate sentence making. Traditional snail mail—the hand-written letter or the postcard that would give the recipient food for his imagination—has been replaced by the cold, dry and terse two-line message.

Man has come to rely on problem-solving technologies to such an extent that when they fail he is in worse shape than if he didn't have them. Imagine spending an entire day without your cell phone, your Internet access or a computer that will not reboot! A slave to technology, man has no longer his mind to turn to when the power is down.

04 GOVERNMENT AND PUBLIC OPINION

Government officials should rely on their own judgment rather than unquestioningly carry out the will of the people whom they serve. Use specific reasons and examples to support your opinion.

1. Key words

an elected representative	un représentant élu
a democratically elected government	un gouvernement élu démocratiquement
a referendum [pl. referenda]	un référendum
to go to the people / to hold an election	consulter le peuple
to confer / to grant authority (to)	conférer / donner l'autorité (à)
to run a country / to govern	diriger un pays / gouverner
under the stewardship (of)	sous la gouvernance (de)
to serve the people	servir le peuple
a government's / public policies	les politiques publiques
to frame / to shape a public policy	élaborer une politique publique
to implement a policy	mettre en œuvre une politique
to carry out / to pursue a policy	exécuter une politique
public opinion	l'opinion publique
to be at the people's service	être au service du peuple
to be accountable (to)	répondre (de)
accountability / to owe one's power to	la responsabilité / devoir son pouvoir à
to exercise one's own judgment	faire preuve de discernement
to make a decision	prendre une décision
to reach a consensus	parvenir à un consensus
to have the ultimate authority (to)	avoir l'autorité suprême (de)
to bring about / to pave the way (to)	provoquer / conduire (à)
political unrest / a coup	l'agitation politique / un coup d'État
an uprising / a riot	un soulèvement / une émeute
a rebellion / a revolution	une rébellion / une révolution
to overthrow / to topple a government	renverser un gouvernement
a puppet government	un gouvernement fantoche
partisan / special interests	les intérêts partisans / spéciaux
to be at the beck and call (of)	être au service (de)
to hoodwink (people)	tromper, mystifier (les gens)
to play a pivotal role (in)	jouer un rôle-clé (dans)

2. Talking points

1. Government should rely on its own judgment.

- Government officials know best. They have inside information, troves of data at their disposal, they rely on forecasters, experts who can anticipate the events and formulate policies.
- The role of government is to lead the people, not to be led by the people. Thus government must be in a position to act promptly and react to crisis. A government sometimes has to act in the name of national security.
- The will of the people is often confused with the power of lobbies and special interests that orchestrate campaigns in favor of or against some measures. Government should not fall for it.
- What is "the people"? A decision will always divide the people into two camps: a majority and a minority. Whatever decisions are taken—be it the ban on smoking, road safety, the repeal of a ban on same-sex marriage, to give but a few examples—they will necessarily be against the will of some people.

2. Government should carry out the will of the people.

- According to the democratic principle, a government is nothing but the voice of the people – Government of the people, by the people, for the people (Lincoln). The role of government is to take people's interests at heart and into account. It is to be at the people's beck and call. Don't we say that "*Vox populi, vox dei*"?
- Regimes in which the people have no say are assimilated to feudality, dictatorship, or any other form of autocracy which abuses authority and tramples on people's rights. A dictatorial regime pays lip service to the voice of people.
- Not paying heed to the *vox populi* will lead to uprisings, rebellion, revolution and the overthrow of government.
- A system of checks and balances is essential to sound government, as well as a bill of rights to preserve individual liberties.
- A government is a contract between the people and the elected officials. It is based on a mandate given by the people to elected officials. This contract is the expression of the will of the people. It gives some leeway to the government but brings the certainty that should the contract be broken, elected officials can be impeached and removed.

3. Possible answers

1. Government should rely on its own judgment.

The links between people and government have been questioned throughout the centuries. Several models of government have been tried only to prove that, according to Churchill, "Democracy is the worst form of government, except for those other forms that have been tried from time to time." The present assertion seems to make light of any nuance and establishes a clear-cut distinction between a government being run by officials following their own judgment regardless of what the people think and a government that should be of the people, for the people and by the people. Yet, relying on its own judgment is in my eyes the only way to wise government.

Government knows best. It can count on the brightest minds to deliver the sharpest and most insightful opinions and advice. It can rely on experts before making decisions in the interest of the country. Thus, a government will decide to invest in the building of nuclear reactors to anticipate the depletion of fossil fuels. It will order carmakers to build fuel-efficient cars to help fight global warming. Similarly, a government will raise the retirement age to cope with the looming pension crisis that so many people dread and would rather ignore, especially the labor unions and other entrenched interests.

The role of government officials is to lead the country. A government must know how to anticipate events and deal with crises. Can we imagine a government going to the people whenever a decision must be made? In times of crisis—be it a natural disaster, a terrorist threat or war—a government must be in a position to react quickly. In 1957, President Eisenhower did not hesitate to send the federal guard to Little Rock to enforce the Supreme Court's *Brown v. Board of Education* decision. Almost a century before, President Lincoln had proclaimed the emancipation of the black slaves, against the fierce opposition of public opinion in the South.

Likewise, it is often better for the people not to be informed of decisions which, should they be made public, might thwart a government's action. When J. F. Kennedy learnt that missiles with the ability to strike the United States were being deployed on Cuba, he kept the information secret for 13 days and left it up to his close advisers to hash out an answer. Never was public opinion consulted or informed of what was being hatched behind closed doors. Kennedy took his decision on behalf of national security.

Lastly, we may question the expression used in the proposition, to wit 'the will of the people', and wonder what is meant here. It is often confused with the power of lobbies and special interests that orchestrate massive campaigns in favor or against some measures. In addition, in a democracy, the people are always divided into a majority and a minority. Whatever decision elected officials may take will divide public opinion into two camps: those who are for, and those who are against.

2. Government should carry out the will of the people.

Should officials unquestioningly carry out the will of the people whom they serve? According to the basic principles of democracy, government is nothing but the voice of the people. "Government of the people, by the people, for the people," said Lincoln in his 1863 Gettysburg address. A government is the result of the people's will freely expressed in the polls. It derives from the people. Indeed, in a democracy, there are many means to consult the people, in addition to general elections: a whole array of measures permit the people to express their opinion at any time, be it referenda or popular recall for elected officials. It seems logical then that the people should have their say in policy decisions.

Many decisions taken by elected officials have been made in the past, regardless of the will of the people, and they did hurt the country. In 1964, when President Lyndon B. Johnson decided to escalate the war in Vietnam, he took advantage of an incident in the Gulf of Tonkin in which the U.S. Navy had been attacked to ask Congress to pass the Gulf of Tonkin Resolution, basically asking Congress for a blank check to wage war in Southeast Asia. Congress overwhelmingly voted in favor of the war. It took several years and 58,000 U.S. casualties for the people to eventually make their voices heard through mass demonstrations before President Nixon decided to bring the boys home and put an end to the only war that the U.S. has ever lost.

The role of government is indeed to take people's interests at heart. Government must be at the people's beck and call, not the other way round. This is an intangible democratic principle. All other forms of government that do not take into account the people's voice are autocratic and dictatorial. In those regimes, the people have no say in the matter. Power then can be used and abused. One case in point is what happens when the voice of the people is stifled: people, tired of corruption and having their rights violated, rise up in arms and take to the streets. They topple the leader, hound him and overthrow any puppet government that has been put in place.

It is necessary to avoid extreme positions. A constitution—similar to the American one—should enshrine such hallowed principles as checks and balances. Separation of powers, which already existed in Ancient Greece and the Roman Republic allows each branch of power to remain independent while exercising a control over each other. In such systems elected officials are closely held in rein, and, so it seems, the will of the people is not flouted.

A government is a contract between the people and the elected officials. It is based on a mandate given by the people. This contract is the expression of the will of the people. It gives leeway to the government but brings the certainly that should it be broken, elected officials will be removed. It offers thus a fine balance between the necessity to listen to the people while allowing government to conduct its business.

05 REVITALIZATION THROUGH NEW LEADERSHIP

In any profession—business, politics, education, government—those in power should step down after five years. The surest path to success for any enterprise is revitalization through new leadership. Use specific reasons and examples to support your opinion.

1. Key words

to step down / to resign (from)	démissionner (de)
to leave office / power	quitter le pouvoir
to stay in power	se maintenir au pouvoir
to hang on to / to cling to power	s'accrocher au pouvoir
to hold on to one's position	s'agripper à son poste
to give up / to relinquish power	renoncer au pouvoir
to set a time limit (to)	imposer une limite dans le temps (à)
a tenure / a turn at the helm / a term	un mandat
tenure in office	l'exercice d'une fonction
to retire / retirement	prendre sa retraite / la retraite
to be forced / eased into retirement	être poussé à la retraite
to quit from choice	partir de son plein gré
to be tossed / tufted out	être mis dehors
to transmit expertise / know how / skills	transmettre un savoir faire / des compétences
to guide / to mentor junior colleagues	guider / superviser les jeunes collègues
to hand over the reins (to)	transmettre les rênes (à)
to serve for a limited time	servir pour un temps limité
to bring in fresh blood	faire entrer des jeunes
to free up jobs for younger people	libérer des emplois pour les jeunes
to make room for younger workers	laisser la place aux jeunes
to pass the torch to another generation	passer le flambeau à une nouvelle génération
a changing of the guard	une relève de la garde
a change in leadership	un changement de direction
the turnover in leadership	le renouvellement des élites
to have adverse effects	avoir des effets négatifs
a career change	une mobilité professionnelle
to move on to another job	prendre de nouvelles responsabilités
a term limit	une limitation du nombre des mandats
the fast pace of innovation	le rythme rapide de l'innovation
entrenched powers	les pouvoirs bien établis

2. Talking points

1. Revitalization is the key to success.

- We live in a dynamic world in which change is the key word. It is a necessity to keep up with change through new technology; progress is impossible without change, and those who cannot change their minds cannot change anything. The pace of innovation forces people to update their skills and worldviews. As Darwin said, "It is not the strongest of the species that survives, nor the most intelligent that survives. It is the one that is the most adaptable to change."
- An older generation may fall into a routine and be caught by surprise if unexpected events arise, whereas a new generation will bring new ideas, impetus and initiatives.
- Being risk adverse, the old guard may be reluctant to make the bold decisions to stay ahead of the curve.
- In democracies, revitalization is offered to elected officials through regular elections; it has proved a healthy process. On the contrary, absolute power corrupts absolutely—a dictator for life brings disaster on to his country. Misuse of power, corruption, nepotism are the consequences of autocratic and entrenched regimes; therefore revitalization is a means of preventing abuse of power.

2. Revitalization through new leadership is a wrong-headed solution.

- There is a primacy of experience and wisdom over inexperience and misjudgment — an experienced leader is invaluable for the welfare of a company (*videlicet* Steve Jobs) or of a country (Churchill, De Gaulle, Roosevelt).
- All too frequent change is detrimental to long-term corporate policy and vision; it may send the wrong signal to the investors who will grow wary of putting money in a company with unstable management.
- A firm or a government needs stability to be able to pass measures and build the future, to formulate, develop and implement strategies and bring about change.
- A leader should be held accountable for his/her results; too short a term might prevent it and thereby lead to disaster.

3. Possible answers

1. Revitalization is the key to success.

We live in a changing world where the necessity for our elites or leaders to step down after a limited period of time has been gaining traction. There are indeed many arguments that underlie how revitalizing such changes can be, for the firm, the institutions and the country at large. Yet, it might be added that there are cases when the argument does not always hold.

Innovation has brought about fast-paced change. In the past it used to take one generation for change to take root, as was the case when the plane, the steam engine, the automobile or the computer ushered in new revolutions in transportation and communications. Nowadays, a revolution happens almost overnight—to wit the digital birth of Google, Facebook, PayPal or Twitter. Keeping up with change is essential if a society is to stay ahead in the race to progress. The pace of innovation forces people to update their skills, adapt their worldviews. Innovation creates a climate conducive to fostering ideas. In that respect, a change of the guard is a prerequisite to progress. A young generation brings with it new ideas and new impetuses.

An old generation is more likely to favor the status quo than foster change. Any idea of change is abhorrent to management because it entails a loss of power. Politically speaking, the status quo will help men to stay in power if they are shrewd enough to avoid the pitfalls that are likely to go hand in hand with revolutionary ideas such as moving up the mandatory retirement age, advocating a ban on strikes or allowing shops to open on Sundays. Change is not always seen in a positive light. Nor are the leaders who want to ramrod reforms.

In the same way, an older generation of leaders will tend to fall into a routine, follow habits and shun from taking initiatives. A new generation, on the other hand, will bring in fresh blood and out-of-the-box ideas. Revitalization is associated with boldness and initiative, whereas apprehension and foot dragging are synonymous with risk-adversity and conservatism.

Politically speaking, revitalization is a necessity. It is the rule in democracies whose elections are a way for the people to change the guard and introduce new personnel and ideas. On the other hand, entrenched regimes such as juntas or dictatorships are absolute forms of power. A dictator for life brings disasters on to his people and rouses its wrath, paving the way to uprisings, rebellions, revolutions or civil war, as was recently seen during the Arab Spring. Misuse and abuse of power, corruption, and nepotism are the hallmarks of regimes that have been ruled by autocratic, change-adverse leaders. Revitalization is the engine of progress. As Churchill once said, "To improve is to change, to be perfect is to change often."

2. Revitalization through new leadership is a wrong-headed solution.

Change is not always beneficial. Let us consider the example of education. In such a field, experience and knowledge are the essential qualities of a good teacher. In other words, it would be hard to change the top professors every five years as they owe their tenure to the aforesaid qualities. The older a teacher, the more knowledgeable and experienced he/she becomes. Although it might be rightly argued that the older teachers get, the less energetic they are, the less engaged in students' success they may be. To my mind, this is a moot point as with age comes respect coupled with the nimbleness of a brain capable of seeing the broad picture.

In the same way, revitalization in a firm's management is not always welcome. Too often, senior executives may be tempted to toss out older workers and make room for new talent. But the history of a company, its corporate culture and traditions are essential to preserve its soul. Thus, many companies have decided to hire back retired employees to transmit knowledge and know-how to the younger workers and thus ensure a smooth transition from one generation to the next. Similarly, a leader's experience and wisdom are duly appreciated at the helm of a firm. Age sometimes is associated with security.

Frequent change can be detrimental to long-term corporate policy and vision too. Indeed, it often takes more than five years to build a company policy, to pass measures, to formulate, develop and implement strategies. In that case, there is no wonder cure that revitalization can bring. On the other hand, a high turnover of the leadership might send the wrong signals to the investors and stockholders who will grow wary of putting money in a company with unstable management.

Last but not least, it is vital that leaders be accountable for their actions. Be it the company's CEO or the party leader, approval or disapproval of his/her action is best expressed in the boardroom, at the ballot box—or through recall referenda, as in California, for example—or in court. Can we imagine that a leader might be free to wield power and bring ruin to his firm without being held accountable to the stockholders? If, on one hand, a long tenure can be harmful, on the other hand, time is necessary to assess a leader's actions and decide whether to change the guard or not.

There is no clear-cut solution to revitalize leadership. All extreme solutions should be avoided to strike the right balance at the top. One way would be to allow change in an incremental way i.e. gradually ease the old guard out, yet have them on hand to mentor the newcomers. A balanced act requires a mix of people, on the one hand the younger generation to put forward bold ideas, on the other the old to urge caution and restraint.

06 PRESERVATION VS DEVELOPMENT

In your country, is there more need for land to be left in its natural condition or is there more need for land to be developed for housing and industry? Use specific reasons and examples to support your answer.

1. Key words

to develop land	mettre la terre en valeur
land development	la mise en valeur de la terre
pristine / unspoilt / virgin (land)	(la terre) vierge
urban sprawl / to expand (into)	la périurbanisation / s'étendre (à / dans)
the housing problem	le problème du logement
a housing estate	un grand ensemble, une cité
to speed up urbanization	accélérer l'urbanisation
to be thrown off one's land	se faire exproprier de sa terre
to build a city on a human scale	bâtir une ville à l'échelle humaine
rural exodus / a real estate bubble	l'exode rural / une bulle immobilière
to encroach (upon) / expropriation	empiéter (sur) / l'expropriation
an indigenous tribe	une tribu indigène
real estate value	le prix de l'immobilier
to exploit land	exploiter la terre
wanton exploitation	l'exploitation anarchique
to tap / to harness resources	exploiter des ressources
to build factories	construire des usines
to create / to generate jobs	créer des emplois
finite land resources	des ressources foncières limitées
a natural habitat / biodiversity	un habitat naturel / la biodiversité
an extinct / threatened species	une espèce disparue / menacée
sustainable development	le développement durable
deforestation / the rain forest	la déforestation / la forêt tropicale
arable land	la terre cultivable / arable
to poison the aquifers	empoisonner les nappes phréatiques
underground water	les nappes souterraines
to thwart a food crisis	éviter une crise alimentaire
to feed the world	nourrir la terre
a growing population	une population en expansion
to meet the needs (of industry)	faire face aux besoins (de l'industrie)

2. Talking points

1. Land development is a necessity.

- Land development is vital to meet the growing needs of a population—be it housing, motorways, schools and universities or sport facilities.
- It is necessary to ease the land pressure and rein in skyrocketing real estate prices. This means freeing more space for construction building.
- Rent control has been unable to provide housing for all. A cap on rents reduces the quality and quantity of housing available. By limiting the price of housing, rent control can increase demand and reduce available supply, causing a shortage. Rent control deters investment, and raises rents on tenants who are excluded from its protections.
- New land must be developed, for industry as well—building factories, workers' houses, shopping centers, schools and colleges. Such activity will generate jobs and curb unemployment.
- To foster a country's expansion of its communications network – building high speed train lines, new airports, more motorways, it is necessary to develop land. The building of the Transcontinental Railroad in the U.S. is a case in point. Between 1862 and 1869, the Central Pacific and the Union Pacific Railroad Companies raced toward each other from Sacramento, California on the one side and Omaha, Nebraska on the other, struggling against great risks before they met at Promontory, Utah, on May 10, 1869.

2. Land must be preserved in its natural condition.

- The wanton destruction of nature must be controlled. Man must put an end to the deforestation of the Amazon rainforest, the overgrazing of meadows wrested from woodland, the encroachment of agricultural land upon wild and pristine soil.
- Sustainable development is a necessity if we expect our children to survive in an eco-friendly world. Therefore, the need for land development must be carefully balanced against the preservation of the environment.
- Cities must be built on a human scale and not transformed into concrete jungles or ghost towns waiting for tenants unable to meet the rent. Urban sprawl and some property developers' building spree are harmful to the welfare of man and turn places where he should grow harmoniously into nightmare environments.

3. Possible answers

1. Land development is a necessity.

The western world and emerging countries are fast developing, yet they are subject to limited land supply. Arguments have been bandied about on how to best allocate the land available. While there are people who believe nature should be respected and natural reserves expanded, others believe it is essential to develop the land to meet the demands of a growing population. Land use ought to be expanded for several reasons.

First, faced with a booming population, government need to cut vast swaths of land for housing projects. Countries are hungry for land to be able to meet the expanding needs of immigrants coming from abroad and the countryside and eliminate housing shortages. The situation is all the more pressing in China, as rural exodus has taken on biblical proportions where the situation of newcomers in urban centers has become dire.

Land development is a priority to put an end to inflated real-estate prices. Whereas some cities have tried rent control or rent stabilization as it is also called, set price controls on the renting of residential housing, it turns out that this rent ceiling has been unable to stanch the flow of newcomers to a city. By opening up new land for development, the pressure on value is bound to ease up.

Another argument in favor of land development is the necessity for a country to grow and therefore for industry to develop. Indeed, with a world going global and economies competing at the international level, it is crucial for industry to keep up with the pace of economic development. Be it for local consumption or international trade, industry needs space to expand. It also needs workers and employees. This means more housing, more schools and colleges, as well as more shopping malls. Without the land needed for growth, cities may wither and die, or be relegated to the economic backwaters. Countries may suffer economic recessions.

At the same time, a modern country needs modern communications infrastructures. Building them often means evicting farmers, destroying parts of villages to make way for motorways or train lines. The interstate highway system, which crisscrosses America, meant trampling on the property of many people. The 75,440 km public works project, the largest in history, needed 35 years to be completed. The construction of the U.S. Transcontinental Railroad also gobbled vast amounts of land. Today, the same can be applied to the building of high-speed rail. The development of air transport has also led to the construction or expansion of airports. In many cases eminent domain has been used, often at the expense of landowners.

A country expects to grow and therefore must cater to the housing needs of a booming population hungry for work. On the global level, world trade and competition require that industry continue to expand, to keep up with technological progress.

2. Land must be preserved in its natural condition.

Wanton destruction of nature is a recurrent argument put forward by the preservationists, anxious about deforestation, intensive slash and burning agriculture or the disappearance of precious rural land in the name of progress.

To start off, it is necessary to find the right balance between economic development and respect for the environment. The many natural disasters that we have been witness to, namely logging and overgrazing in the Amazon Forest, the plundering of rare timber from forests in Thailand or Myanmar, the building of transcontinental roadways to the benefit of the very few have swallowed thousands of acres and driven to extinction hundreds of species, thus depriving the world of much needed sources of pharmacology and of oxygen. In the same way, farmers hungry for more land to feed their growing cattle ought to be reined in. Land used for food staples must be allowed to lie fallow every few years—or be returned to its original nature—so as to regenerate and avoid desertification or another Dust Bowl, such as the one that swept over the U.S. in the 1930s and forced thousands of families to seek a better future in California.

Sustainable development is a necessity if we want our children to survive in an eco-friendly world. To that effect, land must be preserved. The more the earth is left in its natural state, the better it is for the ecosystem. In particular, parks must be protected and expanded in cities, following the model of Central Park in New York City. The rampant development of industry must be brought under control, otherwise the attendant evils that go with development—pollution, greenhouse gas emissions, unsanitary living conditions, global warming, extreme weather—will ruin not only the health of people but also the quality of the landscape.

Cities must be built on a human scale. They should not become concrete jungles—with ever taller and impressive housing or office towers, broader avenues to allow for car traffic and fewer pedestrian precincts for passers-by. A city must have a human face with plenty of green areas for children to play and relax in after school, for people to walk around and trees to grow. A city is an organic whole that needs air to breathe, space to move and sunlight to blossom as well.

When all is said and done, it boils down to a simple equation: what matters more? Short-termism and the hectic race to development, or long-termism i.e. a balanced development, the protection of our natural ecosystems and the preservation of wildlife making the earth a healthy place to live? There are no clear-cut answers. Maintaining a fine line between the need for laggard countries to catch up with economic development and for industrialized countries to keep ahead of the curve all too often means espousing radical solutions at the expense of the environment.

07 LIVING LONGER

In general, people are living longer now. Discuss the causes of this phenomenon. Use specific reasons and details to develop your essay.

1. Key words

life expectancy	l'espérance de vie
to live a long life	avoir une longue vie
to prolong life	prolonger la vie
longevity / life span	la longévité / la durée de vie
the mortality rate	le taux de mortalité
to grow old / to age	vieillir
old age	la vieillesse
health care	la santé
the progress of medicine	les progrès de la médecine
technological progress	le progrès technologique
an advance / a breakthrough	un progrès
a chronic disease	une maladie chronique
a deadly / terminal illness, disease	une maladie mortelle
to die young	mourir jeune
to provide / to effect a cure	fournir un traitement / amener à la guérison
to find a cure (for)	trouver un remède (à)
a medicine / a drug	un médicament
the fight against cancer	la lutte contre le cancer
nutrition / nutritional content	la nutrition / la composition des aliments
to eat healthfully	manger sainement
low-fat food	de la nourriture maigre
to have a medical checkup	faire des examens médicaux
to prevent heart disease	prévenir les maladies cardiaques
eating habits	les habitudes alimentaires
a balanced diet	un régime équilibré
to avoid smoking / drinking	éviter de fumer / boire
to develop a disease	contracter une maladie
a healthy lifestyle	un style de vie sain
to exercise regularly	faire de l'exercice régulièrement
to keep one's weight down	ne pas prendre de kilos
to wear a helmet / safety belt	porter un casque / une ceinture de sécurité

2. Talking points

1. Essay 1

- We have seen a general increase in life expectancy around the world, especially in the western countries where living conditions have greatly improved.
- Medical progress—as well as more accessible and affordable health care—has prolonged man's life. Vaccination drives have eradicated epidemics. New treatments have helped in the fight against cancer and diseases that were once terminal.
- Better health care and access to medical services have prolonged life. Universal and mandatory health coverage allows patients to get treatment at little or sometimes no cost, including in developing countries (with the help of charities and foundations). Better hygiene—like washing one's hands—have stopped the spread of germs. Protecting oneself from the sun prevents skin cancer.
- Changes in lifestyle have prolonged life. We are adopting healthier eating habits; we are encouraged to lead an active life. Snacking while couch surfing, quaffing fizzy drinks is frowned upon. The development of organic food and the adoption of a more varied diet are key to man's longer life. Similarly, we are more attentive to nutritional content in foodstuffs.
- Governments in the West have launched campaigns against smoking and drinking, which both cause many deaths, be they related to cancer or driving.

2. Essay 2

- One of the main reasons why people live longer lives is that they do not die young. Childhood diseases have been virtually eradicated. Better sanitation and housing conditions have reduced the infant mortality rate as well.
- Working conditions have changed too. Work is no longer what it used to be—manual, menial, back breaking. The automation of certain tasks and the introduction of high tech robots have changed the very nature of work which has become less tiring than it used to be.
- Labor legislation now allows man to rest and therefore to improve his health and to live longer. Laws now protect the sick or pregnant worker. Safety rules on work conditions are more stringent too.
- A better lifestyle and some exercising have made man more active and therefore have helped to ward off heart disease.

3. Possible answers

1. Essay 1

Over the past centuries, life expectancy has risen dramatically amongst the world's wealthiest populations from around 50 to over 75 years. This increase can be attributed to a number of factors including improvements in public health, nutrition and medicine.

There is no question that medical progress has prolonged man's life. Vaccinations and antibiotics have greatly lowered the infant mortality rate and deaths in childhood. For example, polio and smallpox have been eradicated in the west and major advances have been made in the rest of the world. At the same time, researchers and doctors have made considerable strides in the fight against cancer to such an extent that some types can be entirely cured today. Similarly, breakthrough treatments against Aids, for example, have allowed stricken patients to live longer lives.

Better health care services have been a major factor behind prolonging life. Since the National Health Service (NHS) was founded in Britain more than 50 years ago, for example, life expectancy has increased by 10 years. In 1948, 40% of British people died before reaching pensionable age, but by 1996 this was reduced to just 7%. Mandatory health coverage in western countries today allows people who are sick to access clinics and hospitals at little or no cost, thus saving and extending lives.

Another major factor to explain why we are living longer today is our knowledge of the steps we can take to ensure that we lead a healthy lifestyle. This is especially true where nutrition is concerned. Several health campaigns—on TV, the Internet and other media—have showed, beyond the shadow of a doubt that healthy living is first and foremost a matter of eating habits and lifestyle. People are encouraged to take up some form of physical activity. Eating green vegetables has become trendy, along with growing organic food. Schools no longer allow sodas and other fizzy and sugary drinks in their vending machines. Pizza is out, broccoli is in. Similarly, the packaging of the food products we purchase now display the nutritional content, using color coding to determine whether this is good for us, or harmful to our health.

Government has also started to wage war on alcohol and cigarette consumption. Advertising campaigns on public transit systems as well as on TV and the radio have warned people against the dangers of drinking, smoking, drinking and driving. Smoking has been banned from public places, restaurants and transportation systems. Stringent laws regulating drinking and driving have been adopted. Those measures have helped keep cancer rates down as well as they have curbed the number of car wrecks and road casualties, thus increasing man's life span.

All in all, better and affordable health care, healthy eating and living as well as the fight against smoking and drinking have been instrumental in saving or prolonging lives.

2. Essay 2

In industrialized countries, a large majority of the population can expect to reach old age. Older people outnumber children and teenagers. Developing nations are rapidly catching up: with the exception of countries with severe HIV problems, life expectancy figures are rising much faster than in industrialized countries. Besides medical advances, which have led to an increase in man's life, there are several reasons why people live longer lives.

The main reason for people's increased life expectancy is very simple: we don't die young. This sounds a stupid thing to say, but it's accurate. The reason why there are a lot more people living into old age is because a lot more of them do not die in the first few months or years of life from what used to be infant killer diseases such as measles, whooping cough and the mumps. In part, this is because of mass vaccination. Increased standards in public sanitation and housing, better nutrition, etc., have also played a major role. It used to be that 50% of infants died before they were five years old. This same figure still holds for parts of the developing world but not in the industrialized world where a baby born today has a life expectancy of three decades more than one born two hundred years ago.

One major reason why people live longer is that working conditions have changed altogether from one century to another, from one decade to the next. Work used to be manual, backbreaking, and grueling. Farmers would toil from sunup to sundown. Factory workers used to slave away six days a week in appalling conditions. The life of a miner at the bottom of the pit was fraught with danger and accidents were frequent. Changes in the law, the introduction of paid and sick leaves and better safety legislation in addition to a reduced work week have helped man to live healthier and longer lives. Today, workers are entitled to a two-day weekend every week. Thanks to government generosity, they can go on holiday to rest, recuperate or pick up some physical activity like hiking, sailing or riding their bikes. Labor law has been therefore a huge engine for change for the better, helping people to live longer.

Other reasons why we live longer lives today are related to lifestyle habits. Better information and awareness campaigns have encouraged people to work out, to go swimming, thus reducing the risk of heart disease. A bit of exercise does people a lot of good. Stretching in the morning, for example, increases blood flow to your muscles providing an extra shot of oxygen and preparing people for a new day. Using the stairs as often as possible instead of the elevator, taking a walk with friends, walking the dog a bit longer than usually – are ways for people to be more physically active and therefore to live longer.

Because sanitary and working conditions have improved, many people are now living deep into their 80s, which was unheard of a few decades ago.

08 SAVING OR SPENDING MONEY

Is it better to enjoy your money when you earn it, or is it better to save your money for some time in the future? Use specific reasons and examples to support your opinion.

1. Key words

to budget money	budgétiser
the household budget	les dépenses du ménage
outside the budget	hors budget
to establish / to balance a budget	établir / équilibrer un budget
to save money / savings	économiser de l'argent / les économies
to cut corners / to pinch pennies	faire des économies
to tighten one's belt	se serrer la ceinture
to pull in one's horns	y aller doucement
to scrimp / a saver	économiser, lésiner / un épargnant
a savings bank	une caisse d'épargne
to put money aside	mettre de l'argent de côté
to spend money	dépenser de l'argent
to waste / to squander money	gaspiller de l'argent
to make a down payment (on)	verser un acompte / des arrhes
expenditure / expenses	des dépenses
to keep track of one's expenses	surveiller ses dépenses
emergency money	de l'argent en cas d'urgence
a piggy bank / a kitty	une tire-lire / une caisse
to trim one's expenses	réduire ses dépenses
to square the accounts / books	équilibrer les comptes
thrift / thrifty	les économies / économe
to make ends meet	joindre les deux bouts
a tight budget	un budget serré
to have the wherewithal (to)	avoir les moyens / les ressources (de)
rent / utilities	le loyer / les charges
to live beyond one's needs	vivre au-dessus de ses moyens
to buy on impulse	acheter impulsivement
an impulse purchase	un achat impulsif
an overdraft / to be short of money	un découvert / être à court d'argent
to indulge / to splurge (on)	se faire plaisir / dépenser une fortune (pour)
to be a burden (on)	être un poids (pour)

2. Talking points

1. Saving one's money

- It is better to save money in case of emergencies such as unexpected health care treatment or dental costs.
- As we are going through difficult economic times, it is better to save and scrimp for a rainy day than spend money on unnecessary luxuries.
- Saving money towards retirement is necessary, especially in the uncertain times of pension reform, budget deficits and financial collapse.
- It is better to save one's money for solid investment such as a house or a car rather than borrow to be able to afford them. A house is a safe investment that generally pays splendid dividends over the years, at least in some big cities.
- Some people save money for fun activities, like a vacation they plan to take on the Riviera in the summer or in a ski resort during the winter.
- Saving money is a way of being and remaining independent. For example, in case of financial trouble, I do not have to ask my relatives or family to help me out.
- Saving money is investing in the future. Education is an expensive commodity and putting money aside to pay for a child's future tuition fees is a way of preparing for life.

2. Spending one's money as soon as one has earned it

- Spending their money on and with others can make some people happy. They enjoy giving their money away, be it to charity, worthy causes or foundations fighting against poverty or diseases; more prosaically, they can invite friends and relatives for a holiday or some occasions.
- Spending money helps build up a balanced life rich in shared moments and remembrances. Also, money is more wisely spent if it is related to the activities of a certain age period.
- Spending money may give a stronger incentive to people to make more money and enjoy it while it lasts.
- We never know what the future holds in store. Why save money for retirement if our savings are wiped out following a sudden economic downturn or if the company you have invested in is forced into bankruptcy?
- People who save money excessively are considered as misers and scrooges. In addition, they are not contributing to the economy and may even do harm to themselves by not investing in their own health.

3. Possible answers

1. Saving one's money

In a world in which instant gratification is the norm, I believe that people ought to be forward-looking and provident. Who knows what the future holds in store and that is why I find it wise to save money rather than squander it all.

First, It is crucial to have an emergency fund set aside to cover unexpected expenses such as unanticipated car repair, an emergency appendectomy or a sudden job loss. As the word economy has been lagging for some time and even though it may pick up again, people are not immune to downturns and the threat of unemployment.

Another essential reason to save money is retirement. We're living in uncertain times. The great recession has depleted public budgets and widened the deficit gap. Cities are going bankrupt, companies are closing down, outsourcing is the number one rule. Pension legislation is becoming ever more restrictive and with it the money paid out by the state when we retire. Therefore, the sooner you start saving for retirement, the less you will have to save in the future. You can put your money to work for you or make wise investments in blue chip stocks or real estate so that you will be free from want in case another pension crisis arises.

A third reason to save money is for buying things that last, such as a house. Making a down payment on a house will earn much more in terms of returns than any other investment. Buying a home provides a shelter and a place to stay should things turn nasty economically speaking. In addition, you can transmit the house to members of your family when you die, so they inherit something tangible whose value will have accrued over the years. You can also save towards buying a car. You will be amazed at how much money you can free up in your budget if you do not have to make a car payment. You can also negotiate down from the sticker price of the car if you are willing to pay cash at the dealership.

A fourth reason to save money is to have fun. You can save up for your tour of America or for that Caribbean cruise you have dreamed of for so long (avoid holiday rip-offs though). Additionally you can save for fun large ticket items such as a game console or a new sailing boat. Your negotiating power is stronger if you have cash in hand on bigger purchases. Plus, you do not want to be paying off your trip to Europe in five years. Even if you save up for your vacation, you should try to save on your vacation expenses.

A final reason to begin saving money is for your future education. Each year more people return to school to earn their master's or doctorate degrees. You may also consider saving for your child's education when the time comes.

2. Spending one's money as soon as one has earned it

It is commonly said that money does not buy happiness, that there are other values in life and among them thrift. I, on the other hand, believe that there are plenty of things that can make a person happy, and amongst those things, spending one's money when you earn it instead of laying it aside for a rainy day.

First off, there are people who simply love giving their money away. For them, giving is an act of love and generosity that makes them happy. Be it friends, relatives, grandchildren or charities, parting with money is the reason why some people make money in the first place. For example, they buy presents for their children or they invite relatives to spend a week during their holidays.

Spending money improves man's quality of life, social status, and level of enjoyment. It teaches people to give money rather than to keep it to themselves, such as a dinner at a posh restaurant, or an evening at the opera. Actually, there are things that we all do at a certain period in our lives and that cannot be replicated at another. If a retired senior citizen wants to go for a spin in his newly acquired sports car, he may as well give up on such an idea because it is too dangerous for an aging person to drive too fast. But if people spend money on a nice car when they are young, they can enjoy the fun of driving around. As a result, people should spend their money when they earn it.

Someone who makes money and splurges will have a greater incentive to go in for more of the same than if they do not spend it. Suppose a business man has worked hard to make his first million and rewards himself with a trip with his whole family, then he will be encouraged to work as much so he can repeat the experience. If an employer pays his employees handsome bonuses, they will be prone to indulge and have a good time spending it.

Another reason why people should live it up here and now is that they never know what the future holds for them. What is the good of saving money if an economic squeeze will wipe out their savings? In 1929, for example, many citizens who had worked long and hard and entrusted banks with their money, lost their entire life savings within a matter of days. In more recent examples, companies who had gone bankrupt caused their investors and employees to forgo millions of dollars in stocks and pensions. What is the use of setting money aside if, when you reach the age of retirement, you pass away and are forbidden to enjoy it?

There is a final disadvantage to saving money. People who save money excessively and do not spend it become known as misers. They are not giving back financially to society. They become known amongst their friends as takers rather than givers, and are disliked for not giving enough. This condition can go to extremes when someone does not spend enough to take care of themselves. Eventually, what use is money if it is kept locked up in a bank and never enjoyed?

09 SHOULD TEENAGERS WORK WHILE IN SCHOOL?

In some countries, teenagers have jobs while they are still students. Do you think this is a good idea? Support your opinion by giving specific reasons and details.

1. Key words

to have / to hold down a job	avoir / conserver un emploi
an odd job / an after-school job	un petit boulot / après la classe
to have a summer / part time job	avoir un boulot d'été / à mi-temps
a paycheck / to receive an income	un salaire / avoir un revenu
to schedule in	prévoir (dans son emploi du temps)
to balance / to juggle work and study	jongler entre le travail et les études
to work part time	travailler à mi-temps
to develop a sense of responsibility	développer le sens des responsabilités
to act responsibly	agir de façon responsable
to be self-reliant / to fend for oneself	compter sur soi / se débrouiller
to gain experience	acquérir de l'expérience
to acquire some work experience	acquérir une expérience professionnelle
to gain valuable experience	acquérir une précieuse expérience
to capitalize (on) / to leverage	tirer profit (de)
to earn / to make a living	gagner sa vie
to work for pin money	travailler pour de l'argent de poche
a double-edged sword	une épée à double tranchant
to interfere with one's studies	entraver les études
to focus on one's studies	se concentrer sur les études
to hamper studying	empêcher d'étudier
to do one's homework	faire ses devoirs
to get good grades	avoir de bonnes notes
to attend classes	être assidu à l'école
class attendance	l'assiduité scolaire
to skip / to cut classes	sécher les cours
to fail / to flunk one's exams	rater ses examens
to be home for dinner	être rentré pour dîner
to hang out with friends / pals	traîner avec les amis / copains
to be robbed of one's youth	être privé de sa jeunesse
to be burned out	être épuisé / lessivé
to stay out of trouble	mener une vie rangée

2. Talking points

1. Having a job is good for teenagers when they are students.

- Holding a job while going to school develops a teenager's sense of responsibility; it teaches kids how to organize their time and keep up with the homework.
- Having a job teaches money management and the value of money. The young will realize that money does not grow on trees. It teaches the kids to become self-dependent, not to rely on their parents' money all the time.
- Holding a job is an initiation to what "real life" is going to be. Teenagers will learn the value of hard work and be prepared when they are out on their own.
- Having a job helps teenagers develop qualities such as self-confidence along with employability skills such as communication and team-working skills. Working is a maturing experience. When you waiter at the local food joint, or you are a clerk for the bookstore or stack books in the city library, you are in contact with other people. A job teaches teenagers skills they will need their whole lives, such as how to fill out an application, how to interview well, or how to get along with others.
- Holding a job helps teenagers narrow down their choices and, at the same time, develop a clear vision of the job they would like to have. The earlier you find a job, the sooner you might find out what sort of job or sector suits you best.
- Being in work will help teenagers with their CVs later on in life. It is also a head start on other applicants in a fiercely competitive labor market. Employers will look favorably at teenagers who have made some serious effort to get up early and work late while pursuing their studies.
- A teenager's income can help with the family's finances, especially in times of crisis. It will help tie up the family until the parents find their feet again.
- Having a job may help to keep the youth out of trouble.

2. Teenagers should not have a job when they are students.

- Having a job interferes with a teenager's schoolwork and the need to concentrate on his/her studies.
- Working, even part-time, disrupts a teenager's home and family life. The parent-children bonds should not be broken because one's kid is financially independent.
- Having a job means teenagers miss out on the fun of being young; they sacrifice their social life and they have less time for extra-curricular activities. They miss out on what being young is like. Having a pizza or a BBQ at a friend's house is next to impossible because working teenagers are committed to their employers.
- Teenagers may jeopardize their health by tiring themselves out, spending long hours and sleepless nights to catch up on their homework.

3. Possible answers

1. Having a job is good for teenagers when they are students.

Some parents worry about the double-edged sword of being a teenager and holding down a job. On the one hand, teens that work might get lower grades. On the other hand, a teenager who works will probably learn some important life skills. Which will serve them better in the long run? I believe that teens should work while in school.

Having a job after class develops the teenagers' sense of responsibility. They learn how to get organized and disciplined so they can meet both their teachers' and their employer's expectations. They are responsible for getting themselves to work on time, and making sure that they can keep up with their schoolwork. Having an after-school job is a great way to teach teenagers about responsibility.

Having a job is a useful lesson in money management. Teenagers love the idea of having their own money. By allowing a teenager to have an after-school job they learn that money does not grow on trees, that they are things such as the cost of living, bills, and value for money. Teens will also have to figure out how to pay their bills while having a little spending money. They will have to find a place to cash their paycheck each week and even how to manage a bank account, if they are allowed to have one. At the same time, when kids earn their keep, it teaches them not to become dependent on their parents for pin money all the time.

Having an after-school job will give a teenager a foretaste of what life might be like when they are grown up. Having a job shows teenagers that hard work is what it takes to accomplish everything in their life. They can't learn the meaning of hard work if everything is handed to them. Plus working develops self-confidence, and skills such as communication or team working. Work experience gives teenagers an edge when they scout around for entry-level positions in the job market.

Jobs can help teens explore potential career paths and decide what occupation will suit them best in the future. The earlier you land an odd job, the sooner you might find out what you like, and what you dislike doing. It is like a winnowing process: you eliminate what you do not like doing,

In difficult times, holding down a job may also be seen as a lifeline for a family. If a parent is on the dole, the teenagers' income will be a welcome supplement to the meager unemployment benefits. And finally, if teenagers work five evenings a week, they are less likely to get into trouble, or run afoul of the law because they have too much idle time on their hands. That's why it is a rich idea for all teenagers to have a job. It is also a fruitful experience because too many kids expect things to be handed to them on a silver platter. Show a teenager what it means to be a responsible human being today and he/she will thank you for it in the future.

2. Teenagers should not have a job when they are students.

The idea of teenagers having a job goes against common sense. To begin with, having an after-class job interferes with a teenager's schoolwork. School is a child's priority. Getting an education will equip a youth for life. If kids clock in too many hours at work while doing their studies, we can expect that not enough time will be devoted to homework or that they will come to class sleepy and distracted. Grades will drop and the chances of pursuing successful post-secondary studies will be slimmer. There might be a benefit to working in the summer, but after-class work should be banned. During the school year, kids need to focus on their studies.

Working, even part-time, disrupts a teenager's home and family life. After a day's work, teenagers need to reconnect with their family, if only to know that they have their full ear and support. Sometimes having a job may give them the impression that they are no longer part of the family since they are earning their keep and learning to be independent. It is vital that the bonds between parents and children be strengthened through discussions around the dinner table or during family weekend activities.

For some people, having a job means missing out on the fun of being young; they sacrifice their social life, and have less time for extra-curricular activities. No one can think of school without the idea of "jocks", "band geeks", "mathletes", "drama kings" and other types of club-related cliques. A teenager who has a job probably won't audition for the school musical because they have too many rehearsals; sports are a no go as most of them require hours of daily practice; there'd be no time to participate in school-sanctioned charities either; even after-school fields trips to the museum, working on the school's literary magazine would be out. A teen that works won't have as much time to focus on the other aspects of human group work. They may also forgo the joys of dating or the communal pleasures of going bowling with their pals.

One final argument that goes against the idea that it is good for teenagers to have a job is that it may jeopardize their health. If they have to juggle school and work, teenagers may tire themselves out, spending long hours and sleepless nights to catch up either on the real-life work or on their homework. It is a well-known fact that teenagers need a lot of sleep and have trouble waking up in the morning. Should they work under pressure, chances are that they will start losing sleep, peace of mind and, who knows, become more likely to use alcohol, drugs or illicit substances.

Allowing a teenager to work is a touchy issue, especially in the U.S. where they can legally start having a job when they turn 14. So, if parents still aren't sure, they should consider letting their children work on a trial basis just to see how it goes. They can also let them try out regular volunteer work too. But whatever the outcome, kids should be made aware that there is a time for study and one for work and that the choice of a job depends on the quality of one's studies.

10 THE AUTOMOBILE: BOON OR BANE?

Some people think that the automobile has improved modern life. Others think that the automobile has caused serious problems. What is your opinion? Use specific reasons and examples to support your answer.

1. Key words

to open up opportunities	présenter des occasions
the motor car industry	l'industrie automobile
a car loving people	un peuple amoureux de la voiture
to own a car / a car owner	avoir une voiture / un propriétaire
a car user	un usager de la route
a car maker / manufacturer	un fabricant automobile
a motorist / a car driver	un automobiliste
to travel (to / in)	voyager (à / dans)
to go to work	aller au travail
ease of transportation	la facilité de transport
door to door transport	le transport à domicile
to live in the suburbs	habiter en banlieue
to commute to work	aller au travail
a motorway / a highway	une autoroute / une grande route
an expressway	une voie rapide, une autoroute
a car accident / wreck	un accident de voiture
to get into an accident	avoir un accident
road rage	la violence au volant
traffic congestion	les embarras de la circulation
a traffic jam / a snarl / a tie up	un bouchon
car pollution / fumes	la pollution automobile
car maintenance	l'entretien de la voiture
a parking ticket	une amende pour stationnement
to tow away a car	emmener une voiture à la fourrière
public transportation	les transports publics
to car-pool	pratiquer le co-voiturage
car pooling	le co-voiturage
over-reliance on fossil fuel	la dépendance des combustibles fossiles
an oil shock / peak oil	un choc pétrolier / le pic de pétrole

2. Talking points

1. The car: a boon

- The car has introduced a revolution in transportation, helping moving goods and people on long and short distances.
- The car is a symbol of freedom and independence: it has made travelling much easier than it used to be for families and individuals. No need to rely on public transportation to commute to work, for example.
- The car has improved living conditions by allowing people to live far from the city center and yet being able to commute to work.
- The car has fostered an industry that has given jobs to millions of people around the world.

2. The car: a bane

- People have come to rely excessively on the car, thus bringing about health problems (lack of physical exercise). Man has forgotten the pleasure and benefits of walking.
- Cars have been massive contributors to environmental problems, including CO_2 emissions and noise pollution.
- Cars can be a financial burden on a family: maintenance, insurance, repairs, fuel, not to mention parking fees and traffic violations.
- Cars have been the leading cause of fatalities for young people. Road accidents are mounting problems that built-in safety devices have failed to address fully.
- Cars have led to the expansion of the cities and what is known as urban sprawl. Local shops have fallen victims to the car culture, with the construction of shopping malls and retail parks outside the city.
- Research has shown a direct correlation between the amount of traffic on a street and the number of neighbors people know by name. The fewer cars there are, the more likely people are to spend time outside their front doors. If you want to get to know people in your area, take a walk.
- By relying exclusively on oil, the car industry has fostered tension and strife and even war in the oil-rich region of the Middle East.

3. Possible answers

1. The car: a boon

The advent of the automobile has ushered in a revolution in transportation that has gone beyond man's wildest dreams. No one would dare go without a car and except for a few hardliners hanging on to 19th century ways, every family today has a car, and sometimes even two. That the car has improved people's lives goes without saying.

The invention of the automobile has brought about a revolution in the transportation of goods and people. Trucks or vans bring fresh produce to the market. Fish is transported overnight from the coast to the hinterland. Vegetables and fruits that are picked up on Monday are on the consumers' table by Tuesday. A more balanced and varied diet is now possible and overall standards of living have increased as a consequence.

The car has also changed the way people travel. What used to take days to go from one end of the country to another can now be done within 12 hours or less. The car has strengthened family bonds, helping parents and children to be reunited during a weekend or a vacation. Even going to the sea or the mountains is no longer a remote dream for people living far away. The car has shrunk distances and brought people together.

The car is also a vehicle for exploration. Not only can man venture deep into his own land and beyond, he can also do so when he wants. He is no longer the slave of schedules and timetables. Thanks to SUVs, he is free to discover the remote places of a country at his own pace and reach places that only few people could travel to before.

The development of the automobile and road infrastructure has allowed man to leave the crowded city centre and move away to distant suburbs, where he can achieve his dream of becoming a house owner. Families that used to live in cramped conditions downtown can have a house built in the suburbs or the countryside. Where there is no public transportation, people commute to work by car.

Above all, the automobile has spawned an industry that has provided jobs for millions worldwide. Ford, Renault, Chrysler, Nissan, Mercedes have become household names. Car manufacturing has lifted many countries out of poverty and generated a healthy competition for innovation. Automotive progress has gone hand in hand with technological progress. Inventors have found in the car industry fertile ground to imagine ways to have safer and swifter means to move around.

Some people may rue the day when they would move at the pace of the oxen-drawn cart, when the environment was limited to the horizon. Yet, I do believe that the car has been more a boon than a bane, bringing man freedom and independence while ushering in a new industrial and technological revolution.

2. The car: a bane

The ubiquitous car has become a staple of modern transportation in the rich and poor worlds. Yet, I believe the car has caused more harm than good.

People have come to rely excessively on this mode of transportation. They have become over-dependent on the car. They can no longer do without it to such an extent that the Americans have even been nicknamed 'a people on wheels'. Public transportation has gradually disappeared to make way for the private car. The car has thus trumped healthy ways of moving around a city such as the bicycle or walking. People have got used to driving even a few hundred yards to go shopping, go out to dinner or visit friends who live a few blocks away.

Cars have also been huge contributors to environmental problems. Exhaust fumes are responsible for releasing CO_2 into the atmosphere thus worsening global warming, altering rainfall patterns, raising sea levels, expanding deserts and unleashing ever fiercer hurricanes. If man wishes to preserve the environment, he needs to get off fossil fuels, which, right now, means getting out of his car.

In many instances, cars can be a financial burden on a family: maintenance, insurance, repairs, fuel, parking fees (and tickets), traffic violation are the price we have to pay to be car owners. Having a car usually represents a big chunk of a family budget, pre-emptying other expenses for education or sports for the kids.

Because cars are so commonplace, we sometimes forget that they are hugely dangerous machines. No matter how safe roads can be, globally road traffic kills over a million people every year, and injures a further 30-50 million. The costs of looking after the injured is astronomical too, thus increasing the financial onus of strained emergency and health care services.

Cars have led to the expansion of the cities and what is known as urban sprawl. Instead of making transport easy, the car has displaced millions to the outer fringes of the city, forcing daily mechanical migrations that play a key role in worsening pollution. Out-of-town shopping malls have been built at the expense of in-town retail stores. Main street has become a ghost of dollar and charity stores and a dire example of what the car culture can do to city centers.

Though it may be hard to pin a war entirely on the need for oil, it has been a factor in a whole string of conflicts, from WWII onwards. The Gulf wars are the most obvious, the ongoing conflicts in Nigeria, Iraq or Colombia less so. Oil remains a sticking point in the new Sudan. If there has been an international campaign to stop conflict diamonds, perhaps we're all far too implicated to call for an end to conflict oil. It cannot be denied that our over dependence on oil and the rich oil producing countries in the Middle East have generated tension and strife that are likely to go on as long as the electric car has not become the norm. Those are some of the reasons why I have chosen to go on foot.

11 THE COMPUTER: CURSE OR BLESSING?

Some people say that computers have made life easier and more convenient. Other people say that computers have made life more complex and stressful. What is your opinion? Use specific reasons and examples to support your answer.

1. Key words

the computer age	l'ère de l'informatique
computer science	l'informatique
information technology	la technologie de l'information
the advent of the computer	l'avènement de l'ordinateur
computer literacy	les compétences en informatique
to be computer literate	savoir se servir d'un ordinateur
to usher in a revolution	provoquer une révolution
to make life easier	faciliter la vie
portability	la portabilité
wireless access	l'accès sans fil
to connect / connectivity	connecter / la connectivité
broadband connection	la bande passante
an attachment	une pièce jointe
a search engine	un moteur de recherche / pratique
to communicate instantly	communiquer instantanément
to keep abreast of the news	se tenir au courant des nouvelles
to find out the latest news	découvrir les dernières nouvelles
to scan prices	scanner les prix
to design buildings	dessiner des bâtiments
a learning tool	un outil d'apprentissage
to SMS / an SMS	envoyer des textos / un texto
to store / to get information	stocker / obtenir des informations
to process / to retrieve information	traiter / récupérer des informations
to crunch / to store data	traiter / stocker des données
data transfer	le transfert de données
to download / to upload	télécharger
to be hooked on / dependent on	être accro à / dépendant de
parental control	le contrôle parental
to lure / a lure	attirer / un piège
phishing	le hameçonnage

2. Talking points

1. The computer has made life easier and more convenient.

- A computer can perform tasks much faster and with more accuracy than a human being. Thanks to the computer, man can obtain, process, share and store a vast amount of information.
- A computer allows the user to create, edit, print, and store documents so that they can be retrieved later.
- The computer has become our own personal library thanks to which we can access scholarly articles, books or newspapers. Thus, we are better informed.
- The computer helps people remain connected throughout the world, no matter where and when (electronic mail, file transferring and sharing, text-messaging, online chat, gaming).
- The computer has automated some everyday tasks such as managing one's money, booking one's holiday, looking for a job, getting an update on the weather, doing one's shopping, checking the rentals.
- Computers are widely used for education and training purposes (online degrees, MOOCs, continuing education).
- The computer is also a fabulous source of entertainment: be it videos, movies, music, gaming, watching television, listening to the radio, the computer does it all.

2. The computer has made life more complex and stressful.

- The computer has made life more complex for the elderly who have had trouble adjusting to the new means of communication and may find themselves isolated for failing to learn how to use a computer and the Internet.
- By quickening the pace of life, the computer has made tasks more complex but also people more dependent on computer systems. Companies are more vulnerable because of the computer, especially when the system breaks down.
- Some people may develop an addiction to the computer and Internet. They cannot do without a computer. They are hooked on games, movies, e-mails and literally forgo any personal life to be on top of their game all the time.
- Children can be easy targets for some adults who pose as children with similar interests and try to 'groom' them. Sexual offenders chat online with children and then make plans to meet them or slowly filter information about them.
- Children can be the target of cyber bullying and sometimes commit suicide. In other worst-case scenarios, adults are victims of phishing or other online fraudsters.

3. Possible answers

1. The computer has made life easier and more convenient.

The advent of the computer ushered in a revolution in the home and the workplace that nothing can stop. The computer has changed the way we live, play and work and made our life easier and more comfortable.

One of the main advantages of a computer is the speed with which calculations and processes are carried out. Not only are they done faster, they are also done more accurately. Machine tools, robots, surgery are powered today with the help of advanced computer programs and software, thus making tasks more convenient. Thanks to the computer, a large amount of information and data can be obtained, processed and stored in a relatively small space, the memory.

The computer has brought changes in the publishing industry. It allows the user to create, edit, and print documents. Thanks to the spellchecker, errors can be corrected. The layout is done automatically whereas it could not be carried out by the classic Underwood typewriter. Beyond that, the Net has become a vast library where all documents (books, articles, newspapers) can be accessed, read and stored to the benefit of one's own pleasure or research. The computer has become man's own private library. As a consequence he is better informed and more knowledgeable.

Another advantage of the computer is connectivity. The computer allows man to be connected throughout the world, be it via email, text messaging, or online chat services. Voice or video services are additional tools that enable man to enhance connectivity. You can exchange files and documents, watch movies or listen to music through the computer. The computer has acquired all the functionalities of a personal office.

The computer has automated everyday tasks to such an extent that man has forgotten that they are carried out automatically by logging in. For example, when you withdraw money at the cash machine, pay your bills, book a holiday, make a car rental reservation, hunt for a job, check the weather, it is all done automatically. The same applies to shopping. Instead of going to the shops, you can order everything online and have the goods delivered to your home.

Finally, computers have transformed the way we deal with education. Whether it is to look for documents for the class, get an update on current research, talk to a professor about a given subject, the computer is a splendid tool for exchange and discussion. Some forums are devoted to particular subjects and we can therefore keep abreast of current news. Recently, some colleges in the United States have started offering cheap massive open online courses. Thus, the disabled, the sick or those who are isolated can now afford an education thanks to the computer.

2. The computer has made life more complex and stressful.

The elderly people, more particularly, have been hard hit by the advent of the computer and have had trouble warming up with the new hi-tech device. They find the machine's workings complex and difficult to understand. Even words that for the layman might sound common, such as hardware or software, are a foreign language to the elderly. For them, a mouse is a rodent. As a consequence, as they are unable to connect with the younger generation, they find themselves isolated and keep sending handwritten letters while their grandchildren use email or text messaging services.

The advent of the computer age has quickened the pace of life by allowing man to communicate and conduct business more efficiently. This has often resulted in stress. Actually, the time saved in doing online business goes toward other tasks, thus crowding personal and professional schedules further. The stress factor has been increased when the technology we rely on breaks down. We have to call a computer expert to fix the bugs. Similarly, companies that are over-dependent on the computer often find themselves helpless and vulnerable when the system fails.

Another side effect of computer use has been the addiction it has given rise to amongst some people. Youngsters in particular, find themselves exposed to the overuse of the Internet and other social networks. Older people have become hooked on to pornography, watching adult movies for hours on end, or gaming: they cannot wean themselves off the addiction to the poker game or the massively multiplayer online games that they have developed. As a consequence, hardcore gamers forgo their personal life, sacrifice family and friends and, in general face-to-face relationships by spending all their time locked up in the virtual world.

The computer has made life more stressful for parents as well. There was a time when the family would gather together in the living room. In our individualistic work, children today take repair to their rooms; there, they delve into the virtual world, connect instantly with their friends. More alarmingly, some fall prey to all sorts of shady characters trawling the Net, pedophiles masquerading as children and trying to lure their young victims away. If you are old enough to look at porn, you might not notice that it costs a lot of money to watch a clip. And if you are logged in to your parents account, that's their money that is being squandered.

Other dangers have made life more stressful for the parents, such as cyber harassment or cyber bullying: some pupils, cyber hounded by their peers, even commit suicide. Parents, unaware of their children's activities have been helpless in spite of safeguard measures such as parental control devices. There are other crimes such as stealing someone's identity (phishing), embezzling money, faking someone's identity, extorting money from gullible people, being eavesdropped by government or intelligence agencies, or, in some regimes, being arrested for blogging the truth.

12 IS HOMEWORK NECESSARY?

Many teachers assign homework to students every day. Do you think that daily homework is necessary for students? Use specific reasons and details to support your answer.

1. Key words

to ban homework	interdire les devoirs
to do one's homework	faire ses devoirs
to give / to assign homework (to)	donner des devoirs (à)
to review the class material	réviser une matière
to review lessons	réviser des leçons
the learning process	le processus d'apprentissage
to learn by rote / by heart	apprendre par cœur, mémoriser
to train the memory	entraîner la mémoire
to revise for exams	réviser pour les examens
a means of evaluation	un moyen d'évaluation
to cram into sb's head	bourrer le crâne
to pursue a hobby	cultiver un passe temps
to have a part time job	avoir un emploi à mi-temps
to do sports / to play on a team	faire du sport / jouer dans une équipe
an all-round student	un étudiant équilibré
a slow learner	un élève lent
practice makes perfect	c'est en forgeant qu'on devient forgeron
a healthy mind in a healthy body	*mens sana in corpore sano*
no pain no gain	on n'a rien sans rien
to have a solid grasp on a subject	bien maîtriser son sujet
to have an insight (into)	avoir un aperçu (de)
to miss / to skip (over) / to overlook	manquer / passer / négliger
to take time (away from)	prendre du temps (qui n'est pas consacré à)
to engage in activities	se livrer à des activités
to practice a musical instrument	jouer d'un instrument de musique
to fall behind in one's work	prendre du retard dans son travail
to turn in a paper	rendre un devoir
to acquire work habits	acquérir des habitudes de travail
to team work / team work	travailler en groupe / le travail en groupe
a workload	une charge de travail
academic achievement	la réussite scolaire

2. Talking points

1. Homework is a necessity.

- Homework is a way for students to keep up with the class material. It shows whether students have assimilated the lesson or not. It strengthens a student's knowledge.
- Assigning homework is a way for students, especially slow learners, to review the day's material and absorb what they have learned, especially in a crowded schedule.
- Giving homework is a way for teachers to assess whether students have assimilated the course material and, if necessary, review the fundamentals. It has been proved that a process of consolidation is essential after new concepts have been introduced.
- Homework is a way for students to gain additional information and knowledge about a given subject matter. It may pique the students' curiosity and encourage them to learn more.
- Homework is a way for students to acquire skills like researching topics, catalog-searching in the library as well as to enhance habits such as team-working.
- Assigning homework helps the students to develop healthy work habits. They know that they have to turn in their work on time; they learn to be rigorous and disciplined. As a consequence, they mature into responsible adults.

2. Doing without homework

- Students spend too much time in the classroom as it is. Studying at home after class is ineffective for students exhausted by the school day. Besides, if a student works well in class, doing homework is unnecessary.
- Students want a break after a long school day. They need to relax, do sports and get ready for the following day. If they work all day and night, they might develop a negative attitude to school.
- In order to become well rounded adults, students need to do sports or engage in leisure activities. Therefore, it is essential to have some free time after school.
- Having some free time is all the more necessary when students need to work part time. Similarly doing volunteer or charity work is resume-building for those who seek to gain admission to college.
- Assigning homework is a way for teachers to shift the responsibility on the students for the part of the curriculum they have not been able to cover.
- Homework takes away precious family time and puts kids under unneeded pressure. It is an ineffective way to help children become better learners and thinkers.

3. Possible answers

1. Homework is a necessity.

Some people actually think that homework is valuable. However reluctant students may be to do their homework, I do believe it is essential if you want to make progress.

First, homework is like a yardstick: it measures whether students have learned or assimilated the class material. In a crowded daily schedule, it may not be easy for students, especially the slow learners, to remember and master all aspects of the subjects tackled by the professor in class. Doing homework helps students to practice and recap what has been taught in class. Homework therefore supplements and reinforces the work done in class. It also helps laggards or absentees to catch up and keep ahead of the learning curve.

For professors, homework is a way of assessing whether students have assimilated the course material and, if necessary, whether they need to review the fundamentals. Educational research has proved that a process of consolidation is essential after new concepts have been introduced. Making sure students have done their homework correctly is also a way of helping them to keep up with the rest of the class in order that they should not be left behind.

Doing homework is a way for students to gain additional information and knowledge about a given subject matter. It may pique their curiosity and encourage them to learn more. For example, someone interested in the biology of the cell or in 18th century English literature will be encouraged to explore the subject further if they've been asked to write a paper or do a presentation to the class.

By doing homework, students can gain many skills that will be helpful all life long. For example, they may need to do some research in a given field and will have to go to the library, meet professors and also experience team working. Homework helps a child learn to use resources in libraries, such as reference materials or any information (books, serials, audiovisual materials, computer files, maps, manuscripts), or search websites for relevant information. Thus, through homework, students can develop communication, interpersonal and leadership skills that will be useful all life long.

Assigning homework can help students develop healthy work habits. Because they know that they have to hand in a paper or do an oral presentation on a given day, students learn how to manage their time, how to organize the work week but also how to be rigorous and disciplined. For example, if they are doing a team-based project, they know they have to deliver results, learn how to listen to their team members, present arguments in a logical and sensible fashion. As a consequence, they learn to be accountable for their work. Homework can therefore be instrumental in training students to assume responsibility for their own progress.

2. Doing without homework

Giving homework to students has been a bone of contention for several years. While some believe that homework is necessary to memorize the day's lessons and improve one's skills, others would rather let the students off once school lets out. I share this latter point of view for several reasons.

To begin with, students spend an inordinate amount of time in the classroom most of the day, most of the week and most of the year. Because they have spent so much time in class, some teachers are convinced they need not provide homework every day. A school day that starts at 8 a.m. and ends up at 5 p.m. is chock-a-block with various subjects and activities, in addition to focusing, being active participants in the classroom, taking tests or even preparing for exams. Should they study more things outside the classroom after school? If students are keen on listening to their teachers and concentrate their attention on lectures, studying in class should be enough.

Second, I believe that students deserve a break. When they have spent the whole day locked up indoors, they need to let some steam off after the day so as to be in a good shape the following day. They need to relax by watching movies, listening to music or reading, all types of activities that help them become fully developed adults. Without some leisure time after school, students will fail to grow up harmoniously. They may even develop a negative attitude towards school and learning.

Three, students need some time for other pursuits after school and that includes spending time with the family. Some have chosen music and are learning an instrument. Others have opted for sports activities and play on the football team. Others want to indulge in hobbies that are no less personality building than academic subjects. Therefore, it is essential that the teachers leave their students alone once school is over. Don't we all know that "all work and no play makes Jack a dull boy"?

Having some time off after school is all the more necessary as some students have chosen to hold a part time position (thus being able to afford the essentials) or to do charity work for a non-profit organization. Such activities are enriching on a personal but also academic level, especially if the high school student seeks to enter college. It is a well-known fact that extra curricular activities are an asset for admissions committees looking for the student that will be able to make a difference in the program.

Finally, assigning homework to students may not be bad in itself. Yet, doing so every day could mean that the teacher did not take the time to cover all the aspects of the lesson. Teachers may also have been remiss in failing to address all the aspects of a subject for lack of time or ambition. Yet, it should not be up to the student to take the blame for a teacher's inefficiencies when all the teacher has to do is cover the whole curriculum. After all, students expect teachers to fill in the knowledge blanks. That is what educators are paid for.

13 PREPARING FOR A TRIP

Imagine you are preparing for a trip. You plan to be away from your home for a year. In addition to clothing and personal care items, you can take one additional thing. What would you take and why? Use specific reasons and details to support your choice.

1. Key words

to go on / to set out on a trip	partir en voyage
to travel around the world	voyager dans le monde entier
to go overseas / abroad	aller à l'étranger
to miss (people / a country)	manquer (à qn) (gens / pays)
to do without (sth)	se passer de (qch)
to feel lonely / to be on one's own	se sentir seul / être seul
to be homesick	avoir la nostalgie du pays
a smart phone	un téléphone intelligent
a laptop / a portable computer	un ordinateur portable
a digital camera	un appareil photo numérique
a video camera	une caméra
film / a roll of film	de la pellicule / une pellicule
a lens / a tripod	une lentille / un trépied
photography / a picture	la photographie / une photo
to shoot thousands of pictures	faire des milliers de photos
reading / a novel / fiction	la lecture / un roman / le roman
a book lover	un amoureux de la lecture
the complete works (of)	les œuvres complètes (de)
a musical instrument	un instrument de musique
a map	une carte
to stay connected	rester connecté
to keep in touch (with)	rester en contact (avec)
to share experiences (with)	partager des expériences (avec)
to journal / to keep a diary	tenir un journal de bord
to document / to record	enregistrer / documenter
to display / to boost one's creativity	exprimer / encourager sa créativité
to tap into one's creativity	exploiter sa créativité
to stir the imagination	stimuler l'imagination
to broaden man's horizons	élargir l'horizon de l'homme

2. Talking points

1. A camera

- A camera will help me document every single moment of my trip, be they important or not. It will be like a companion to me, a journal of my progress.
- A camera never lies. It provides pride in the pictures taken. Because you see the results instantaneously, it means you can keep the most genuine pictures and throw away those that look cliché or banal.
- A picture is a work of art. As Ansel Adams used to say, “Pictures are not taken, they are made.” Photography is actually a way of expressing how I feel but also share those feelings with people around me so that I can have an impact on how other people see the world.
- Through the art of photography, I can hope to make an impact on other people’s perceptions of the world when I return from my journey. It is a way of sharing one’s ability to create with others. Photography can inspire other people to capture their moments in time.
- Beyond the sharing of memories, photography fulfills a humanistic and somewhat useful role, especially when it denounces the atrocities of war or the fallout of man-made or natural disasters.

2. A book

- A philosophy treatise, a fiction book, a play or a collection of poems will enrich people in many different ways, from the knowledge it provides to the outlook it offers on life. Such books by world-known authors are inexhaustible sources of wisdom and teach life lessons that are bound to last.
- A book stimulates man’s creativity and captivates his imagination as he transcends to a hidden world of fascination with no rules or boundaries.
- A book feeds man’s hungry mind with an endless supply of knowledge and information, thus helping to broaden his mind and sharpen his analytical skills. A storybook or novel allows man to embark on a sentimental journey, exploring feelings he can match with those he is experiencing during his year away from home.
- A book is a way of traveling into the past. So, as he sails across the present time, discovering new countries and cities, the traveler will find himself setting out on two parallel journeys.
- A book will be a relief and a distraction whenever man feels down in the dumps, overwhelmed by the feelings of missing home and his beloved ones.

3. Possible answers

1. A camera

Should I take one additional item along in my one-year journey, I would choose my camera. My most precious equipment is an old Leica digital camera. A gift from my grandfather, it is the most expensive camera I have ever owned. It has exposed thousands of pictures. It is the tool with which I learned how to see; it has been my constant companion for the past few years. Thus, there are many reasons why I would take it along with me rather than a cellphone or a laptop.

The first reason why I would choose a camera is plain to see. A camera is a third eye. It registers, records and documents every aspect of our life. So, if I decide to travel, the camera will be like a mobile diary to me. No matter where I go, the camera will allow me to keep memories of my journey across a continent. It has already taken thousands of portraits of people whose names I can't remember, but whose faces I will never forget. A young girl with her prized pet monkey, a workman taking a break on the Gabriola Island ferry, an old woman posing with pride on her newly swept wooden porch, but also the images of family reunions, graduation ceremonies, wedding anniversaries were trusted to it. My camera will be a reliable companion that will not betray me.

A camera never lies. I have held it so many times it has become an extension of me. It has never failed me. The pictures I will be taking will show the reality as I see it. It will capture moments as I see them. And I will be able to see it instantaneously, discarding the pictures that look too cliché or hackneyed, and keeping in its memory the genuine fragments of the life I will be able to catch a glimpse of.

Another reason why I would choose a camera is because of the artistic value of the pictures, adding another dimension to the chronicle of my exploration across the world. So, it is not so much a description of the world as I see it that I will be able to record but also a world as I make it. As famous American photographer Ansel Adams used to say, "Pictures are not taken, they are made." The pictures I will be taking will therefore be carved in the time I took them but, because they are works of art, they will reach a level of eternity, in the same way as a Monet or a Picasso painting do not belong so much to their authors as they belong to time. The camera then will fulfill another need, allowing me to explore and develop my creativity through a glass lens.

At the same time, I expect my work to create awareness and understanding by evoking reactions and emotions in others. Gordon Parks, for example, used his images to help viewers understand and share the feelings of people from different racial backgrounds, in the hope of changing societal viewpoints. Similarly, by expressing the world around me creatively through images, I hope to get to impact others on its reality, however sad, ugly or beautiful it may be.

2. A book

Torn between taking a cellphone or a laptop, both devices people find convenient when going away for a full year, I believe that the item I'd like to take along on a grand journey would be a book. The benefits of reading are boundless. Given that the technological revolution is gathering pace, reading books has healthy and therapeutic benefits. It might be the complete works of Shakespeare, Milton, Plato or Byron, but it would include it all and be a companion when I set upon that yearlong journey.

Why a book by a playwright, a poet or a philosopher? The first and obvious reason is that such authors enrich you with their knowledge and outlooks on life. Such books are inexhaustible sources of wisdom and provide invaluable life lessons that are bound to last. As you delve into what goes on in the inner world of the great thinkers, you can expand and develop your own mind and knowledge. A book will make you smarter as it will expand your knowledge, enhance your thinking and reasoning skills and turn you into a more interesting person.

A second advantage of a book is that it stirs up man's creativity and captivates his imagination as he transitions to a hidden world of fascination with no rules or boundaries. It unleashes the creative and reflective part of the mind into action. Life is much more interesting when one explores new avenues or ventures into somebody else's imagination and creativity.

Naturally, a philosophy book fills a hungry mind with an endless supply of knowledge and information. It can help man to broaden his mind. A story book on the other hand engages man in a world which is miles apart from his own, where he can have a glimpse of what goes on in the lives of fictional characters, where he can explore his feelings, experience empathy, sympathy and compassion as he brings these people and their experiences to life.

A book can also take you back into history and days gone by. It can give you an insight into the *hic* and *nunc*, the known and the unknown. To such an extent that one will have the feeling of traveling both in the present and in the past. As man goes through new countries and discovers cities, a book can help him draw parallels, make comparisons and enrich his mind.

Of course, there will be times during the journey when you'll be down, missing home or people whom you feel close to. A book can help you relieve loneliness or boredom. Once you become engrossed in a book, you lose all track of time. A book motivates you, takes your mind off worries and gives you a chance to escape into a different world, where fantasy, suspense, and curiosity engage your attention. All in all, a book is an ideal way to while the time away, especially on long journeys away from home. Above all it is a way to unwind and relax away from home as well as gain more knowledge, for the day man stops learning is also the day he stops growing.

14 THE ROLE OF ADVERTISING

Some people say that advertising encourages us to buy things that we really do not need. Others say that advertisements tell us about new products that may improve our lives. Which viewpoint do you agree with? Use specific reasons and examples to support your answer.

1. Key words

to advertise	faire de la publicité
an advertisement / an advert / an ad	une publicité
an advertising message	un message publicitaire
an advertising campaign	une campagne de publicité
the advertising industry	l'industrie de la publicité
false advertising / manipulative	la publicité mensongère / manipulateur
an advertising strip / banner	un bandeau publicitaire
an advertising slogan	un slogan publicitaire
to keep sb informed (about)	informer (qn) de
to provide information (about)	apporter des informations (sur)
to inform sb (about / of)	informer qn (de)
to persuade / persuasion	persuader / la persuasion
to manipulate / to condition	manipuler
to brainwash / brainwashing	conditionner / le lavage de cerveau
consumer behavior	l'attitude du consommateur
to increase consumption	accroître la consommation
hoopla / ballyhoo / hype	le battage publicitaire
propaganda	la propagande
to deceive / deception, deceit	tromper / la tromperie
misleading / catchy	trompeur / accrocheur
a brand / trendy (a)	une marque / tendance
a brand name / impulse buying	le nom d'une marque / l'achat impulsif
brand awareness / recognition	la reconnaissance de la marque
a mass brand	une marque connue universellement
to feature (sb in an ad)	mettre en scène (qn dans une pub)
to lure customers (to)	attirer les clients (vers)
to target / a target	prendre pour cible / une cible
to win customers away (from)	détourner des clients (de)
to display warnings (about)	comporter des avertissements (à propos de)

2. Talking points

1. Advertising encourages people to buy things they do not need.

- Advertising can be used to manipulate people Advertising tries to convince people that purchasing a certain product will make them feel happy, look gorgeous or improve their life.
- Many advertising campaigns deceptively suggest a connection between certain brands and a higher status in life.
- Admen associate glamorous people (models, actors, actresses, singers) with products in order to stimulate the competition among people, especially young people, who are gullible preys to ad messages.
- Young children and teenagers are the choice targets of advertising agencies. They are encouraged to buy products they do not necessarily need but that fashion commands in order to be trendy or that parents order to have peace of mind.

2. Advertising improves people's lives.

- Advertising can inform people about different products and services. Advertising tells people how useful such products can be, how much they cost and thus helps them to make better purchases.
- Advertising saves time by helping consumers to make an enlightened choice of the products they buy, by comparing different brands and pointing out to the advantages of brand X.
- Advertising creates a healthy competition between products and services.
- Advertising can lead to direct feedback from customers. Opinions expressed by advertisers help improve the products and services.
- Advertising informs the customers about the introduction of new products or the replacement of old ones.
- Advertising can be used to educate and motivate the public about non-commercial issues such as Aids, deforestation, family planning.
- Advertising fulfills a useful role in warning people against some dangers such as smoking, drinking or texting and driving.

3. Possible answers

1. Advertising encourages people to buy things they do not need.

Advertising plays a central role in the consumer society we live in. Whereas it may be helpful for people to make enlightened choices among the myriad products they want to buy, more often than not advertising plays a harmful role, twisting people's minds and conditioning customers into buying things they do not need. That is why I consider advertising as being more a bane than a boon.

First, advertising can be used to manipulate people. Advertising tries to convince people that purchasing a certain product will make them look beautiful, happy or will improve their lives. For example, some ads target the gratification and self-esteem of women by producing a catchy slogan of body care products to make them feel special: be radiant, be fresh, be transformed. With most of these products, consumers are exploited as they are promised something special that will transform their skin, their body, weight, faces and so forth. It is not so much that women need the product as the idea that it will turn them into Cinderellas ready for the Charming Prince.

Another example of how admen try to lure you into buying the latest products is that of the smart phone. Basically, there is not much difference between brand X and brand Y. You can read your mail, listen to music, text message or just call people. Most features are the same from one model to another. Yet, cellphone makers will persuade you that Brand X is better than Brand Y, or vice versa. To convince you, advertising will use glamour, or models and not real people to deliver their messages.

Many ads offer examples of psychological manipulation. They are deceptive in so far as they suggest, in a not too subtle subliminal way, a connection between certain brands and a higher status in life. Thus, we often see sexy models in glamorous attire or hunky male athletes driving sports or luxury cars being associated with life in the fast lane as if, by simply luring customers to buy those things, customers could belong to that club too. By copying the lifestyle of the glitterati, the average man will be under the impression that he belongs to a wonder world, far remote from the reality he lives in. Advertising in that respect creates a misleading, deceptive world which gullible people will believe in hook, line and sinker.

The most at-risk people are teenagers and children. Teenagers because advertisers appeal directly to their emotional side and the fact they are in constant competition with one another, especially with regard to their physical appearance. Children because they know that parents will cave in to their whimsical desires, if only to have peace of mind, or peace at home, not because what they are craving is essential to their well-being.

All in all, advertising lures people into buying superfluous things only because admen have for long realized that what matters is to create the need.

2. Advertising improves people's lives.

Advertising has crept into our lives and is now used by every medium, be it billboards, street furniture, television, the radio and, more recently the Internet and social networks. For some, advertising has become all too pervasive whereas for others it fulfills a useful function, that of improving people's lives.

To begin with, advertising has an informative function. It helps to make people become aware of products and services. Unless they do not know what is available out there, consumers will not be able to buy and make the most of these products and services. Advertising thus creates an awareness that helps people remember and recognize products and services and thereby develop a sort of trust (or distrust) in whatever products and services are on offer. By informing the customers about the cost, the use or the replacement of existing products by new, more efficient ones, advertising does indeed improve people's lives, helping customers, especially those who live in remote places, to get the best they can expect from a company.

Advertising is also time saving. Instead of spending hours in the alleys of a supermarket pushing a cart and reading the back of each box, consumers know beforehand, and through advertising, which product fills their needs. Thanks to comparative advertising, man can weigh the merits of various brands and, as a consequence, make a clever, wiser choice.

In the same way, informing consumers about the various advantages of a product or service creates a competition between brands, as companies vie to lure as many customers as possible away from the competition. Advertisements create a healthy rivalry because they teach people about the other firms in the market and help consumers take advantage of price differences.

In the same way, advertising has led to direct feedback from the customers. This is especially true when products fail to hold up to the standards the adverts carry about them. People start complaining, following which companies have to make the necessary adjustments to right the wrongs and please the customers. A better product makes life better, as a catchy slogan once mentioned.

Advertising is not only used for the purpose of selling; it has an educational function and can be used to create and enhance awareness among consumers. For instance, several advertisements have been designed and put out in the name of the public interest, to make people aware of their rights, to increase awareness about health problems such as cancer and Aids, to educate people about the benefits of healthy eating, and so on. Other advertising campaigns have urged motorists to fasten their seat belts, or warned them against the dangers of drinking and driving or texting and driving. Be it outdoor advertising, newspaper advertising, or television advertising, the reach of advertising is far and wide, and helps people in numerous ways.

15 CHILDREN AND ADULTS

People recognize a difference between children and adults. What events (experiences or ceremonies) make a person an adult? Use specific reasons and examples to explain your answer.

1. Key words

to grow [grew / grown]	grandir
the grown ups / to come of age	les adultes / devenir adulte
to transition (into)	devenir
to grow into a man / woman	devenir un homme / une femme
a rite of passage	un rite de passage
childhood / adulthood	l'enfance / la maturité
to graduate from university	obtenir un diplôme universitaire
graduation day	le jour de remise des diplômes
to complete one's studies	terminer ses études
to get engaged / married	se fiancer / se marier
to land one's first job	décrocher son premier emploi
to get one's driver's licence	obtenir son permis de conduire
to go out on a first date	avoir son premier rendez-vous
to buy one's first car	acheter sa première voiture
to become independent	devenir indépendant
to earn one's living	gagner sa vie
to achieve financial independence	parvenir à l'indépendance financière
to draw one's first paycheck	toucher son premier salaire
to move into one's own apartment	emménager dans son appartement
to live independently	vivre en toute indépendance
to serve in the army	servir dans l'armée
to do one's military duty / service	faire son service militaire
to take ownership of one's actions	être responsable de ses actions
a life-changing event	un événement marquant
a momentous event	un événement capital
to develop a sense of responsibility	développer un sens des responsabilités
to shape man's personality	former la personnalité
character building	qui forme le caractère
a development stage	une étape dans le développement

2. Talking points

1. An experience

- To become an adult is not a question of age but a matter of experience. It is not having the vote, obtaining one's driver's licence, getting a job, moving out of the house. Becoming an adult is often a question of the experience you have had, such as the loss of a parent.
- An experience may change a child's outlook on life. Overnight, the child grows from a carefree and innocent human being into a mature and responsible adult.
- Parental loss means the eldest child usually finds himself/herself saddled with unexpected burdens: looking after the siblings, making sure the family stick together, filling the shoes of the missing parent.
- For the eldest child, the loss of a beloved parent may mean doing all the chores that are usually a parent's lot while at the same time trying to come to terms with insuperable grief and being scared and scarred.
- To become an adult under such circumstances also means coping with the emotional emptiness that the dead parent has left behind. Sometimes, it may mean the end of a child's dreams and the awareness that one's potential may never be fully realized.

2. A ceremony

- When is the defining point between adulthood and childhood? Becoming an adult in the legal sense of the word and becoming an adult in the true sense are two different things. It is not just a matter of law, rather a matter of experience.
- High school graduation is such a life changing event, not only because it defines a end (to high school life) but above all because it is the first step in a long process that may take place in a different country.
- Attending college is a rite of passage into adulthood: one has to fend for oneself, sometimes learn a new language if one studies abroad, adjust to a different life and set of values, make new friends in a new academic environment. Becoming an adult is going through the experience of independence and autonomy.
- Going off to college means living on one's own, becoming responsible for one's actions and accountable to oneself only.
- To become an adult means assuming the choices that one has made independent of one's relatives and family. It means taking control of one's life.
- Graduation is the end of innocence and the beginning of experience: winning independence, autonomy and responsibility, which are the hallmarks of what being an adult means.

3. Possible answers

1. An experience

What makes you a grown-up? What marks the point at which you now meet the expectations of being grown up? Graduating from college? Reaching 18? Having a relationship? Getting a job? Moving out of the house? How is it that we can do those things, that we consider to be "adult", but we still feel like kids? Or that we feel like grown-ups but we don't seem to have accomplished any of those things adults are supposed to have done? Becoming an adult is one of those subtle issues that have dogged generation after generation. For my part, I believe that some experiences can forge the character and turn a child into an adult. One such life-changing event is the death of a parent. Even though parents are not supposed to outlive their children, no child is prepared for a parent's passing away. Such an event—how to come to terms with death—can happen at any time and some children have found themselves growing up rapidly and assuming the role of adults when death struck in the family.

In a large family, the loss of a parent means that Katie, the eldest child finds herself shouldering many burdens. For example, she is the one that will have to pick the youngest at day care, hurrying to get back from the school where she is studying in order to become—or so she hopes—a doctor. Looking after the young ones means feeding them their snacks, or taking them to sport when daddy is busy at work and won't be back before 9 p.m., and supervising their homework.

As the eldest child, Katie is also responsible for the shopping and, sometimes, the cooking: rustling a hasty meal before rushing her brothers and sisters to bed. Sometimes she will have time to read stories, but more often than not other chores beckon, doing the dishes, the laundry, the ironing, the cleaning up, in a word assuming the responsibilities of a mother, yet being only a child with no time to heal.

Such an experience is bound to change a young girl's outlook on life too. Gone are the careless games, the sleepover parties, the outing to the movies with her best friend. A night on the town is out of the question for her siblings are clamoring for her attention, be it the homework she can help them with, the lunch box to prepare for the next day's field trip or the appointment at the dentist's. The age of innocence is gone, replaced by the harsh reality of experience.

Possibly the hardest aspect of the loss is the emotional one. How can one expect a young girl barely out of her teens to cope with the loss of practical support and affection? Death changes every aspect of family life, leaving an emotional emptiness. In addition to grieving the loss of a parent, you mourn the loss of the hopes and dreams you had as a child, as well as the potential that will never be realized and the experiences you will never share with people of your age.

2. A ceremony

In most countries, according to the law, we're adults at 18. Yet, in some countries, people can't drink until they're 21. Are they still adults even if they don't have adult privileges? When is that defining point between adulthood and childhood? Becoming an adult in the legal sense of the word and becoming an adult in the true sense are two different things. It is not only a matter of law, rather a matter of experience. There are defining events more than age moments that make you an adult. Let us take the example of going away to college.

First off, going away to college is a form of transition for the high school senior. When he leaves home to a distant campus on the other side of the country, or even on the other side of the globe—think about a Shanghai kid leaving his homeland to go and study in Boston, Mass.—this can be considered as the first step on the road to adulthood. By going away, that kid will have to learn to fend for himself: he may have to acquire the command of a new language, he will have to adjust to the culture of a radically different country as well as make new friends in a system of education that is completely foreign to him. This is a first step towards adulthood in so far as he becomes independent from his home, his parents and his friends. Thus, I believe self-sufficiency and a sense of independence are the hallmarks of adulthood.

Second, he will have to live on his own. No mother to do the cooking, no father to give him a ride to school, no parent to account for every penny he is going to budget for the shopping or the utilities of the flat he is renting. In other words, he must learn to account for himself and take responsibility for his own actions: he will not be able to turn to his parents when a faucet is leaking, or when he has to organize his time between study and sports. Those decisions are his only. Accountability for one's actions is exactly what defines the adult from the child.

Three, when it comes to choosing his major, and therefore steer his life in an academic direction that will define the job he will hold later, he will have only himself to rely on. No relatives to urge him to study biology rather than computer science, take up literature rather than math, or pick up chemistry rather than physics. The ability to make one's own choice is what distinguishes the adult from the child. Whereas the child is toeing the parents' line and more or less complying with what the parents wish he would do academically, the student is alone and his destiny rests in his hands. No one can and will help him, except himself.

That is why I consider leaving home for college as the moment when it all merges together: the sense of independence, the capacity to fend for oneself, the necessity to assume the choices one will make along those four years or more. Going away is actually the litmus test of adulthood, when the student now has all the cards up his sleeve and will have to play with the hand that fate has befallen him.

16 PAYING ATTENTION TO CELEBS' OPINIONS

When famous people such as actors, athletes and rock stars give their opinions, many people listen. Do you think we should pay attention to these opinions? Use specific reasons and examples to support your answer.

1. Key words

to influence people	influencer les gens
to hold sway (over)	avoir de l'influence (sur)
to be in the public eye	être exposé aux yeux de tous
to influence public opinion	influencer l'opinion publique
to listen to / to trust sb's advice	écouter / faire confiance aux conseils de qn
publicity / a publicity stunt	la publicité / un coup de pub
celebrity culture	le culte des célébrités
fame and fortune	la gloire et l'argent
to be infatuated with an idol	être entiché d'une idole
celebrity endorsement	le soutien des vedettes
celebrity addiction	l'attirance pour les vedettes
to gain celebrity status	accéder au rang de vedette
to be obsessed with celebrities	être obsédé par les vedettes
an obsession with stardom	une obsession du vedettariat
to look up to sb	admirer qn
to speak out (against)	s'exprimer (contre)
to voice one's views (about)	exprimer ses opinions (sur)
to be qualified (to)	être qualifié (pour)
to have access to the press	avoir accès aux médias
a platform	une estrade
to attract news media	attirer l'attention des médias
the star-struck quality	ce qui fait le propre d'une vedette
to dispense advice	dispenser des conseils
to be credible / credibility	être crédible / la crédibilité
to develop an expertise (in)	devenir un expert (en)
to weigh sb's opinion carefully	peser soigneusement l'opinion de qn
to be best suited to give advice	être bien placé pour donner des conseils
to make barely a ripple (in)	être à peine mentionné (dans)
to make the headlines	faire la une des journaux
a banner headline	un gros titre

2. Talking points

1. We should listen to what celebs have to say.

- The celebrities have the ear of the media. They have gained visibility and credibility. They play an educational role and therefore people should pay attention when they speak.
- People are hungry for some news about the celebrities. They have developed a special connection with the rich and famous. Therefore when a celeb utters something, however banal, people listen to them.
- Because we identify with some celebs, what they say reverberates with us. We talk about problems because some celebs have mentioned them.
- There are some celebrities who use their fame to bring about change; they are inspirational role models that we should listen to when they talk about the pressing issues that have plagued society, for example environmental problems, poverty, hunger. Since 1999, Bono, singer of the popular band U2, has been campaigning for third world debt relief and helping to raise awareness of the plight of those living in Africa. Angelina Jolie has become a spokeswoman about the living conditions deprived children in various third world countries face.
- Even though some celebs have negative attitudes, they serve as models for things people should not be doing, thus strengthening the role they play in society.

2. We should not pay attention to the celebs' opinion.

- Fame is not equal to truth. One should not blindly follow the opinions of the celebs. Why should I listen to what Eminem has to say on quantum physics, or Martin Sheen on electronics?
- Being enamored with rock stars or obsessed with a teenage idol is a sign of immaturity. Young people often swallow everything a celeb says, hook, line and sinker. Teenagers, especially vulnerable ones, are so infatuated with their idols that they cannot make the difference between right and wrong.
- Some of the messages conveyed by the celebs are fallacious. An extremely thin model encouraging healthy eating habits is a lure for teenagers. Pregnant teenage models send the wrong kind of signals as well.
- Paying heed to what the celebs say can be dangerous. We all have in mind how Oprah Winfrey's endorsement of Barack Obama helped propel him to the presidency. But suppose a celeb backed some radical politician?

3. Possible answers

1. We should listen to what celebs have to say.

We live in a make-believe world in which the celebrities have been playing an increasingly vocal role, at the expense of the scientist, the researcher or the professor. Many a times we turn to them and listen when they express their opinions on topics that may range from banning GMOs to adopting healthy eating habits. Why should people listen to what celebs have to say?

To begin with, celebrities are the end product of the media, be it the written press, the cinema, TV, the Internet. They have been fabricated by the media and the media voraciously feed on to each and every pearl of their wisdom. Because the celebs have gained visibility, they have also acquired credibility. Celebs therefore hold a sway over public opinion. They play an educational role and we should listen when they speak.

Conversely, people are obsessed with celebrities. They are addicted to them. They voraciously devour people's magazines; they are glued to the screen when celebs are the guests of talk shows. The media feeding frenzy is mutual. Stars have the ear of the media as the media seek to sate man's appetite for news of and opinions by their favorite celebs.

Because we identify with some celebs, what they say reverberates with us. We should listen because some of the celebs' problems might be ours. When Larry King had a heart attack and told his audience how it prompted him to stop smoking, people listened. The same goes for Michael J. Fox when he talked about Parkinson's disease or Angelina Jolie when she had a mastectomy to thwart off the risks of developing breast cancer. When Britney Spears was brought to the hospital and evaluated for bipolar disorder, we felt differently about our own depression. So the impact of celebrities can be positive as well as negative.

On the other hand, only celebrities can give publicity to some problems that plague society. Environmentally conscience topics, such as global warming, have received publicity because of celebrities. Al Gore, DiCaprio and Hanks are strong believers in living a "green" lifestyle. These celebrities have vocalized support for "going green," and have endorsed hybrid cars. Their advocacy for environmentalism can influence people in adopting a more eco-friendly lifestyle, while strengthening the environmental movement. Other celebs take pride in abstaining from drugs and alcohol. They promote chastity as an alternative to teen sex that could result in an unplanned pregnancy.

True, some celebrities make the headlines going through their own trouble, to wit a politician caught with his pants down and trying to squirm out of it. We frown upon such attitude. But overall, celebs provide clean role models for kids who are desperate for a reason to say no to peer pressure.

2. We should not pay attention to the celebs' opinion.

What is it about celebrities that makes them so irresistible? Is it that they lead such different lives? Is it that they have the ability to buy whatever they want? Or is it that they seem to lead such a glamorous life? Everyone has their own reason for wanting to take a look into the life of their favorite A-List celebrity, and there is no stopping the media machine. In a sense, celebrities are man's new gods. We fantasize that our lives could become like theirs that we too could be beautiful, desirable, talented, rich. At the same time, we secretly want to see them fall so that we know that even our gods have feet of clay. That is why we should be wary about paying attention to what they say.

Actually, celebs speak out on every kind of topics. Rock stars talk about politics, athletes protest against war. But how qualified are they? A musician's qualification is playing his/her own instrument, not expatiating on the evils of nuclear power. Likewise, athletes may run faster or jump higher than the average Joe but that does not turn them into experts on hybrid cars.

Young people are particularly vulnerable to the star culture. They want to ape their style and lap up everything they say. With so many teen girls influenced by the airbrushed models they see on their favorite magazines, it stands to reason that celebrities can influence what girls say about their own bodies. So, what celebs say may sometimes lead to serious problems such as anorexia, and, even worse, depression.

The sad fact is that we are more enthralled by celebrities who have bad reputations than celebrities who are role models. As parents or mentors, we have to be careful about what we allow children to see and listen to. Some parents seem to believe that all celebrities are worthy of being role models. Unfortunately, this is far from the truth.

Celebrities have been involved in political issues throughout history. Should we listen to what celebrities say and do? In the 1930s, Charles Lindbergh used his name to support a movement to keep the United States out of the "foreign entanglements" that would eventually become World War II. Jane Fonda was the anti-war voice of the Vietnam era. Vanessa Redgrave has been a controversial supporter of the Palestinian cause. Is it a celeb's business to discuss political matters?

Our obsession with celebrities goes back a long way, more precisely to 1835 when Madame Tussaud opened her first shop to exhibit the waxwork figures she had created of the celebrities of her time. The minute the doors opened, it was a huge success. Even now, you will still see a long line outside of Madame Tussaud's locations. There is nothing educational about the experience. The only thing we get from visiting a place is the feeling that we've got closer to our favorite celebrities, when, in reality, we have done nothing else than pay a fee to see a waxy imitation of the person we idolize. That is a good enough reason not to pay attention when those waxy figures get to talk. Empty shells have always uttered empty words.

17 A VANISHING RESOURCE

Many parts of the world are losing important natural resources, such as forests, animals, or clean water. Choose one resource that is disappearing and explain why it needs to be saved. Use specific reasons and examples to support your opinion.

1. Key words

the health of the planet	la santé de la planète
deforestation / reforestation	le déboisement / le reboisement
the Amazon forest / Amazonia	la forêt amazonienne / l'Amazone
the rain forest	la forêt tropicale
to cut down / to fell trees	couper / abattre des arbres
the lungs of the earth	les poumons de la Terre
slash and burn techniques	les techniques de brûlis
overgrazing / intensive farming	le surpâturage / l'agriculture intensive
biodiversity / the fauna and the flora	la biodiversité / la faune et la flore
to log / logging	exploiter / l'exploitation des forêts
to harvest wood / lumber	récolter le bois / le bois en grumes
photosynthesis	la photosynthèse
soil conservation	la conservation des sols
a vanishing / disappearing species	une espèce en voie de disparition
a protected species / to be home to	une espèce protégée / abriter
to be on the brink of extinction	être sur le point de disparaître
to be threatened with extinction	être menacé d'extinction
on the list of endangered species	sur la liste des espèces menacées
to be driven to extinction	être amené à disparaître
to become extinct / to exterminate	disparaître / exterminer
to stave off extinction	éviter la disparition
to kill off / to wipe out a species	exterminer / anéantir une espèce
to shrink / to dwindle	se réduire / diminuer
animal trafficking	le trafic d'animaux
ivory / a tusk	l'ivoire / une défense
to smuggle / smuggling	passer en / la contrebande
Antarctica / the floe	l'Antarctique / la banquise
a source of fresh water	une source d'eau pure
the melting of the ice cap	la fonte de la calotte glaciaire
an unspoiled wilderness	une étendue sauvage inexploitée

2. Talking points

1. Saving the rainforest

- The rainforest absorbs CO_2 and therefore helps fight against global warming and greenhouse gas emissions. It is useful for carbon storage. Forests are essential to regulate the Earth's climate.
- The rain forests are the world's lungs. We need the rain forests to produce oxygen and purify the atmosphere to help us breathe.
- The rainforest is an ecosystem that is home to biodiversity. Saving the rainforest means preserving one of the world's largest living species reserves.
- The rainforest is one of the world's richest bio pharmacies. It provides us with many valuable medicinal plants. Destroying the rainforest is paramount to taking away medicines critical to treating major illness and the source of many of the medicines currently used.
- The rainforest is essential to recycle water that is essential for drinking and irrigating crops.
- Rainforests are home to indigenous peoples who have lived there for thousands of years. Many of these people have a culture of harvesting and maximizing the use of the plants within the rainforests. As the people and tribes die out, so does the knowledge of how to reap the rainforest's benefits.

2. Preserving Antarctica

- Antarctica is central for science because of its profound effect on the Earth's climate and ocean systems. Antarctica drives the world's climate, and has a central role in regulating the earth's environmental processes, including the world's atmospheric and oceanic systems, global tides and sea levels. Its preservation and well-being is therefore vital to the health of the rest of the planet; any impact on Antarctica's environment could have global effects.
- The Antarctic has a crucial role to play in our understanding of global climate change and how man's activities have affected those shifts in weather patterns.
- Antarctica is one of the few pristine, untamed, virgin places left on earth. It is the destination of thousands of tourists seeking a taste of what life might have been like before man stepped in to damage the earth.
- Antarctica belongs to no one, yet it belongs to all of us. Because of this, it should be preserved as an example of how nations can unite and save a vital resource.
- Antarctica is the world's greatest reserve of a most precious commodity: fresh water.

3. Possible answers

1. Saving the rainforest

Deforestation is proceeding at an unprecedented rate all over the tropics. Over the past forty years, nearly half the world's tropical rainforests have been cleared. In Brazil, Mexico, Costa Rica, Malaysia, Indonesia, Zaire, and many other tropical countries, forests are succumbing to the chainsaw and the torch. The Ivory Coast and Ghana, until recently major timber exporters, will soon be logged out completely and, like Nigeria, will have to start importing timber. Yet, I believe forests in general and the rainforest in particular play an essential role in maintaining the world's natural balance. They should be preserved.

To begin with, the rainforest helps to fight against global warming and greenhouse gas emissions. The rainforest absorbs CO_2 and is therefore useful for carbon storage. The importance of forests stretches far beyond their own boundaries. Forests help to regulate the Earth's climate because they store nearly 300 billion tons of carbon in their living parts—roughly 40 times the annual greenhouse gas emissions from fossil fuels. When they're destroyed through logging or burning, this carbon is released into the atmosphere. The destruction of forests is responsible for up to a fifth of the world's greenhouse gas emissions—more than every plane, car, truck, ship and train on the planet combined.

The tropical rain forests are rich with plants and animals. Rain forest plants include many of the things we eat such as chocolate, sugar, or bananas. Cinnamon, vanilla, and many spices come from rain forests, too. In addition, plants from the rain forest provide us with many other things. The rubber in tires comes from the rubber tree. Some of the chemicals from rainforest leaves, flowers, and seeds are used to make perfumes, soaps, polishes, and chewing gum. Others kill germs and fight diseases such as cancer. All in all, the rainforest can be considered as the world's biggest pharmacy, even though many plant species have not been discovered and exploited yet.

Rain forests are essential to recycling water. Almost half of all the world's rain falls on rain forests. Plants trap water in the soil and then slowly release it into the air, where it evaporates. Clouds form and rain falls, filling rivers and streams. That water is later used for drinking and irrigating crops. Where rain forests have been cleared from the land, much less rain falls. The land becomes hard and dry. Animal and plant life disappears. Forests regulate water flow and rainfall so we depend on them to grow our crops and food. The loss of forest in one part of the world can have severe impacts in another; forest loss in Amazonia and Central Africa can severely reduce rainfall in the U.S. Midwest, for example. The rain forests thus play a central role in the preservation of biodiversity and the sustainability of the environment. They should be saved.

2. Preserving Antarctica

Remote, hostile and uninhabited, Antarctica is one of the few territories that remain unchartered to this day. Home to many species, it also plays a key role in understanding the weather phenomena that affect the world. That is why we should preserve it.

The Antarctic is essential to observe how our world works, and man's impact upon it. When man deals with the Antarctic, the Earth's climate and ocean systems are affected. The Antarctic has a crucial role to play in our understanding of global climate change. The untrammeled nature of the region provides a living laboratory where scientists can measure the effects of changes in the environment. The four kilometer-thick ice sheet is a unique record of what our planet's climate was like over the past one million years. Ongoing research is crucial to understanding and monitoring global warming, ozone depletion and atmospheric pollution. In fact, Antarctica's greatest value might well be in the information it provides on the functioning and health of our planet. The discovery of the ozone hole above the Antarctic in 1985 alerted man to the potentially dangerous changes in the environment caused by human activities. This discovery led to the first measures to control pollution on a global scale.

Antarctica is a continent of superlatives. It is the coldest, windiest, highest and driest place on earth. It is one of the few unspoiled places left on earth, in addition to being the world's natural laboratory. The nutrient-rich Southern Ocean is home to a diverse and fragile ecosystem consisting of 75 million marine species, including whales, seals and many other bird and fish species found nowhere else on earth. Its frozen wastes have sparked the public imagination for generations, and around 30,000 tourists now visit the Antarctic each year to experience what life looked like in the Earth's last great wilderness. However, Antarctica is fragile and increasingly vulnerable and should be handled with care, lest we destroy part of the laboratory.

Although many nations have laid claim to parts of Antarctica there is no government here other than an agreement reached from the Antarctic Treaty System. It means there can be no petroleum or mineral exploration and no hotels or ski slopes for tourism. As of now Antarctica belongs to no one and it belongs to everyone. No place on earth can claim this. That is an additional reason why it should be preserved.

We know that water is going to become a precious commodity; yet, what most people do not know is that seventy percent of the world's fresh water and ninety percent of he world's ice is in the glaciers in Antarctica. It is our bank, our legacy to future generations. If we mess up that legacy by building, drilling and mining, we potentially mess up one of the most important resources to sustain human life. If that ice melts due to climate change we have lost our ability to keep that water resource.

Antarctica is essential to man. It should be made clear that it is not for sale. If the continent fell in private hands, it would sound the death knell of life on the planet.

18 A GIFT OF MONEY

Your school has received a gift of money. What do you think is the best way for your school to spend this money? Use specific reasons and details to support your choice.

1. Key words

to donate / a donation	donner / un don
to contribute money (to)	mettre la main à la poche
a contribution (to)	une contribution (à)
to benefit (from)	tirer parti (de)
to lack resources	manquer de ressources
to support a project	soutenir un projet
to fund a project	financer un projet
to invest (in)	investir (dans)
a gift of money	un don d'argent
classroom equipment	du matériel pédagogique
to update equipment	moderniser l'équipement
educational technology	la technologie éducative
classroom furniture	du mobilier de classe
to outfit / a computer lab	équiper / une salle informatique
a white board	un tableau blanc
a digital textbook	un manuel numérique
to award / to give a scholarship	attribuer une bourse
a deserving student	un étudiant / élève méritant
merit-based	fondé sur le mérite
need-based / means-tested	attribué en fonction des besoins
a disadvantaged student	un élève défavorisé
a low income family	une famille aux revenus modestes
to pay out of pocket	payer de sa poche
to be excluded from education	être exclu d'une formation
to be shut out from the school system	être exclu du système scolaire
to miss out on education	ne pas avoir la chance d'aller à l'école
to lag behind / a laggard	être à la traîne / un traînard
to close the achievement gap	combler le fossé de l'échec
academic achievement	la réussite scolaire
to afford / affordable	se payer / abordable
a dormitory / a gym	une résidence / une salle de gym

2. Talking points

1. A scholarships fund

- State support for schools has decreased substantially. Although it looks like some countries may have weathered the worst of the recession, many states are still reeling from the economic slump and most have made large cuts in public service funding—including education. As a result, public schools have increased tuition, meaning you're probably going to pay more now.
- Scholarships would provide educational opportunities to children from low-income families and allow parents/guardians to choose the best schools for their children and prevent the kids from dropping out.
- Handing out scholarships to underprivileged kids whose families often can ill-afford an education would be a way of promoting equal opportunity.
- Scholarships make education and career goals easier to obtain. A student on a scholarship would not have to worry about material things and would work serenely.
- To be awarded a scholarship is an achievement that speaks volumes about a student. College admissions committees or potential employers will know they have a talented candidate. So, a scholarship looks good on a resume.
- Thanks to scholarships, students from low-income families could envision a future that will be better than their parents'.
- To award merit-based scholarships is the best way to encourage students to excel in their domains and achieve top marks.

2. A computer room

- If a school was given a gift of money, it should be best spent on a computer room and computer equipment, especially if the school is located in a deprived area.
- In poor districts, low income children do not necessarily have the means to afford a computer or get a foothold into the digital age.
- Computers are great teaching aids. They allow students to develop a wide range of skills that will best prepare them for the future.
- A computer room is a great place to interact with other students in a friendly, collaborative way. Thanks to computers, children learn how to work together.
- Computers are windows open to the world. They allow students to communicate not only with their own classmates but with keypals from all over the world, thus expanding their horizons and outlook.
- A computer is a learning tool that enables students who are lagging in some domains to find the resources and answers to the questions they may ask themselves, especially if the teacher does not have the time to address each student's problems.

3. Possible answers

1. A scholarships fund

Should my school receive a large amount of money, I believe it would be best spent on setting up a fund that awards scholarships to deserving and disadvantaged students, be it for academic, artistic or athletic reasons. This fund would be all the more welcome as state support for schools has started to wane because of the great recession. Students would benefit from such scholarships in many ways.

The first benefit would be an educational one. Most underprivileged students attending my school have to work to help their families make ends meet. Yet, working while in school is the number one reason why people drop out. Being awarded a scholarship that pays for education and living expenses would actually minimize the risk of dropping out and not getting the degree a student seeks. By reducing financial concerns, scholarships would also mean more time for studying and learning, which can lead to better grades and retention of knowledge and increase chances for continuing on to college.

Another reason to hand out scholarships is to promote equality. Many students come from low-income families. Even though they may be talented, they are not given the same opportunities as kids from well-off backgrounds and whose parents can pay for their tuition fees and living expenses. So, awarding scholarships would by all means show that, by dint of hard work, every one has a chance of completing their studies and accessing higher education.

Three, by removing financial barriers, scholarships make education and career goals easier to obtain. Because scholarships are free money, students can focus on their academic goals and careers instead of thinking about how they will repay loans. If students know they have financial security, they will work in much better psychological conditions than if they have to worry about how their parents will pay the electricity bill.

Earning a merit-based scholarship can actually make a student a more attractive candidate for admission to college or potential employers. Employers who understand the competitive nature of the scholarship will recognize it as an accomplishment. Generally, a merit-based scholarship demonstrates that you have exceptional ability in the academic, athletic or artistic realm. Competitive scholarships are accomplishments worth listing on a resume; they can help a student stand out when searching for a job.

Giving merit-based scholarships is the best way to encourage students to excel and achieve top marks. It is also a way for deprived students to escape the poverty trap or the economic condition their parents are in. If students know that by dint of hard work they can obtain a scholarship that will improve their chances not only in education but in life too, they will push themselves to achieve the top marks and get the best jobs.

2. A computer room

In deprived areas and inner cities, where money is scarce but students eager to learn, I believe the best way to spend a gift of money would be to buy equipment and set up a computer room, outfitted with the latest computing technology. I believe that is how the school and the student community would benefit from such a gift of money.

The first reason is plain economics. In the low-income districts where some schools are located, not many families can afford to buy a computer, let alone have an Internet connection. What little money the parents make is spent on the basics: food and renting. Going to the cinema is unheard of. School is a place where you spend most of the day and prepare for the future. So, buying computers would be a godsend for those kids raised in the digital era but unable to have modern technology at home.

Computers would be a great help in learning. Students are keen on discovering and experimenting and computers offer just that. They allow people to surf the wide web looking for information, digging for resources, downloading books and videos, making contacts, retrieving documents that might all be useful for class work. At the same time, a computer is a splendid tool to learn programming, design games, write programs, in a word, acquire the skills necessary to be operational in the computer age.

Computers are also a way to learn collaborative work. Through the school intranet, students can first keep abreast of each other's work. In addition, computers allow for a fair distribution of tasks among students with some working on the sociological aspects of a problem, others on the technical or the historical one. Computers therefore are tools to learn how to work together by pooling resources and sharing information. They put all the kids on an equal footing and therefore help each team member to move at the same pace.

Beyond the school limits, computers are also a unique way to interact with other schools. Thanks to computers, students can reach out to other kids in the town, the state or beyond. They can connect with students of their age but who are on the other side of the country or live in another continent, get and exchange information, in other words they can broaden the somewhat limited horizon of the backcountry town where they live. A computer room therefore is a window open on the rest of the world.

More importantly, a computer is a useful tool to learn at your own pace. Whereas in the classroom, teachers do not always have time to address each of the students' requests, and verify they are moving along at a crisp clip, in the computer room wired students will be able to find answers to the problems they may stumble across in the classroom but that the teacher cannot address for lack of time. A computer room would thus be a great equalizer of the students' level, pulling them upward and showing that there are creative solutions if only they have the resources at their disposal. A computer room is definitely the best investment possible for a school.

19 IS HUMAN ACTIVITY DOING HARM TO THE PLANET?

Some people believe that the Earth is being harmed (damaged) by human activity. Others feel that human activity makes the Earth a better place to live. What is your opinion? Use specific reasons and examples to support your answer.

1. Key words

harmful / harmless	nuisible / inoffensif
the living conditions	les conditions de vie
the Stone Age / the Ice Age	l'Âge de la pierre / de glace
prehistoric times	la préhistoire
a sustainable world	un monde durable
the progress of technology	les progrès de la technologie
to hurt the planet	faire du mal à la Terre
to exhaust natural resources	épuiser les ressources naturelles
to protect the environment	protéger l'environnement
to go on holiday	partir en vacances
holidays / a holidaymaker	les vacances / un vacancier
to deplete / depletion	épuiser / l'épuisement
deforestation / to cut down trees	le déboisement / couper des arbres
to overgraze / to overfish	pratiquer le surpâturage / la surpêche
slash and burn	la culture sur brûlis
to pollute the atmosphere / water	polluer l'air / l'eau
global warming	la réchauffement climatique
the greenhouse effect	l'effet de serre
greenhouse gases	les gaz à effet de serre
carbon dioxide emissions	les émissions de CO_2
to throw waste (into)	jeter nos ordures (dans)
urban sprawl / car congestion	la périurbanisation / les embouteillages
loss of habitat	la perte des habitats naturels
the extinction of species	la disparition des espèces
to wipe out / to kill off a species	exterminer une espèce
to be driven to extinction	provoquer la disparition
the melting of the polar ice caps	la fonte des calottes glaciaires
the retreat of glaciers	le recul des glaciers
nuclear / biological weapons	les armes nucléaires / bactériologiques
cyberwar / hacking	la cyberguerre / le piratage informatique

2. Talking points

1. The Earth is being harmed by human activity.

- Deforestation is one of the major threats to the survival of the Earth. The disappearance of forests, such as the rainforest or the old-growth forest, is a matter of grave concern.
- Pollution, caused by man's activities (mining, extracting, hydraulic fracturing) is a threat to the survival of an energy-hungry planet.
- The accumulation of greenhouse gases and CO_2 emissions is harmful to the planet. Global warming has already led to extreme weather conditions such as storms, droughts, flooding, sea level rise.
- Human activities have caused much harm to the fauna and the flora. Many bird and fish species are on the verge of extinction or have already gone extinct.
- Human activities have led to the development of cities and the expansion of suburbs, thus bringing about traffic congestion, encroaching upon rural land and the loss of the countryside.

2. Human activity makes the Earth a better place to live.

- Human activity has greatly enhanced man's life in many domains. From the Stone Age to modern times, progress has made our lives easier and the Earth a better place to live; home appliances, electronic devices, food supply, solar heating, wind energy, in every domain technological advances have improved man's life on Earth.
- Human activity has transformed the way to travel today. We have moved from the horse to the hybrid car, thus opening up our horizons and making it easy to move goods or people from one place to another.
- Thanks to human activity, it is easier to communicate today. Conversely, the cellphone or other means of communication such as test messaging or chat rooms have made the world a better place to live by bringing people together.
- Human activity has fostered change in the way we work. Automation has relieved man of some backbreaking tasks and freed time for leisure and entertainment. Yet, we have also become aware that we have only one earth. We have taken steps to preserve our planet and learn from the lessons of the past.

3. Possible answers

1. The Earth is being harmed by human activity.

The past centuries have seen a quickening of the pace of industrialization to such an extent that whole regions are now endangered by human activity. In plain words, the Earth has become a fragile ecosystem, threatened by man. Clear evidence abounds.

The Earth's woodlands are under a great deal of pressure. The rainforests are rapidly disappearing due primarily to illicit activities such as gold mining, logging, timber harvesting, and the hunger for land. Tropical and old-growth forests are being damaged by the lumber and paper trade.

Pollution is another major threat. Industrial activity has made the air more difficult to breathe and the water we drink less pure. Factories, especially coal-fired plants, belch out noxious fumes into the atmosphere. Extracting coal or oil, and today fracking, are evidence of man's unquenchable thirst for fossil fuel energy. As for the nuclear industry, recent incidents have proved how hazardous it has been to tap that kind of energy.

Because of an increase in temperatures, due to man's activities, the planet is slowly heating up. The accumulation of greenhouse gases has led to global warming along with extreme weather phenomena: storms, droughts, flooding are common occurrences. The rise in the sea level is jeopardizing coastal areas and low lying islands scattered in the middle of the oceans.

The toll of human activity has been harsh on the fauna and flora. Countless bird and fish species have been driven to extinction. Overfishing has made the oceans a wasteland. The sparkling blue waters of the Mediterranean Sea are home to over 700 varieties of fish and almost 10 per cent of the world's marine species. Its coastline is one of the most densely populated in the world and the human pressure on this sea is magnified each summer with the influx of holidaymakers. Western civilization developed around these shores but now human activity is having a profound effect on this endangered sea and some species, amongst which the bluefin tuna, are fast disappearing. On the other hand, overgrazing and intensive farming have given way to dust bowls: coupled with droughts, large swathes of land have gone arid and caused dust storms which, at times, have engulfed cities.

Finally, man's activities have had a huge impact on the urbanization of the planet. Lured by the prospect of jobs and driven away by poverty, millions of migrants have flocked to the cities hoping to have a better life than in their impoverished rural areas. As a consequence, cities have boomed, suburbs have expanded, highways have been built in a mad race for progress and money. The list of evils caused by man reads like a doomsday catalog. Short of vigorous action in the near future, the Earth as we know it will no longer be able to cope with technological progress.

2. Human activity makes the Earth a better place to live.

Even though some people think industrial and technological progress has made the Earth a worse place to live than it once was, I believe that it has improved living conditions, be it in everyday life, communications, transportation and the workplace.

Remember when your ancestors had to go down to the river to do the laundry? Or when man would take up his rifle and go hunting so as to bring home some bacon for the evening meal or wood to stoke the fires? Or when expeditions across the oceans were fraught with hazards? Well, those times are now gone, thanks to progress. The housewife has now plenty of appliances to do the cooking, the washing or the cleaning up. Man is no longer forced to go hunting to find the food that will sustain his family during the freezing winter months: there are refrigerators to keep the meat bought from the local butcher's and most of the energy is supplied by the local nuclear plant.

Progress has extended to other activities such as transportation, making the Earth a better place to live. We used to travel on horseback, that is, when we traveled. Crossing a continent was quite an adventure. Yet, we would usually spend our lives in the same place and hardly ever venture beyond the village boundaries. Besides, dirt tracks were impassable most of the time, especially in winter and spring months when the snow turned to thaw. Today, the advent of the car, the train and the aircraft has changed the way we travel and where we go. Superhighways crisscross the country and flying overseas has become quite common, be it for pleasure or business. High-speed rail has shrunk distances and allowed people to get together easily. The revolution in transportation has made life on earth a better place.

Advances have benefited the way we work and communicate too. The telephone was quite a breakthrough; the old landline will soon go the way of the horse, to be replaced by the ubiquitous cell phone or smart phone. We now get in touch with people or stay connected through the Internet and social media. Whereas news would take days or weeks to reach us, a mere computer click can keep us updated on the latest news. The idea that parents can talk to their kids at any time anywhere has made many a parent's life much more reassuring and comfortable.

Human activity has naturally fostered changes in the way we work. Machines, automation, computer-aided robots have eliminated the menial, backbreaking tasks and given man time to enjoy his leisure and entertainment. Farm work has become industrialized too. Above all, we have become aware that we have only one earth and taken steps to develop clean energies, passive buildings, fuel-efficient vehicles and environmental preservation in general. Man has learnt from the lessons of the past. And because he is now applying those lessons, the Earth is a better place to live.

20 STUDYING MANY SUBJECTS OR ONE?

Some universities require students to take classes in many subjects. Other universities require students to specialize in one subject. Which is better? Use specific reasons and examples to support your answer.

1. Key words

a set / a range of courses	un ensemble de cours
a set curriculum	un programme établi
a core curriculum	un tronc commun de connaissances
core requirements	des prérequis
to specialize (in) / specialization	se spécialiser (en) / la spécialisation
to complete a curriculum	terminer un programme
a syllabus / a remedial course	un programme / un cours de ratrappage
basic / fundamental subjects	les sujets de base / fondamentaux
a prerequisite / compulsory	un prérequis / obligatoire
a mandatory course	un cours obligatoire
a foundation course	une année préparatoire
optional / prescriptive	facultatif / normatif
an elective / elective (a)	un cours facultatif / facultatif
to pick and choose	sélectionner
to impose (to)	imposer (à)
to leave little / no choice	laisser peu / pas de choix
to force to study	contraindre à étudier
to adopt a hands-off approach	choisir de ne pas intervenir
to assume responsibility (for)	assumer la responsabilité (de)
to leave it up to the students (to)	laisser aux étudiants le soin (de)
to be intellectually curious	être curieux intellectuellement
to arouse / to awaken curiosity	susciter la curiosité
to satisfy one's curiosity	satisfaire sa curiosité
to prepare for a career	se préparer à une carrière
to broaden one's scope	élargir sa perspective
a broad knowledge (of)	une connaissance étendue (de)
to be well-rounded	être complet / généraliste
a workforce training program	une formation professionnelle
an all-round student	un étudiant complet
Grasp all, lose all	Qui trop embrasse mal étreint

2. Talking points

1. Studying many subjects

- To ask students to choose from a wide range of subjects is a way of empowering them and helping them to be accountable for their own choices.
- It is not advisable for students to specialize early in their academic career while they have only a vague idea of what professional path they want to follow. Allowing students to choose amongst a wide range of electives will help them to make a more enlightened choice, and possibly guide them towards pursuing a career they may not have thought about previously.
- Studying a wide range of subjects will equip students with a solid bedrock of general knowledge that will be helpful all life long.
- Studying a wide array of subjects will prepare the students better for a career, where, more often than not, they will need to have more than general knowledge in one single area.
- Studying different subjects will help students to be more rounded and responsible adults. As well, they will become more informed citizens.

2. Choosing one subject

- Students are hard put to study so asking them to choose from different subjects means exposing them to the risk of failing them all, whereas focusing on one topic is likely to be a chance of success for them. A jack-of-all-trades is master of none.
- Subject matters have become more and more complex over the years, requiring the students to specialize early in order to know the subject in-depth.
- Students who take a rigid core curriculum have higher college retention rates than students who do not take the core, regardless of gender, family income, and racial/ethnic background.
- Students who take the core curriculum in high school are less likely to need remedial coursework in college than students who do not take the core.

3. Possible answers

1. Studying many subjects

The idea that higher education is primarily about gaining various skills and knowledge has been gaining currency over the past decades, especially at a time when students watch the ranks of the jobless grow steadily. The sort of dabbling in which many students have historically engaged may seem like a luxury in an era when vocational interests might seem to trump all others. Yet, I believe that studying a wide range of subjects is the right thing to do for students today.

To begin with, requiring students to choose from a whole range of subjects rather than specialize early is a way of empowering them and helping them to be accountable for their own choices. After all, it should not be up to the college to impose subjects on students. It is up to the students to be responsible for the choices they make.

Second, it stands to reason that asking students to specialize early in their academic career is premature. Most students have a blurred idea of an area of specialization. Giving students time to explore subjects and figure out their academic paths will actually result in making better choices of their major, and ultimately, wiser career choices. In addition, choosing amongst many elective courses outside the prescribed plan of coursework will give them a more 'well-rounded' education. Electives will allow students to discover subjects that might interest them and change the direction they wish to take with their education. A student who takes an elective class in drafting, for example, might discover a love of design and engineering that leads to a career he or she might not otherwise have imagined. Therefore, it is necessary to give students the time and freedom they need to learn both what they like and what they're good at. Additionally, studying different subjects will help students make more enlightened and responsible choices and become better-informed citizens.

Three, giving students the freedom of choice in their subjects is bound to equip them with a solid bedrock of general knowledge that will be beneficial all their lives long, be it in the personal or professional sphere. Actually, it is essential that a physicist know about biology, or an economist about music and art. In a world that is getting complex, acquiring a general knowledge will stand you in good stead in society.

Studying a sweeping array of subjects is necessary to establish a solid career. For example, a doctor studies different fields before choosing to specialize in one. He must have notions on hematology, cardiology, but also in biology and psychology. A civil engineer must possess a background in math and physics but also computer science if he/she wants to design bridges. To run a business, a manager must possess skills in accounting, corporate and labor law, human resources, economics in addition to knowledge in the products the firm is specializing in.

2. Choosing one subject

Whereas some universities encourage students to choose several electives, I for one believe that focusing on one single subject is quite enough. Actually, there are many reasons why it is preferable to remain focused rather than embrace too many subjects.

First, not all students are hard-working enough, or even smart enough, to study many subjects at the same time. If too many subjects jostle for a student's attention, he/she is bound to spend too much time on them all—and waste it—rather than concentrate on one subject and be successful at it. As the saying goes, a jack-of-all-trades is master of none. By diluting his/her efforts among several subjects, the distracted student will fail to grasp the content of one. Because topics tend to be ever more complex, chances are that he will fail all the subjects instead of planning on studying one in-depth and being successful at it.

Second, subjects have become more and more complex today. Be it calculus, trigonometry, literature, economics, civil engineering, the knowledge and the skills required to be in full command of a domain have increased to such an extent that it takes much longer to tackle those topics than it used to. Because so much progress has been made in science, it is hard to even know all of a single one. Doing research has now become specialized to such an extent that it has become next to impossible to broaden one's scope beyond the limits of one's specialty. That is why doctors specialize in dermatology, cardiology or gynecology, for example. When learning a foreign language, the student will focus exclusively on that language. When practicing penal law, the attorney will devote his time and attention to that branch of law only. We need specialists that know what they are talking about, not generalists with a smattering of knowledge in every field.

Students who follow one rigid core of set courses, instead of many electives chosen at random, have better chances of moving up to the following year than those who try to embrace too many courses. 'Grasp all, lose all', as the saying goes. College work is quite demanding and requires full attention. On the other hand, one year of tuition is quite expensive and if students spend too much time following a syllabus that is too big for their breeches, they are likely to drop out and lose not only one year but four years of college, let alone the possibility to do graduate work.

That is why I believe that students who take the core curriculum are less likely to need remedial coursework in college than students who do not take the core. By strengthening your fundamentals and making sure you have the required skills, you are more likely to succeed in other domains than if you decide to choose many electives without a precise idea of what you can do with them and where they can lead you. Therefore, doing one subject equates academic success, which is not the case if you follow several subjects.

21 IS GRAFFITI AN ART FORM?

Some people think that graffiti is an art form and therefore should be protected and preserved. Other people think graffiti deface the walls of cities and should be systematically removed. Use specific reasons and examples to support your opinion.

1. Key words

graffiti (ni) [sg. graffito]	les graffiti
a graffitist / a graffiti artist / a tagger	un graffeur
a tag / tagging / street art	un tag / le tagging / l'art de la rue
to be tagged with graffiti	être recouvert de graffiti
graffiti culture / to beautify	la culture du graffiti / embellir
street art / urban art / an art form	les arts de la rue / une forme d'art
a style of graffiti / stenciling	un style de graffiti / le pochoir
to produce graffiti	faire des graffiti
to be a target for graffiti	être la cible des graffiti
an art critic / artistic value	un critique d'art / la valeur artistique
to be worthy of display	être digne d'être exposé
to display one's work	exposer son œuvre
an art gallery / a museum	une galerie d'art / un musée
to scrawl / scrawling	gribouiller / le gribouillage
to paint / to spray paint	peindre / peindre à la bombe
an aerosol can / a mural	une bombe aérosol / une peinture murale
spraycan art / subway art	l'art aérosol / les graffiti dans le métro
to deface / defacement	dégrader / les dégradations
to desecrate / to vandalize	profaner / vandaliser
vandalism / a vandal / an eyesore	le vandalisme / un vandale / une horreur
to be used as a gang signal	être utilisé comme signe par les gangs
to mark territory / a marking	marquer un territoire / une marque
gang-related activity	les activités liées aux gangs
to be reviled by authorities	être la bête noire des responsables
to be associated (with)	être associé (à)
the anti-establishment	les mouvements contestataires
the punk rock movement	le mouvement punk rock
the hip-hop culture	la culture hip-hop
to be covered with graffiti	être recouvert de graffiti
to scrub the walls / to buff	gratter les murs

2. Talking points

1. Graffiti as an art form

- Graffiti art is an ancestral art form: it was widespread in Ancient Egypt, Ancient Greece or even with the Mayans. It was found on the walls of ancient ruins and sepulchers. Cave paintings can also be compared with graffiti. Graffiti art is an avatar of such art and has an established history of development in style and technique, from the 1960s to present times.
- Graffiti art forces man to raise the question: what is art? Many artists have used unconventional objects to express their creative talent. Graffiti art has now been recognized by the art world.
- Graffiti is a way of addressing issues and conveying a political message. Graffiti on end walls of terraced houses in Belfast or on the Berlin Wall—the largest canvas in the world—bear witness to the Troubles or the political situation during the Cold War. Street art can be a way of making a statement. Often, graffiti is part of a subculture that rebels against authority and the square society.
- Like any other art forms, graffiti is a means of expression to which the public reacts. Graffiti art brightens up a street or a monument and provides the viewer with another way of looking at a building. Graffiti art is definitively art when both the artist and the audience agree on the works ability to provide maximal aesthetic satisfaction.
- Street art is a form of self-expression. The art as "writing" is a creative method of communicating with the general public. What it communicates is the artist's identity, expression, and ideas. Judgments are based solely on one's artistic ability.

2. Graffiti art is no art.

- Graffiti art is a way for people to achieve fame and gain name recognition at the expense of recognized art forms. Doing graffiti can be dangerous (heaven spots on the high end of skyscrapers, on the sides of bridges, on trains or subway cars) yet the more daring, the greater the name recognition.
- Graffiti artists have no respect for old buildings and other monuments they take pleasure in defacing. Graffiti is unsolicited art; it is an act of vandalism that shows little respect for people's property.
- Graffiti usually spread in pockets of poverty. It means that a district has been abandoned and is going to rack and ruin. It is a sign of urban decay, not urban renaissance. It makes an area look dirty and unsafe, all the more so as graffiti are often related to gang-warfare and the defense of a gang territory.
- Graffiti are a form of visual pollution that affects the eye of the beholder. They are offensive and ought to be cleaned up.

3. Possible answers

1. Graffiti as an art form

Street art, also called graffiti art, appeared in the late 1960s and has developed since. Yet, it has never been readily accepted as art, in the same way as those works that are found in a museum. Yet, I believe that it is genuine art, notwithstanding its lack of form or other mainstream aesthetic elements.

First, most of the opposition to street art comes from its definition and location: tags, markings, which relate to self-identification and sometimes define gang territory, cannot qualify as graffiti *per se.* Street art means tagging to enhance walls, bridges, subway cars, factories, monuments with bold, unexpected and unconventional colors and shapes. However illegal its practice may be, it does qualify as art. Actually, graffiti is an ancestral form of expression that was common on cave walls in prehistoric times, in Ancient Egypt, on the walls of Pompeii houses. Graffiti require skills to complete and represent realistic or abstract scenes just like on a traditional painting.

Graffiti force man to raise the question: what is art? Marcel Duchamp was an artist whose works included a bicycle wheel and a urinal. He literally took these everyday items and exhibited them. Marcel taught us that really anything could be art, so there is no reason why graffiti, though disrespectful, shouldn't be art, even though it may call the street its home. Graffiti artists like Banksy, Jean-Paul Basquiat, Keith Haring or Plantrees have thriven and become mainstream today.

Graffiti art is a way of addressing issues and conveying a message. Picasso denounced the horrors of the war and the sufferings it inflicted on civilians in *Guernica*—thus bringing the Spanish Civil War to the world's attention. Delacroix painted *Liberty Guiding the People*, commemorating the July Revolution of 1830 that toppled Charles X. Likewise, graffiti artists get a message across through the murals or the walls they illustrate. In Belfast, graffiti bear witness to the Troubles and glorify paramilitary groups such as the Irish Republican Army, giving the inhabitants a sense of identity. The Berlin Wall, also called 'the graffiti Mecca of the urban art world' was a visual political forum. Street art is a way of making a statement and spreading a point of view.

Above all, street art is a means of expression. The graffitist first does a sketch, then plans out characters and selects colors. Next, the artist selects his or her "canvas" or surface and does a preliminary outline, followed by a filling in of colors and ornamentation, and then the final outline is completed. Graffiti can also be analyzed according to lines, color, and structures in order to produce a narrative. Graffitists intend their work to be apprehended as art that can communicate feelings and ideas to the audience. In all, graffiti artists make cities look more vibrant and beautiful. They help brighten up the urban environment.

2. Graffiti is no art.

Street art should not be elevated to the status of art. Actually, graffiti is a cheap form of considering art and therefore street artists should not be on the same footing as Monet or Rembrandt.

Street art is first and foremost a way for some people, especially those who have been unable to exhibit their works in galleries or museums, to achieve fame and name recognition. Doing graffiti is an act of boldness and recklessness. It means artists trying to elude the police, for street art is illegal, and publishing their works on monuments, bridges, or trains to attract the attention of the public. Even if you're Picasso, you're not allowed to paint on other people's walls.

Sometimes, graffitists will run risks at the expense of their own lives, when climbing to the top of skyscrapers to present their bubbling, scrawling and squiggling. And naturally, the more unconventional the tagged place, the better the name recognition.

Actually, street art is vandalism at its worst. There is no need to be a rocket scientist to figure out that tagging public or private property is an act of vandalism. Defacing a building shows little concern for other people and is plain illegal. For some artists, it is actually seen as a challenge to the law, to authority, the square society that has nothing to do with art but everything to do with rebellion against the world, however justified the visual message may be. Markings are a way to claim space from ever-increasing corporate control.

On the other hand, graffiti are often gang-related. Gangs, so as to define their territory, will tag every wall, every sign, every bridge that defines their turf as a way of saying to rival gangs that there is no trespassing beyond that tag. Sometimes, graffiti may be used as a subtle form of racism too, difficult to detect as they are linked to local codes. A spatial code or a color scheme, for example, could mean that there is a youth group in an area that is engaging heavily in racist activities. Honestly, graffiti here has nothing to do with art.

Graffiti flourish in dodgy and poor districts that have been long abandoned, and whose population has fled from because of violence, gang warfare, drug trafficking and other of the evils associated with low lifes. Thus, graffiti usually herald or reinforce urban decay. They make a neighborhood look dirty, uncared for and unsafe. It is a way of saying to strangers that they enter a district at their own risks. When graffiti is synonymous with dereliction and decay, violence and violation, it seems difficult to raise its status to that of art.

Finally, graffiti are visual pollution. It means the authorities are indifferent to the plight of the inhabitants where walls and buildings have been defaced. Graffiti are a license to turn a district into an eyesore and the residents into second-class citizens, whose living environment is of little concern for the taggers or the city managers.

22 UNIVERSITY FOR ALL

Some people believe that a college or university education should be available to all students. Others believe that higher education should be available only to some students. Discuss these views. Use specific reasons and examples to support your opinion.

1. Key words

higher education (HE)	l'enseignement supérieur
to enter higher education	faire des études supérieures
to attend university	aller à l'université
college access / preparation	l'accès / la préparation à l'université
to make college education compulsory	rendre la formation universitaire obligatoire
to graduate from college	être diplômé de l'université
a college degree	un diplôme universitaire
to be in the interest of a nation	être dans l'intérêt d'un pays
to provide the tools to compete	fournir les outils pour être compétitif
to widen / to broaden access (to)	élargir l'accès (à)
to open the doors (to)	ouvrir les portes (vers)
pay inequality	l'inégalité des salaires
to be employable	trouver un emploi
to equip one's citizens (with)	armer ses citoyens (de)
social / upward mobility	l'ascenseur social
to take people out of poverty	extirper les gens de la pauvreté
to require a college degree	exiger un diplôme universitaire
to put a burden (on)	alourdir
to deny access (to)	refuser l'accès (à)
equal opportunity for all	l'accès à l'égalité pour tous
to reduce social inequalities	réduire les inégalités sociales
to put on an equal footing	mettre sur un même pied d'égalité
educational equality	l'égalité devant l'enseignement
a cultural capital	un capital culturel
a vocational program	un programme de formation professionnelle
on-the-job apprenticeship	un apprentissage sur le tas
to go into an apprenticeship	entrer en apprentissage
to drop out of college / a drop out	arrêter ses études / un décrocheur
to be academically gifted	être doué pour les études

2. Talking points

1. Everyone should have access to HE.

- Education is a right. All high school kids should have access to HE, regardless of background, origin or even academic results. Educational sinners should have a path to redemption at least through the community colleges.
- HE education is a chance. Everyone has potential to be developed to its maximum. Denying access to higher education would constitute a violation of their rights to a better future.
- HE is a unique opportunity to rise up in society. It opens the doors to a better future and allows kids to climb the social ladder.
- Denying access to HE to some students is likely to create two categories of students, the qualified and the unqualified, the bad and the good, and, as a consequence lead to a nation torn between those who can and those who can't. It would severely harm a nation character building.
- Education for all is a way for a country to solve social problems. Being educated means acquiring knowledge, discipline, and determination. Additionally, HE is a way of reducing inequalities. A college degree is also a passport for a better salary.

2. Access to HE should be restricted.

- The desire to send all kids to college rests on a snobbish premise that middle class values trump working class values. HE is not for everyone and does not necessarily offer wellbeing.
- There is a need for a diversified workforce, not a unified one. A college degree for all is not the best way to prepare the workforce for tomorrow's challenges. College degrees are not necessary for many jobs. Of the 30 jobs projected to grow at the fastest rate over the next decade in the U.S., only seven typically require a B.A.
- Many subject matters learned at school are never used in one's professional life. Why study quantum physics, dead languages or advanced chemistry when what you need is good communication skills? High school graduates would be better served by being taught how to behave, problem-solve and communicate in the workplace.
- Not all students are fit for higher education. College demands qualities that not everyone possesses, so the selection should be strict, all the more so as there are already too many students wasting their time at college.
- A college education does not necessarily lead to a job. Plus the cost of education makes it difficult for students to become autonomous rapidly. That can mean a lot of tuition to pay, without a degree to show for it.

3. Possible answers

1. Everyone should have access to HE.

Education plays a central role in a nation's character building. Facts show that the rise and fall of a nation depends on the quality of the education it provides for its citizens. The higher the quality is, the more successful the nation will be. That is why I believe that college education should be available to all.

First, as education is a universal right, access to higher levels of education should be available to everyone, regardless of their background or previous academic performance. If you're telling kids 'You can't cut the mustard, you shouldn't go to college or university,' then you're shortchanging them from experiencing an environment in which they might grow. That is why everyone should have a chance to access HE.

HE education is a chance. Education is the primary, and probably the only road to opportunity. Everyone has potential to be developed and cultivated to its maximum. Denying students access to higher education would kill their chances of such development and would somehow constitute a violation of their fundamental right to a better future. Therefore higher education should be available to all students, because it opens doors to a better future. The higher the education, the more chances in the future students can grab.

If education is a right for all, on the other hand denying some students access to higher education would create a kind of discrimination between "good" and "bad" students. In the long term, those who can get access to higher education would likely feel superior to those who cannot. This kind of feeling would be detrimental to a nation's character building.

Above all, the only way for a country to tackle and solve its social problems—drugs, crime, poverty, unemployment—is by providing education to all, and that includes the less privileged students. Education instills the knowledge, rigor, discipline, and the habits of life that lead to personal renewal and social mobility. It would be a mistake to miss out on that opportunity. Higher levels of education for all are bound to reduce social inequalities, as they will put everyone on a more equal footing. Actually, people with college and graduate degrees generally earn more than those without them, and face lower risks of unemployment.

As the saying goes, a rising tide lifts all boats. If a country raises the educational level of its population, chances are that the country will be ahead of the progress curve and foster an economic climate in which there are only winners.

2. Access to HE should be restricted.

Debates over college access, preparation and completion generally start with the unspoken premise that every kid should be able to go to college. Parents impart in their children a sense that college is the path most likely to provide for a secure and successful adulthood. Yet, the premise is starting to change, as policymakers and the public wonder if the push for access has gone too far. Should everyone go to college?

The desire to send all children to university is driven by a snobbish belief in the supremacy of middle-class values over traditional working-class aspirations to gain money and have a happy family life. If someone has had a rotten time at school and wants to be a bricklayer, a game warden, or a hair stylist, why send them to university? Higher education is not for everyone and it does not necessarily offer wellbeing. Just because you don't go to university does not mean you do not want to be educated.

A country needs a diversified workforce. In the same way as there are various TV channels, there are various paths to the job market and going to college is only one of them. A country needs to vary the routes to rewarding careers, because if all men are created equal, they do not have the same personality, the same style, the same type of intelligence, the same motivations. The academic-only approach imposes a kind of sameness on young people that is inappropriate to the job market.

Plus, a large majority of workers never use the advanced math, chemistry or language skills they learned in school. The traits that employers value most are non-academic: attitudes, communication skills and work experience. For many students, the key to getting a job is having been trained to do a job.

Four, not all students are fit for higher education. College requires qualities that not everyone possesses. HE has special requirements, especially intellectual ones, which, supposedly, not every student can meet. Therefore, HE would better be reserved only to tightly selected students. Actually, colleges and universities are chock-a-block full of students who do not really belong there, who are ill prepared for college and uninterested in breaking a mental sweat.

The argument that four years of higher education will translate into a better job, higher earnings and a happier life has been pounded into the heads of schoolchildren, parents and educators. But there's an underside to that conventional wisdom. No more than half of those who began a four-year bachelor's degree program will get that degree within six years. In addition, the cost of a college education is such that students are saddled with debt they have trouble paying back, thus hampering further their material independence.

Students unlikely to be successful pursuing a higher degree should therefore be steered toward intensive, short-term vocational and career training, through expanded high school programs and corporate apprenticeships.

23 ONLINE DATING

Some people think that online dating is a convenient way to meet people. Others think that it should be restricted because it is a fraud. Which view do you agree with? Give examples and reasons to support your point of view.

1. Key words

cyber dating / online dating	les rencontres en ligne
an online dating agency	une agence de rencontres en ligne
a dating site / website	un site de rencontres
a digital matchmaker	un entremetteur virtuel
to meet sb via the web	rencontrer qn sur Internet
to sign up for a site	s'inscrire à un site
a lonely hearts club	un club de rencontres
to find love / a lonely heart	trouver l'amour / un cœur solitaire
to be single / a bachelor	être célibataire / un célibataire
to get married / to tie the knot	se marier / passer la corde au cou
a marriage partner / a profile	un partenaire / un profil
a bogus / misleading / fake profile	un faux profil / un profil trompeur
a bait profile	un profil fait pour attirer
to make initial contact	établir un premier contact
to find romance / a soul mate	trouver l'amour / l'âme sœur
to broaden one's circles	élargir son cercle
an arranged marriage	un mariage arrangé
to hunt for one's beloved	être en quête de l'amour
a casual encounter (in a bar)	une rencontre fortuite (dans un bar)
to prey on women	s'attaquer aux femmes
to undermine marriage	saper le mariage
to cheat on one's spouse	tromper son époux / épouse
to masquerade as single	passer pour célibataire
to produce successful unions	conduire à des mariages parfaits
a matching algorithm	un algorithme de compatibilité
to refine matching techniques	affiner les techniques de compatibilité
a matchmaker	un entremetteur / une entremetteuse
to narrow potential choices	restreindre les choix potentiels
to fill in a detailed questionnaire	remplir un questionnaire détaillé
to provide a detailed list of criteria	fournir une liste détaillée de critères

2. Talking points

1. Online dating is useful.

- Internet dating sites offer the shy person a way to cautiously approach a stranger without fear of rejection or social awkwardness, as most services are anonymous.
- The web offers the ability to create large pools of potential partners that would be hard to replicate in the real world. Such sites act as deal breakers. You get to find out more about the other person before arranging to meet. Texting back and forth tends to eliminate people who tell off-color jokes, write ungrammatically or who are otherwise unsuitable.
- The web offers the sheer convenience of being able to trawl through hundreds of profiles without having to leave the comfort of one's home.
- Online dating sites provide the possibility for millions of isolated single men and women to get in touch with one another.
- Often busy people have little time to look for a soul mate. Online dating sites provide a convenient shortcut to soul matching.
- Dating online is safer than trying to pick up a date at random in a bar. You can get to know more about the other person than in real life.

2. Online dating is a fraud.

- Many sites' claims of matchmaking prowess are often greatly overblown. One of the drawbacks to dating sites is their ability for a profile to be misrepresented and to lie about personality and characteristics (appearance, social and economic status, or, in some cases, age and gender).
- Dating websites do not take robust action to protect those who seek romance from falling into the clutches of crooks, cads and worse, fraudsters, voyeurs and sexual predators. Spammers use dating sites to cull email addresses to add to their spam lists. Plus electronic privacy is easy to violate when you give someone personal information about yourself such as a telephone number or email address.
- Virtual matchmaking is bound to fail, as shown by scientific studies: couples that have been paired off through dating sites have a short lifespan.
- Dating sites may encourage extramarital affairs and promote infidelity, thus playing havoc in some couples.
- Dating sites can be compared to meat markets where men and women go shopping for what they think is the ideal mate, encouraging people to view partners as commodities that can simply be traded in for better versions at the click of a mouse, thus debunking the old-age notions of love and romance.

3. Possible answers

1. Online dating is useful.

In a world where isolation has become a recurrent problem, the web offers singles myriad advantages over more traditional routes of finding a partner or a mate. Actually, there are several reasons why those dating sites are necessary and useful.

One of the reasons why people start an online search for dating possibilities is that they are unable to find that sweet, charming, down to earth person while they are heavily intoxicated at the bar. Internet dating sites have become a way of avoiding the awkward approach and the face-to-face reality of rejection. So, if someone doesn't accept a message on the site, just move onto one of the next possible matches and continue the search.

Second, unlike in real life, dating sites offer a vast pool of potential partners. An online dater can browse through thousands of profiles before hitting what people consider as the closest match. Online dating allows people to pick and choose the characteristics that they are looking for and narrow down options based on personal criteria. It is similar to selecting the toppings on an ice cream without going through a blind taste test. This can be in the form of a specialized online dating site for specific religions, profile screening, as well as customized questionnaires developed to weed out those that do not fit within certain parameters such as age, height, musical tastes, hobbies, etc.

Another advantage of online dating services is that they allow people to trawl through hundreds of profiles without having to leave the comfort of their home. They can dress as casually as they like, and log on at whatever time is suitable for them.

Dating sites are particularly helpful for all those people who are isolated such as farmers who live in rural communities where chance encounters with the love of one's life are few and far between. At least, through those sites, they can access a virtual community of like-minded people and break the loneliness they are trapped in.

Another category of people for whom dating sites can be useful is business people, or, more generally, all those that live a frantic life with little down time and leisure. Those people are usually hard put to actually go out and meet Mr or Ms Right because they are too busy. Internet offers a quick way to make acquaintances with people, cut the conversation or the small talk to a minimum and get on with the business of life.

Finally, I believe online dating is safer than trying to pick up a date at random in a bar. The site will arrange to winnow a list of potential matches and thus save you the trouble of going through the paces when you meet someone. Also, because those paying sites are touchy about their reputation, they will make sure you get 100% satisfaction by providing all the necessary information you need about the other person.

2. Online dating is a fraud.

Dating online has generated much controversy. Some people have seen it as the real thing to find one's perfect match. Yet, those sites are way overblown and can be compared to fraud in many cases.

Going into some of the arguments against online dating is the ability to cast false impressions. The picture is chosen, obviously, to emphasize attractiveness. It may be a few years out of date. Not all of the information provided is reliable. Exaggeration is more common than outright deceit, although outright deceit certainly does occur from time to time. Still, this is a lot more information than you have about a blind date, let alone someone you meet at a public place such as a singles dance or a bar.

Anonymity in using a dating site can offer both protection but also create unidentifiable danger. It is easy for anyone to pass off as an astronaut, a surgeon and many other endearing and alluring professions and turn out to be a sex offender or a serial killer. Financial scammers use such sites to lure unsuspecting victims into parting with their money. Sites cannot run background checks on each and every customer. It is this ability to lie that is one of the overriding concerns caused by online dating.

While many dating sites claim the ability to find your perfect match, social scientists aren't buying it. Research suggests that, while it is possible to predict whether two people could enjoy spending time together in the short term, it is (nearly) impossible to scientifically match two people for long-term compatibility. The strongest predictors of a good, functional relationship are how a couple interacts, and their ability to handle stress—two things that science says current dating website algorithms can't predict and online profiles can't demonstrate.

Some people have criticized the very existence of dating services, saying that they encourage extramarital affairs or promiscuity and promote infidelity. Truth is some men will not balk at using those services to meet women and cheat on their wife. Dating services are thus transformed into procurement agencies where you can actually meet people for an evening of fun on the town you happen to be passing through while on a business trip.

Yet, what makes those sites irksome is the fact that it can be compared to a vast market place where people of both sexes go shopping, for an evening, or for a life. What matters is matching interests, tastes, colors, financial records, etc. Whereas when you actually meet someone in real life, chances are that there will be true chemistry between the two people: the meeting will naturally blossom into romance and, who knows, into marriage, thus respecting the several steps that lead from courtship to wedding in the most traditional form, but also the most respectful. A computer's cold, drearily functional approach to assessing compatibility will always fail to capture the indefinable spark that triggers romance.

24 SHOULD VOTING BE MADE MANDATORY?

Some people think that voting should be made mandatory in all democracies. Others think that the right to vote ought to be exercised freely and without constraints. Which of these two policies do you think is better? Use specific reasons and examples to support your opinion.

1. Key words

the right to vote	le droit de vote
polls / the polls	le scrutin, les élections
compulsory voting	le vote obligatoire
to vote (for) / a voter	voter (pour) / un électeur
a non voter	un non-votant
the electorate	l'électorat
a constituency	une circonscription électorale
election day	le jour du scrutin
to exercise / to give up a right	exercer / renoncer à un droit
to abstain from voting	s'abstenir de voter
to be denied the right to vote	se voir refuser le droit de vote
to disenfranchise	priver du droit de vote
disenfranchisement	la privation des droits civiques
to cast a ballot	mettre un bulletin dans l'urne
an absentee ballot	un vote par correspondance
an absentee voter	un électeur votant par procuration
proxy voting	le vote par procuration
a voting booth	un isoloir
an election	une élection
a general election	une élection législative
a presidential election	une élection présidentielle
voter turnout	la participation électorale
to bring out voters	encourager la participation
to expand / to increase turnout	augmenter la participation
to fail to vote	ne pas aller voter
turnout decline	la baisse de participation
an elected official	un responsable élu
political inequality	l'inégalité politique
participatory effort	l'effort de participation

2. Talking points

1. Voting should be made mandatory.

- Even though some people think that being required to vote is a violation of autonomy, so is mandatory taxation, jury duty and the requirement to educate children.
- Mandatory voting is a most decisive means for arresting turnout decline and closing the socioeconomic voting gap. Compulsory voting prevents disenfranchisement of the socially disadvantaged.
- Elected political leaders in compulsory systems can claim a higher degree of political legitimacy than those of non-compulsory systems with lower voter turnout.
- The outcome of an election where voting is compulsory reflects more fairly the will of the people and prevents wealthy, radical or extremist groups from seizing power.
- Mandatory voting means that government will do its utmost to remove barriers to voting (working day, reaching out to disabled people, restrictive employers, etc.).
- Mandatory voting, including the possibility to cast spoilt or blank ballots removes the possibility that some people may be intimidated or bullied into voting for a candidate.
- Mandatory voting requires that all voters do some research on the candidates so as to make an informed choice.
- To be able to enjoy the benefits of a democracy, compared to, say, a dictatorship requires participatory effort.

2. The right to vote should be exercised freely.

- It seems anti-democratic to mandate participation. One of the greatest freedoms is the freedom to be left alone. Compulsory voting may infringe upon other rights, including the right to exercise one's religion freely or the right to free speech.
- If people don't care enough about their country and community to vote, they are not capable of casting an informed vote.
- Most people believe that more voting causes better government. Yet, higher turnout does not cause higher quality government.
- Some people opposed to compulsory voting are nonvoters by principle. Either they think the system is corrupt (for example, because of districting, gerrymandering, the inordinate role played by money, negative campaigning, advertising), or, on the other hand, they are satisfied with the way it works.

3. Possible answers

1. Voting should be made mandatory.

Since Athens required that all citizens should participate in assembly work, putting to shame those who refused to do so, many countries have gone democratic and shed some blood for it. Because so many have fought for the right to vote, it stands to reason to make it mandatory.

Voting turnout can be quite low in some countries, for example during the mid-term elections in the U.S. Making voting mandatory would arrest turnout decline and close the socioeconomic gap that sees that only well-informed citizens vote. Some categories of people who are usually underrepresented—the homeless, the uneducated, the young, the unemployed or the deprived minorities—would be granted a say in public affairs. On the other hand, elected political leaders in compulsory systems would claim a higher degree of political legitimacy than those of non-compulsory systems with lower voter turnout. The victorious candidate would represent a majority of the population—not just the politically motivated individuals who vote without compulsion—and not under-represent sections of society that are less active politically.

One core advantage of mandatory voting would be to reflect more truly the will of all the people. At the same time, it would prevent power from being monopolized in the hands of a minority, a faction, or some extremist group. So, a high turnout would be likely to mitigate the risks of political instability brought about by a charismatic but sometimes dangerous leader. Mandatory voting would make sure every voter does some research on the candidates so as to make an informed choice.

Mandatory voting would mean that government would do its utmost to lift barriers to voting, thus removing the possibility that some people may be intimidated or prevented from voting. Employees would be given a free day should polling take place on a weekday. Mobile polling stations would be made available to the disabled, the elderly or the sick.

In particular, mandatory voting should include the possibility to cast spoilt or blank ballots. Similarly, a 'None of the above' ballot would help people express their dissatisfaction with the choices offered and send the message to the political parties that they need to improve their method of selecting their candidates. Should 'None of the above' win a majority of the votes cast, it would be back to the parties to figure out how they can improve their chance of putting forward an acceptable candidate.

Finally, enjoying the benefits a democracy instead of, say, a dictatorship, requires participatory effort. Democratic citizens owe it to one another to vote so that, together, they can constitute and perpetuate democracy and collectively enjoy the benefits of living in a properly functioning society where every vote counts and is accountable for.

2. The right to vote should be exercised freely.

A handful of countries across the world have made voting mandatory. Yet, few enforce it, thus giving the lie to the idea that forcing people to vote actually works. One of the tenets of democracy is actually the freedom to exercise one's rights. And that includes the right to vote. That is but one reason why voting should not be made compulsory.

To start with, it is anti-democratic to mandate participation. One of the greatest freedoms is the freedom to be left alone. In addition, compulsory voting may infringe upon other rights. For example, the Jehovah's Witnesses believe they should not participate in political events. Mandatory voting is also a violation of the right to free speech. Doesn't the right to speak also imply the right not to speak?

Second, if some people don't give a hoot about their country and community, they will not be capable of casting a thoughtful, informed vote. Others may be well informed, but have no preference for any particular candidate, and no desire to voice support to the incumbent political system. If we force everyone to vote, the electorate will become even more irrational and misinformed. They will fulfill their electoral duty at random, without taking pains to know more about the candidates and will cast their ballots for anyone, a phenomenon aptly called the donkey vote. Still, others will willfully skew their ballot to slow the polling process or disrupt the election. So, if we made voting mandatory, we should also quiz every voter to make sure they have done the research and listened to the debates, which is a tall order.

Many people believe that more voting causes better government. This is an article of faith, not fact. For example, the turnout rate for presidential elections in the U.S. has hovered around 50% since the 1960s. It hasn't caused bad government, nor have higher turnouts in other countries entail good government. Social scientists have shown that higher quality government tends to cause higher turnout. But higher turnout does not cause higher quality government.

Some principled voters prefer not to get involved in the present political system for other reasons. For example, they consider that the system is corrupt, violent, biased. They think politicians make hollow promises, do not listen to the people anyway and should not be trusted. Therefore they prefer to minimize their participation and not lend credibility to it. For example, voting in most House elections in the U.S. is pointless because districting ensures that the incumbent will always win. And when there is a competitive election it's often decided by money, in other words the biggest advertising budget wins. Is that what you call democracy? Conversely, it may also be argued that non-voters remain on the sidelines because they're satisfied with the way the system works.

25 UNPAID INTERNSHIPS ARE A DISGRACE

Some people think that unpaid internships for college students are useful. Others think it is a disgrace. Which of these two policies do you think is better? Use specific reasons and examples to support your opinion.

1. Key words

an internship / an intern	un stage / un stagiaire
a work placement	un stage en entreprise
to intern / to do volunteer work	faire un stage / faire du bénévolat
an unpaid intern / unpaid work	un stagiaire / du travail non rémunéré
a paid position	un emploi rémunéré
to be paid nothing / to pay wages	ne pas être payé / verser un salaire
to start at the bottom	démarrer au bas de l'échelle
youth unemployment	le chômage des jeunes
an entry-level job	un travail de débutant
a steppingstone (to)	un tremplin (vers)
on-the-job experience	une expérience sur le tas
a trade (UK) / labor union	un syndicat
to be unionized	être syndiqué
to organize interns	syndicaliser les stagiaires
to offer valuable experience	offrir une expérience précieuse
to violate wage / hour laws	violer les lois sur les salaires / horaires
minimum wage	le SMIC
to be entitled to the minimum wage	avoir droit au SMIC
to be exploited / to work for free	être exploité / travailler gratis
employment / labor law	le droit du travail
a résumé line	une ligne sur le CV
to strengthen a college application	renforcer ses chances d'admission
to gain experience	acquérir une expérience
to become independent	devenir indépendant
to contribute value to an organization	apporter une valeur ajoutée à une entité
respect for work	le respect pour le travail
to displace other employees	remplacer d'autres employés
to run errands	faire des courses
to do menial tasks	effectuer des tâches subalternes
to be exploited at will	être taillable et corvéable à merci

2. Talking points

1. Unpaid internships play a useful role for college students.

- An internship is a great way to get work experience that will strengthen a student's graduate job applications as well as add one line to his/her CV.
- An internship is an extension of the classroom. Whereas in the past people were apprenticed, today, they do internships, thus complementing school or college work, which is more theoretical.
- An internship, even though it is unpaid, will provide the intern with valuable insights into an industry. It will prove how good he/she is and may lead to interesting opportunities within an industry. Unpaid interns are more likely to find permanent work than students who have never done an internship at all.
- An internship will help young people make a lot of connections in the field they want to work in during their professional life. Work experience teaches valuable skills that most schools do not: among them are how to speak, how to listen, and how to show up on time. Such advantages outweigh being paid or not.
- As interns are likely to get more from the internships than the employers, it stands to reason that the work should be free. Be it as it may, the experience an intern gains is invaluable and cannot be quantified.

2. Unpaid internships are a fraud.

- Unpaid work is biased towards the well-off students who do not have to earn a salary to pay for tuition or living expenses. Thus, the system works against class mobility as only the comparatively privileged can afford to make the investment of accepting an unpaid internship. Even apprentices of the past would receive room and board from their masters. Medical students in their residency are essentially apprentices, but they are paid. The same could be said of law clerks.
- Unpaid interns replace paid workers, which undermines the trust, the expertise, and other things that are typical of seasoned workers. Plus, it displaces experienced employees, making them redundant.
- Unpaid internships can be compared to child labor: interns are not paid, yet they have to do all the menial work for free.
- Unpaid internships are against the law that demands that work should be rewarded. It is time employers stopped exploiting at will gullible and obedient interns. It is time employers stopped breaking labor law.

3. Possible answers

1. Unpaid internships play a useful role for college students.

Internships have become an established steppingstone to employment for students and graduates starting their careers. However, many internships are unpaid, particularly in sectors such as the media. So, how to decide whether an unpaid internship is a valuable opportunity or a waste of time that could be better spent earning some much-needed cash? Are unpaid internships ever justified?

First off, an internship is a great way to get work experience that will strengthen a student's job applications as well as add one line to his/her CV. An internship will show an employer that a student already has some work experience and that he/she is not a beginner. It will show many qualities too, such as the ability to team work or communicate with other people. An internship is therefore a nice complement to the academic experience, establishing skills beyond the classroom.

Second, internships are an extension of the classroom. Most unpaid internships require that a student receive academic credit. In a way, internships can be compared to apprenticeships in the olden days: an internship is a learning experience. It is another form of homework grounded in the real world. This fully justifies why internships should be encouraged.

An internship, even though it is unpaid, will give a student valuable insights into an industry. Some sectors, particularly the media, are hard to get access to (unless one has strong connections). Offering his/her services free will probably get a student a toehold in a firm, and once they have their foot in the door, who knows what will come next in terms of employment. Unpaid work may pave the way to paid employment if they manage to capitalize on the skills that they have gained during the internship. If interns work hard, people will notice. They will be rewarded. So, it is worth spending some time working for free rather than waiting for a paid internship that may never materialize.

Interning helps students make a lot of connections in their fields that they wouldn't otherwise make—connections that could come into play in the future. While they may not be getting paid, interns are getting other benefits: meeting important people who can be mentors, role models, references, and future employers. These positions will help them figure out what they want to do in the long-term.

Interns get more from their internships than their employers. It is expensive to train interns; actually, employers see interns as longer-term investments. Paid or not, interns take a company's time, money, and other resources. Also, many interns don't have a lot of experience under their belt – sometimes none. In that case, they are a risk to hire. This way, they get a foot in the door and the company gets to see what they can do while taking as little risk as possible.

2. Unpaid internships are a fraud.

Unpaid internships have become one of the thorniest issues today, all the more so as the economy is tanking and a job that pays is hard to come by. Therefore, many young people are willing to try everything, including unpaid work to enter the workforce. Yet, I believe this is wrong and unpaid work should not be allowed.

First off, unpaid work is biased towards the rich kids. Some college students just can't afford to take on tuition payments, school, a paying job, and unpaid work in the name of "experience." So the well-off kids gain all the hands-on, practical experience, get to build their resumes, and come out on top after graduation, all because they could afford to work without pay. Does that sound fair?

Unpaid internships are prejudiced against women, thus strengthening gender stereotypes. If, on one hand, internships bring more women into the workplace (three-quarters of unpaid interns are female) it also means that there are more women working for no money. Female interns are said to be "compliant" and "silent"; they do not argue nor do they challenge authority. Thus, the unpaid internship may just be another way to marginalize women and contribute to the pay gap between the genders. The wage gap still exists–and unpaid internships are not the way to fix it.

Unpaid interns replace paid workers, which undermines trust, expertise, and other things that are crucial to the operations of an industry. An employer will be very much tempted to hire unpaid interns to replace workers that are expensive to the firm. Yet, an intern has little experience. An intern cannot replace an experienced worker. Not only that, but interns are prone to be hired for free thus displacing experienced workers for whom work is a necessity to provide for their families.

Not paying interns for their work (whatever it is, running errands, bagging food, making photocopies, delivering pizzas, fetching coffee) can be compared to child labor. For a long time (and this is still the case in many poor countries today), children were hired to do the backbreaking and menial jobs that adults would not, be it mine work, carpet weaving or brick processing. They had no rights and were deprived of education. Modern interns might be compared with children, slaving away for free.

Worse, depending on how people look at unpaid internships, this is either massive exploitation of young people by powerful corporations, which worsens inequality, or a valuable opportunity for on-the-job training at lower cost than a degree or certificate at a college or university. Unpaid internships—similar to indentured servitude—violate some fundamental labor and overtime laws. They are a modern-day scandal. They allow unscrupulous employers to exploit the hopes and dreams of young people desperate to get a foothold on the career ladder. It is time the authorities put an end to this practice and made sure interns were paid in compliance with minimum wage laws at least. It is time interns stopped being exploited at will.

26 SUPPORT FOR THE ARTS OR THE ENVIRONMENT?

A company is going to give some money either to support the arts or to protect the environment. Which do you think the company should choose? Use specific reasons and examples to support your answer.

1. Key words

to preserve the environment	protéger l'environnement
environmental protection	la protection de l'environnement
air / marine pollution	la pollution atmosphérique / marine
to be harmful (to) / to do harm (to)	causer du tort (à) / nuire (à)
to disturb an ecosystem	perturber un écosystème
a source of livelihood	une source de subsistence
global warming	le réchauffement planétaire
the greenhouse effect	l'effet de serre
extreme weather conditions	des conditons climatiques extrêmes
the food chain	la chaîne alimentaire
the extinction of species	la disparition des espèces
biodiversity / wildlife	la biodiversité / la faune sauvage
the fauna and the flora / natural beauty	la faune et la flore / la beauté de la nature
to preserve / to conserve a landscape	préserver un paysage
to go green	se convertir à l'écologie
to invest in green technologies	investir dans les technologies vertes
funding for the arts	le financement des arts
an arts organization	une association artistique
a theatrical production	une production théâtrale
philanthropy / philanthropic	la philantropie / philantropique
corporate largesse	la générosité des entreprises
corporate sponsorship	le mécénat d'entreprise
to elevate one's brand image	améliorer son image de marque
to enhance company / product image	améliorer l'image de la société / d'un produit
product promotion	la promotion d'un produit
to build a cultural legacy	bâtir un héritage culturel
to donate for cultural causes	faire don à des causes culturelles
a patron of the arts / a sponsor	un mécène
to enjoy the arts	profiter des arts
to visit a museum	visiter un musée

2. Talking points

1. Protecting the environment

- Business has a responsibility to care for the environment. Mitigating the effects of air or water pollution has many benefits.
- Investing in the preservation of the environment (through energy-saving policies) means saving money for a company.
- An eco-friendly business that creates environmental awareness in its employees provides additional benefits.
- Supporting the environment (through eco-investing or green investing) gives a company a positive eco-friendly corporate image and encourages people to buy its products. It also attracts investors.
- Companies that behave irresponsibly and recklessly towards the environment are bound to stir up the anger of customers alike. Conversely, an eco-friendly business will attract investors and possibly be in a sounder financial situation.
- To protect the environment is in the interest of industry. An industry taps the earth's resources and harnesses its power. If industry destroys nature, it destroys itself.

2. Supporting the arts

- Support for the arts has been on the wane over the past years, especially because of the great recession. Sponsoring the arts means that a company does not only care for profit. It shows that it cares about educating people and raising cultural standards thus softening its image in the eyes of public opinion. Sponsoring events is also a way of encouraging new talent.
- To sponsor the arts is part of a company's promotional toolkit: it is a way for a company to communicate about itself and advertise its services in a positive, forward-looking way. Art sponsorship can also help improve employee motivation, provide media coverage and redress or mend the brand image of a company, battered by problems or scandals or dogged by a bad reputation.
- To support the arts is a way for a company to connect with the past and show continuity with the present. It shows involvement in the community as well.
- A company that sponsors artists shows that it is creative and able to reach out to prospective clients.
- Art events can be an opportunity for a company to enhance its connections, entertain choice customers or clients while showing a dynamic image of itself.

3. Possible answers

1. Protecting the environment

Because of their impact on the environment, businesses have an obligation to try to mitigate the effects of their activities in an effort to protect scant land and water resources. Many businesses act voluntarily to reduce their environmental footprint. For example, industries that produce hazardous waste are mandated by law to regulate their businesses. In any case, reducing their environmental impact is a sensible approach to business that can have many benefits.

First, businesses benefit by protecting the environment through cost savings. Efficiently run businesses that generate minimal waste, by recycling the water they use or insulating their facilities save money. Initiatives, such as using more energy-efficient appliances may involve an initial investment. However, this investment can often result in significant energy savings that will reduce costs.

Second, an eco-friendly business creates environmental awareness in its employees, providing additional benefits. Employees can be encouraged to turn the heating down at night, switch off computers, monitors, printers, copiers and lights at the end of each working day, refill printer cartridges instead of buying new ones, reduce paper use by printing double-sided or use email instead of sending memos and faxing documents. They can also substitute incandescent lamps with compact fluorescent lamps (CFLs) or remove excess fluorescent lights and install reflectors.

Businesses that follow green practices portray a healthy message to consumers. They may be more likely to support a business that takes its role in the environment to heart. Companies that are better at managing their environmental impact may attract investors. This is the case with eco-investing or green investing, which is the practice of investing in companies that provide environmentally friendly products and adopt sound green practices. Such companies profit from new technologies that support the transition from carbon dependence to more sustainable alternatives.

Conversely, industries that behave irresponsibly, maliciously, or uncaringly towards the environment are likely to rouse the wrath of customers. Companies that are slow to mend their eco-harmful ways will find that customers shy away from their products. For example, oil companies that have caused spills have been boycotted by motorists. A company with little or no GHG emissions has a better risk profile compared with a business that has an adverse impact on the environment. Industries with better environmental discipline have a tactical advantage over polluters. And naturally, green stocks have a built-in cost advantage for a company. As investors become increasingly environmentally conscious, we see capital flowing to these companies, which in turn provide for increased investment performance for well-run green companies.

2. Supporting the arts

Caught between the demands of industry and an uncertain economy, arts programs occupy a vulnerable and shrinking niche. Yet, for arts institutions, corporate donations are a lifeline without which many would cease to exist. The awkward symbiosis is the result of shriveled government funding for the arts and spiraling costs. Although research shows countless benefits when exposed to the arts, art programs are frequently the first to go when budgets are stripped. Art is essential for all and that is why I believe it should be supported by the corporate world.

First, a company that supports the arts shows that it does not only care for profits, the balance sheet or the bottom line but that it can fill an educational function too. Sponsoring the arts proves that the company is concerned with raising people's cultural standards and awareness. At the same time, they show that art can be a source of beauty and pleasure, therefore softening the ruthless image that most people usually entertain about the corporate world. In the same way, a company can build up its corporate reputation and leave behind a cultural legacy by seeing budding talent nurtured through sponsorships and an enhanced local arts scene.

Second, sponsoring the arts is a way for a company to communicate about itself. It is good for the brand image. Association with an arts festival enables brands to differentiate themselves from the competition by projecting an up-market or premium image.

A company that commits to sponsoring the arts plays a useful role in preserving the past. Funding the restoration of a castle or sponsoring an exhibition of old masters is thus a way to say how essential it is to be involved while at the same time sending a positive advertising message to its customers that it cares by giving back to society.

A company that sponsors artists shows that it has a creative side. If science and technology help to answer questions of "what" and "how," the arts and humanities give ways to confront the intangible, to contemplate the "why," to imagine, to create. With some creativity, companies can open up unexpected avenues to reach prospective clients through support of the arts.

Arts events present opportunities to entertain, engage and network with prospective clients while deepening and strengthening the existing relationship in a setting that highlights the company's creativity and vibrancy. When a firm sponsors an exhibition or helps restore some ancient ruins or refurbish monuments (the Hall of Mirrors in the Palace of Versailles, for example), it attracts the attention of the clientele who have been invited to the première or a private preview and the public who visit the places. It heightens the premium that people can put on a company, especially if this is a company whose activities are not usually looked favorably upon such as energy utilities or health insurance organizations.

27 GREATNESS AND HISTORY

The greatness of individuals can be decided only by those who live after them, not by their contemporaries. Use specific reasons and examples to explain your answer.

1. Key words

history / French history	l'histoire / l'histoire de France
a historian	un historien
a historic site	un site historique
a historic occasion	une occasion historique
historical (=concerning history)	historique
a historical event / perspective	un événement / une perspective historique
artistic greatness	la grandeur artistique
to assess the greatness (of)	évaluer l'importance (de)
to confirm greatness	confirmer la grandeur
to achieve greatness	parvenir à la grandeur
to be destined for greatness	être destiné à devenir célèbre
to shoot to / to rise to fame	devenir célèbre
with the benefit of hindsight	avec du recul
to withstand (centuries of)	résister (à des siècles de)
to pass the test of time	résister au temps
the impact (of)	l'impact (de)
to make a contribution (to)	contribuer (à)
the benefit of historical perspective	le bénéfice du recul de l'histoire
to pass judgment (on)	juger, évaluer
to earn one's place in history	mériter sa place dans l'histoire
to secure a place in history	s'assurer une place dans l'histoire
to make history	entrer dans l'histoire, marquer l'histoire
to arouse controversy	soulever la controverse
controversial (a)	polémique, controversé
posthumous success	le succès posthume
a legend / legendary	une légende / légendaire
a living legend	une légende vivante
to become a legend in one's lifetime	devenir une légende de son vivant
to be celebrated	connaître le succès
to be ahead of one's time	être en avance sur son temps
to catch on	devenir à la mode

2. Talking points

1. Man has achieved greatness in his lifetime.

- The political sphere offers countless examples of people who achieved greatness in their lifetime, especially when history came calling. For example, Elizabeth Cady Stanton and Susan Brownell Anthony spearheaded the women's emancipation movement in the U.S. that spread rapidly and extended to Europe.
- In some sports, victory is synonymous with instant greatness and a place in the hall of fame. People love a hero. And heroes make people dream. Bannister was the first man to run the mile under four minutes, Federer clinched a record grand slam titles.
- The entertainment industry has produced countless artists who have become world-known in their own time. Not only did they secure a place in their present time, they also managed to set standards which are hard to meet in history. Luck, the media and the power of the image, spin doctors and image-makers helped elevate some artists to the status of icons.
- The high tech world offers many examples of inventors and entrepreneurs who have been recognized by their contemporaries. They came up with the right device or idea and have not waited for history to pass judgment on their greatness.
- The art world is replete with artistic genius—painters, composers, writers and architects—who managed to achieve fame in their lifetime. Their work found an echo in the people's hearts and minds.

2. Greatness is not measured by what a man accomplishes in his lifetime.

- Some inventions and theories are ahead of their time. Their impact on the world can only be felt after the death of their inventors or authors.
- Scientific theories need time to mature and be confirmed. Understanding the full potential of a discovery or a groundbreaking theory takes time. A. Wegener's research on continental drift was not accepted until after his death.
- Art can be ahead of its time for social reasons (it is offensive to public taste) or artistic ones. The artistic talent and creativity of Vermeer, El Greco, Manet, and Cézanne were only given recognition posthumously. It was after his death that the world came to know about da Vinci's unequaled genius in painting. There are examples galore of writers and poets whose genius was not recognized by their contemporaries: W. Blake, H. D. Thoreau, E. Dickinson, F. Kafka, E. A. Poe, P. Verlaine, A. Rimbaud are cases in point.
- A great man's personality or social institutions—such as the Church, the scientific community at large, lobbies or trade unions—can also play against contemporary recognition. The authors of a theory can also sink into oblivion.

3. Possible answers

1. Man has achieved greatness in his lifetime.

There are several domains in which history has determined an individual's greatness. Through a combination of determination and vision, and sometimes luck, these men made things happen and were recognized for the greatness of their actions.

Explaining someone's rise to fame often defies logic. Some people achieve greatness because they fill a void in the political sphere. They are the right people at the right place and the right time. George Washington, a war hero, was the people's logical choice as first U.S. president. Civil rights leaders knew that their time had come after hundreds years of bondage. M.L. King, Gandhi, Mandela did not have to wait for history to pass judgment on their actions to make history.

People's thirst for greatness—and jingoistic feelings too—have turned men into heroes. Sport is a field where fame has not waited for the test of time. Legends are born when a country recognizes itself in those ephemeral heroes on the field and track, the court or the slopes. Fabricating such instant heroes is a deep-seated craving for man who yearns to dream and make the impossible possible. This is true when those people break records or barriers.

The entertainment industry has provided countless examples of artists who have risen to stardom in their own time. The power of the image, some well-orchestrated advertising campaigns, banner headlines, the 'hard-to-catch' cat-and-mouse game played by some stars but also their scandal-rife private lives have led to the rise of hero worship the world over. Greatness is often compounded by the power of the media, especially TV, the tabloids and people's magazines.

Technological progress has been a powerful boost to fame. The groundbreaking contributions by Bill Gates or Steve Jobs ushered in the digital age and turned America into the world's technological powerhouse. Not only were those technology savvy and visionary men able to anticipate the demands of time but they could also see far beyond what could be expected from technology.

Genius is another trademark of instant fame. Art, which is often judged at face value, is replete with examples of greatness immediately recognized and later confirmed. Michelangelo's greatness was acknowledged by the Pope. Europe's monarchs testified to Mozart's genius by granting him generous commissions. In the literary field, Mark Twain's works brought nationwide attention in his lifetime. *Adventures of Huckleberry Finn* solidified Twain as a noteworthy American writer. Architects I.M. Pei's or F.L. Wright's feats became instant hits with the public and established their greatness as the masters of modern architecture. In many cases therefore, man did not wait for history to achieve greatness, yet history also played a part in their greatness.

2. Greatness is not measured by what a man accomplishes in his lifetime.

Several reasons, scientific, social or personal, may explain why the greatness of man has not always been recognized in his own time. This is especially true of the scientist, the engineer, the discoverer and the artist.

For a start, some discoveries are ahead of their time and therefore pre-empt worldwide recognition. C. Columbus did not know he had found a new continent and thought he had reached the Indies. Now hailed as the one who stumbled upon America, he only became famous after he died. Henry Ford's impact of the assembly line on the American economy could not have been predicted in his own time.

Scientific theories need time to mature, to be proved or disproved. They need to withstand the rigorous scrutiny of time. When scientists discover and lay down the fundamentals, it is only much later their potential is fully understood and leveraged. Copernicus was the first to formulate a comprehensive heliocentric cosmology that displaced the Earth from the center of the universe. His theory was published in the year of his death, 1543, though it had been proposed several decades earlier.

Many famous artists had to deal with rejection and criticism in their lifetime, running afoul of public taste. It took three centuries for Vermeer to be recognized as a master painter of the Dutch Golden Age for his use of light and the unusual characters that populated his works. After his death, some of his paintings were sold with the names of other artists on them to make them more valuable. Despite his post-Impressionist genius, Van Gogh only sold one painting in his lifetime. As he presciently observed, "I can't change the fact that my paintings don't sell. But the time will come when people will recognize that they are worth more than the value of the paints used in the picture."

Some great men's cranky personality can also play against them. Nikola Tesla, an eccentric Serbian inventor, is best remembered for his contributions to the field of electromagnetism. Yet, a tragic and controversial figure, Tesla was marginalized by the scientific community later in life and died nearly penniless in a New York hotel aged 86. The authors of theories or of inventions can also sink into oblivion. The Wave Theory is more remembered for its name than its author, Ralph Nelson Elliott.

Institutions such as the Church, for example, have prevented some scientists from achieving fame in their own time. While Galileo proved that Copernicus's heliocentric theory of our solar system was correct, he was accused of heresy by Pope Urban VIII and put on house arrest until his death. Even though he didn't know it, Galileo was studying and experimenting with scientific ideas that today are considered essential, including kinematics and strength of materials.

Many factors explain why it is difficult to achieve greatness without the benefit of historical hindsight. History is one, yet man's personality and achievements often do not fit in with the time of man's vision, or the vision of his time.

Achevé d'imprimer en juin 2014 par Normandie Roto Impression s.a.s., 61250 Lonrai
N° d'impression : 1402327 - Dépôt légal : juin 2014 - Imprimé en France